❖

ABSOLUTE
HAPPINESS

❖

ABSOLUTE HAPPINESS

The Way to a Life of Complete Fulfillment

Michael Domeyko Rowland

Hay House, Inc.
Carson, CA

Copyright © 1993, 1995 by Michael Domeyko Rowland

Published and distributed in the United States by:

Hay House, Inc.
1154 E. Dominguez St.
P.O. Box 6204
Carson, CA 90749-6204
(800) 654-5126

Book Design: AeroType, Inc., Amherst, NH

The author of this book does not dispense medical advice or prescribe the use of any technique as a form of treatment for physical or medical problems without the advice of a physician, either directly or indirectly. The intent of the author is only to offer information of a general nature to help you in your quest for emotional well-being and good health. In the event you use any of the information in this book for yourself, which is your constitutional right, the author and the publisher assume no responsibility for your actions.

Library of Congress Cataloging-in-Publication Data

Rowland, Michael Domeyko, 1949-
    Absolute happiness : the way to a life of complete
        fulfillment / Michael Domeyko Rowland.
       p.   cm.
    ISBN 1-56170-219-6 (tradepaper) : $12.95
    1. Self-actualization (Psychology) 2. Happiness. I. Title.
BF637.S4R69   1995
158'.1—dc20   95-1312
                                    CIP

ISBN 1-56170-219-6

99 98 97 96 95   7 6 5 4 3

First Published in November 1993 by Self Communications Pty Ltd
AUSTRALIA
Second Edition, October 1994

Third Printing, September 1995, by Hay House, Inc., Carson, CA

Printed in the United States of America

This book is dedicated
to my wife

Paulina,

who contributed so much to the research and
writing of this book, and without
whom I would never have begun it.
She gives me the constant experience of
love, kindness, friendship, and makes me
Absolutely Happy.

C O N T E N T S

ACKNOWLEDGMENTS

First of all, I would like to express my thanks to the editor of this book, Astra Niedra. She has done an excellent job, worked long hours, and given much of herself and her intelligence to make this as good as it can possibly be.

I would also like to thank my friend and partner, Dr. John Coroneos, who has totally supported the work we do without question and with great generosity. Without his support, this book would not have appeared.

There have been many people over the years who have taught me so much and to whom I will always be grateful: my late father, Vivian, who was always kind and thoughtful and who gave much of his time in his later years, helping greatly and assisting me with all the administration; my mother, Eugenie, who gave totally of herself, going without so that I could receive a good education and have the best opportunity life has to offer. She always made me believe that I could do anything that I wanted and encouraged me to go for the best experiences available.

There have been many teachers who have greatly assisted me and taught me so much about the secrets to gain Absolute Happiness. The first one to really inspire me was Dr. John Mumford, who has a tremendous knowledge and scientific approach to the mind, Consciousness, and spirituality. Drs. Hal and Sidra Stone gave me some brilliant insights into the human mind and personality and whose teachings I have included specifically in this book. There are many people who are grateful to them for the advances that they have both made in the field of understanding and awakening to more awareness.

There are countless others whose work I have studied, whose contribution to the well-being of humanity will echo throughout this century and the next, people such as Dr. Stan Grof, Dr. Ken Wilbur,

Dr. Ken Dychtwald, Dr. John Lilly, Dr. Alexander Lowen, Dr. John Pierrakos, Da Free John, Nisargadatta Marahaj, Gopi Krishna, BKS Iyengar, and, from a thousand years ago, Abhinava Gupta, and too many more to list.

I also must thank two great masters of Yoga, who both personally initiated me into their systems, the Maharishi Mahesh Yogi, and Swami Satyananda of Bihar.

But most of all, I am truly grateful to the man who embodied all the highest teachings of the ages and was a living result of Absolute Happiness. He was Paramahansa Muktananda of Ganeshpuri. I consider it the most fortunate occurrence of my life to have met him and to have spent so much time studying his teachings and living within his school. He was an extraordinary being, a man who lived in the state of consciousness he taught others to access, as well as giving them the means to discover their essential nature, their highest essence. To him I offer my heartfelt thanks for traveling the world, revealing to all who were interested what he had discovered and what he made available for all of us.

— Michael Domeyko Rowland
    Bondi Beach, Australia, 1995

❖

<u>P A R T   O N E</u>

THE EXTRAORDINARY EXPERIENCE THAT LIFE HAS AVAILABLE FOR YOU

❖

What an extraordinary experience this thing called life really is. What possibilities, adventures, joy, peace, knowledge, and exquisite happiness awaits those who discover its great secrets.

Most people live at a tiny fraction of their potential and believe that this is all there is. But a handful realize that there must be so much more to living—that life is not restricted in any way. You are an expression of life and, as you will discover, the only limitations are those that you put onto yourself.

From now on, you can leave behind the ways of the many and join the path of the few. Stand back for a moment, look, examine, and accept that there is far more available for you than the mundane, the mediocre, and the dull. You can now leave the cocoon of any past limitations and move on to the full power and expression of who you truly are.

Once the goal becomes clear and you truly take the first step, an exhilaration of power and energy will surge through your system.

Absolute Happiness can then be yours.

CHAPTER 1

FULFILL YOURSELF
BEYOND ALL EXPECTATIONS

What Life Really Holds for You

W hat you are about to read in this book will amaze and liberate you in a way that you may never have dreamed possible. Read it very carefully. It holds many secrets that you need to know, that you *must know* if your life is going to go in the direction you want it to and if you wish to expand yourself to a life of pleasure and excellence that you may never have even imagined.

Perhaps you have wondered about how to live a life filled with enjoyment, success, and well-being in each and every area. Maybe you have considered and believed that there is far more to living than merely paying off the mortgage and indulging in pastimes that do only that: pass the time.

Well, there is. This other way, hidden from you for so long, is a stunningly simple and powerful means to maximize your potential and live your life to the fullest. Once you have grasped this knowledge, the world becomes your playground, your feelings pulsate with joy, and your life fulfills you beyond all expectations. It is called *absolute happiness*, and it can be yours as a permanent experience.

Some of the greatest minds in the world have spent their lives exploring and searching for the keys to living an exquisitely happy life. They were recognized as the great sages and genius artists of every culture. They were the wise ones, the true individuals, the masters of their path, who sought the truth; and the truth—that life can be an ever-increasing experience of absolute happiness—set them free. They experienced how it happened, and then they passed on the secrets to anyone who wished to learn.

Realizing that happiness was a result of certain actions within the human system, these great beings, the researchers of the highest happiness, set about exploring and mapping the way that the human system works. They realized quickly that the external events of life were only triggers or catalysts to inner experiences, and so they went directly to the source of these experiences, focusing on their own body, mind, and spirit.

Not only did they master the art of ordinary happiness very quickly, but they discovered, to their amazement, states of happiness that were so rich, profound, and exquisitely fulfilling that they were unable to describe them in words. They could only point the way and show how, to those who were interested. I have been fortunate enough to meet and study deeply with such people.

Over a period of 25 years, I have collated and personally applied, with great results, the information that I will now pass on to you, so you can move through the levels of happiness, to absolute happiness, as quickly as you choose. I suspect that it is impossible to discover the way to absolute happiness on your own, without guidance from those who have trodden the path before you. So here is the path.

The Most Important Experience

Consider this for yourself: isn't it true that the most important experience in your life is how you feel? It doesn't matter how many material possessions you have, how many sexual encounters you can enjoy, how important you are in your job or peer group. If you don't *feel* good, then what is it all for? These other things don't deliver anything but temporary satisfaction.

What would you rather feel: miserable, or ecstatically alive and filled with good humor? An obvious choice, isn't it? I am going to show you how you can have the ecstatic bliss and enjoyment and full aliveness, as well as the material possessions, relationships, and creative opportunities that you want. You don't have to be poor to be happy, nor do you have to be rich. You can *be* and *do* whatever you want; it is all available to you. It will merely be up to you to decide what you want. This is the teaching and inspiration that I have gained, and am happy to be able to pass on to you.

The secret of how to live like this already exists within you, within your own mind. Don't waste time only struggling in the world trying to achieve your aims. Work with your mind first, then take the actions. Mind is the creative power. It is your own mind that will allow you to dictate your destiny.

Imagine that! Being able to live out something without unpleasant effort, struggle, and time-consuming irrelevancies—you would then feel no hesitation in grasping life with both hands. You will find that life does a flip, and instead of you being involved in trying to make things happen in the way you want them, things actually start to come to you, in ways that will amaze you.

This is the goal. This is what has been known, by the few, for thousands of years in secret societies, ancient schools of learning, monasteries, and the royal courts of some cultures. Sages, wise people, and geniuses all knew how to do it. This is the power within you that has remained untapped and unused because you have never been told how to access it and because it has been deliberately suppressed by those who would keep you small and powerless.

Now you will know. Possibly for the first time, your eyes will open. Perhaps deep down you also want to know the secrets of life and to be able to enter the absolutely happiest state possible for a human being. It is always obtainable once you know how to access it. Then, knowing, you may choose. And when you do, choose wisely and well, for whatever you want will come to you. You will truly become the creator of your life.

Let Your Dreams Fly

As you proceed through this book, realize that you have in your hands something that can change your life radically in the most positive way possible. Let your dreams fly; don't be held back by the past anchors and internal saboteurs. This will be the time to let them all go. Prepare yourself, if you wish, to jump into a new dimension of living. Create whatever you want—materially, physically, emotionally, and spiritually.

The way is not difficult, nor is it any longer hidden. No special qualifications are required. It is open to any human being, from any lifestyle, any life experience. You can become the controller of your fate, the master of your experiences. No one but you will decide what you can do. No one but you will rule you from now on. You will see what there is to do and how it can be done.

Fasten your seat belt for the ride of your life, for you are about to discover your hidden power and your higher intelligence, which together will bring you absolute happiness. All this is available. All this can be yours. A few have done it before; now it is your turn to join them.

So, to action.

❖ ❖ ❖

CHAPTER 2

DEFINING HAPPINESS

A New Experience of Your Own Power

The purpose of this book is to crack the nut of happiness once and for all. Happiness, in the way that it will be explained here, involves a variety of different levels, from the ordinary and most familiar happiness, right up to and including the highest experience of absolute happiness with its ecstatic, blissful, and euphoric states of pleasure and fulfillment. This includes the so-called spiritual states. As you will see, these states are very down to Earth and readily accessible.

All of them can bring you to a new level of living and a new experience of your own power, and they can awaken a series of unexpected abilities to bring you success in all your endeavors. Happiness is the key to a brilliant life. Understand this and you understand everything.

Every issue in life can be solved and understood if you ask the right questions and pursue the truth. This also applies to happiness. And it doesn't matter where you start from. You can be a totally negative and disappointed person, or you can have your life working in the way that you want. I speak from personal experience, and I want to share with you what I have discovered because it will save you years, or even a lifetime, of trying to find out for yourself.

Fulfill Your Desires!

Happiness is a word we use to describe feelings of pleasure, joy, excitement, fulfillment, satisfaction, and many other emotions that signify that we are filled with positive energy. Everyone wants a happy life, regardless of the particular word used to describe this state.

Ordinary happiness (something that evades many people) essentially means that you can *fulfill your desires*—in other words, get what you want. However, there are some people who will immediately say, "When you get what you want, it doesn't make you happy." This instant negative response only shows just how deeply the belief that "life is an unhappy experience" is ingrained in some people. If you have such a belief, or even a hint of this type of negativity, dump it now. It is useless and will only become a self-fulfilling prophecy.

Of course, there will be things you go for in life which, on achieving them, don't make you happy. But that is only a result of wrong or misinformed choices. It is nothing to do with happiness itself. You can leave behind the making of wrong choices once you have understood what is revealed here.

Becoming happy, or fulfilling your desires, requires an intelligent, conscious approach. It is not a result of random emotions or luck. If you want happiness, then you follow definable steps that bring predictable results. It is never a haphazard or chance affair. Becoming happy is as easy as driving a car, and anyone can drive a car once they know what all the pedals and switches are for and are shown how they work.

The Way to Happiness

Fortunately, there is a way to become very, very happy. It requires that you know three things:

First, a complete understanding of what happiness actually is.
Second, why you are not already permanently happy.
Third, the unavoidable steps you must follow in order to create the maximum happiness.

Happiness is not something to do with the lower mind, where you struggle with thoughts. It is so much easier than that. Happiness is something that becomes deeper, richer, and more euphorically blissful the more you get into it, like a tree that grows stronger and more luxurious as the years go by. It is also accurate to say that there is an ordinary state of happiness that deepens and expands to absolute happiness when the application of the correct procedures bear fruit. But few people know of any other experience of happiness beyond the ordinary level. This book will change all that by giving you the means to experience the many delicious states of happiness. Best of all, the methods to becoming happy are completely free, as well as being easy to assimilate into your life.

Now let's look at the subject carefully so we can discover all the answers.

What Exactly Is Happiness?

With anything in life, if you can define and identify exactly what it is you want, then it is quite easy to achieve it. Most people have difficulty obtaining their goals because they have not clarified for themselves all the details. It is normal to be general in one's desires—for example, "I'd like an interesting job" or "I want a good relationship." But much more detail and consideration is required if you want to be certain you'll attain them. You will be surprised at how quickly you can fulfill your desires when you focus your attention on defining them precisely.

It is the same with happiness. Your first step is to find out what it really is. I have met few people who have ever truly considered exactly what happiness actually is. There are many who have thought about what the things are that *make* them happy, but hardly any who have really looked at what the *internal function* is within themselves that they then identify as happiness. It can seem a bit of a mystery. But if you don't completely understand how happiness arises in your own self, then you will not know what it is that you are looking for. And to be looking for something without knowing what it is, is a very difficult task indeed!

Let's define it precisely.

Happiness is a *feeling*. It is something you experience within your skin. It is not something outside yourself. You never experience your own happiness outside the boundaries of your body. This is why it is useless to try and find happiness in the outside world. It is an inner result of certain processes within your mind. Mind, as you shall soon see, is the most potent force in your life. It decides whether or not you are going to become and remain happy.

Happiness usually arises because of your reactions to a variety of external triggers and the resulting internal activities of your mind. For instance, seeing your newborn baby for the first time, winning a lottery prize, getting the job you really want, and watching a brilliant sunset—all of these external triggers cause your system to react with various degrees of happiness. But *always* the feeling will be within you. The external triggers, regardless of what they are, are always that—external.

All of these examples are, of course, temporary in their triggering effect. When the newborn baby wakes you up for the fourth time in the middle of the night, prior to the most important interview of your career the next morning, happiness is rarely the feeling that arises. And once the prize is won and the money spent, there is no power left in it to bring you any happiness. When you have been in the job for a period of time—it may be weeks or years—it just becomes the job you do—enjoyable, but rarely making you jump for joy on the office steps every morning. And, of course, the sun sets.

I am convinced, as is anyone who looks deeply into themselves, that happiness is *our natural state*, and all negative feelings and emotions are a result of wrong computations within our minds, and misconceptions about what life is and how it works. Our early conditioning has "wired" us incorrectly. This causes a series of blockages to our energy system, and it is our energy system that is the key. Feelings and emotions are a flow of energy, as is happiness. When you block your energy system, you restrict your inner experiences. Most importantly, it is, once again, your mind that is the master. It controls your inner energy movements. What we need to do is rearrange our programming, dissolve the past, clear out delusions and misinformation, and awaken a new consciousness within us, if we wish to enjoy the various levels of happiness that are available to each and every human being.

Ordinary Happiness and Absolute Happiness

Happiness, at the ordinary level, occurs when your life is going in the way you want it to. It is a result of clearing your mind of its various blockages. The removal of all negativity, the clearing of it from your personal mindset, allows you to enjoy a life of success, achievement, excellent relationships, and fulfillment in every area of your daily experience. Success, by the way, means to be able to live in the way that you choose. It doesn't necessarily mean you have to have millions of dollars or be famous or special in any way whatsoever. And anyone can become successful regardless of their background or life circumstances. We will deal with this kind of happiness in the first parts of the book.

Absolute happiness is a deepening and increasing of ordinary happiness. It is your birthright and your natural state. It becomes deeper and richer every day. It really fills you with an indescribable joy, far beyond any ordinary level of pleasure and enjoyment. Yet, amazingly, it is available to anyone who wants to experience it.

When you glimpse it, there suddenly arises within you a sense of extraordinary personal power and a realization that you have "come home." You remember the feeling clearly from sometime in the distant past, even though you have been out of touch with it for decades. It is a sense and feeling, a direct experience, of absolute peace, absolute centeredness, absolute clarity, and a continuing, ever-deepening, pulsation of love. This we will clearly explain in the second half of the book.

Happiness Is the Free Flow of the Life Force

To sum up, happiness is something that is ever present within you. It is released, not created, and it does not require anything from the outside world. It is very much an inner pulsation. Happiness is essentially an energy flow that occurs when you remove the negativities and blocks from your mind and so open yourself to more of the life force. This can also sometimes occur through various events in the outside world triggering your body and mind to release its contractions enough, so that more of the force can flow through you.

When you laugh a lot, you are happy. What has happened here? It is the outside trigger (what it was that caused your humor) that prompted you to open up. Anything threatening, or which you perceive as threatening, causes you to close down and eventually become frightened, aggressive, or even violent. On the other hand, the less threatening the outside catalyst, the more you open up. Therefore, we could say that something that makes you laugh is completely nonthreatening.

In romantic love, we see this taken to an extreme. The person who is the object of love to you is totally caring, kind, generous, sweet, and so on. You feel so completely nonthreatened that your whole psychological armoring, which is usually in place to protect you, drops away and you feel a surge of energy go through you. It is so intense and pleasurable that it is identified as love. You have opened up to an unprecedented degree, and this has dissolved the protective wall in the subconscious that contracts your whole system, releasing the powerful charge of loving energy.

The people who have examined what gives the most pleasure to a human being realized pretty quickly that the ancient sages were absolutely right: to become happy you have to unlock and release your energy system. This is not an intellectual pursuit; it is never just a head trip.

What is vital for you to understand, is exactly what the effects will be in your body and mind as you awaken your natural power. This is why it is necessary to totally and completely understand your mind, your emotions, and what you are as a human being. Misunderstanding these effects is the single cause of an unhappy life. Life is constantly trying to bring you to your natural happiness, so pay very real attention to this.

As you open your system up to more of the life force, to more happiness, you will observe the programs of your mind revealing themselves. This is amazingly interesting. The negative ones will be unraveled and dissolved. You will see the structure and the configuration of your emotions. You will also discover your inner universe, which you only glimpse in dreams. Finally, all the higher and more profound aspects of your identity will be brought into consciousness. It is a thrilling and deliciously fulfilling journey that will provide you with extraordinary states of pleasure and ecstasy, and these will often arise without any external cause.

You will flush out any blockages that may be within you, so awakening the free flow of the life force, the energy within your system, once again. Most people's systems have been blocked up since childhood. But life always wants to flow freely so we can enjoy ourselves to the maximum. And it uses its force of healing to clear out anything that stands in its way.

Realize that you are a very rich and interesting being, even if your life sometimes seems mundane and mediocre. In the process of becoming happier, you will need to understand what you are and where you are going. As you proceed through this book, I am going to first give you an overview and then explain individually all the elements of the amazing jigsaw puzzle of who and what you are. Once they have been defined, they will then all fit together to form the whole picture of how you can achieve the happiness you desire. As the picture is coming into place, I will also give you a variety of highly effective techniques, interspersed throughout the chapters, that you can use to take you to the state of absolute happiness.

First, though, let's begin with the ultimate prize, because if you truly know where you are going and why, you will always arrive at your destination.

❖ ❖ ❖

CHAPTER 3

BECOMING A FULLY ALIVE BEING

Awaken to Your Most Natural Self

I f you take away the trappings of your everyday life, all the involvements you have and all those normal things you do, and you just
remain present with yourself, what you are left with is the key to discovering your innermost essence. It is necessary to know precisely what
this is so that you can enjoy the greatest happiness. It is, in fact, the ultimate source of happiness.

All civilized human beings have been cut off from their essential self
by the demands of their civilization. If you look to the animal kingdom
and you see wild animals running free, without any of the trappings of
civilized life, then you can get a glimpse of where you have come from.
Because, as anyone who has brought up a young child knows, we are all
born wild and free and are tamed and trained by the culture and society
we grow up in.

We have a natural self, a free spirit, that is unhindered and uninhibit-
ed, even though it is bound and harnessed by the programming in the
mind. This "free spirit" part of ourselves is fully alive. Unfortunately, it
has been buried and so repressed by the demands of civilization that it is
very hard to find anyone who is not bound by their mind.

It is always an interesting experience to go to a pedestrian crossing in
a large city and watch the crowds of people as they wait for the "walk"
signal and cross the road. What a revelation it is to see, in the expressions on their faces and their body language, just how far we have gone
from our natural state, our state of full aliveness. The effect that the conditioning process has had on most people is revealed in their physical

expression—and it usually displays a shocking ignorance and misunderstanding of the human condition.

This unavoidable—and it is unavoidable—process of being civilized has cut us off, not only from our natural power, but also from the full use of the faculties of mind that we have over and above the members of the animal kingdom. Some people believe that the secret to feeling fulfilled and becoming fully alive means to go back to living like humans in pre-civilization days. But to return to the state of the savage will not deliver the desired results. This is very important to understand. Avoidance and dropping out from society is a sad delusion; it will never take you to where you truly want to go. The way is *forward* to the greater expression of your true nature by becoming more and more alive and moving to a "trans-civilized" state, a state higher than both the savage and the civilized human. You need to have the human opportunities and involvements as solid foundations in order to climb to the peaks of happiness latent within you.

Don't avoid the civilized reality in which you live and its requirements. If you do, you will waste your life. And also remember that nothing will satisfy you more than the discovery and complete expression of your powers. The normal state of the average human being is something you can pass through and use as a step ladder to the fully alive experience of absolute happiness.

Experience Full Aliveness

The most powerful urge, and even craving, in our lives is for full aliveness. We need to feel the pulsation of life surging through us to really be in harmony with ourselves and our environment. This is a literal statement. Life is an energy; it is something tangible and something that can be felt and experienced within your own system. It is exquisitely beautiful and, when allowed to move through you unhindered, it is deeply and totally transforming and fulfilling.

When you are fully alive, you can do almost anything. You find that quite naturally many talents spontaneously arise: creativity, vitality, humor, communication skills, personal power, magnetic attraction, sexual potency, high intelligence, intuition, social responsibility, natural love, and many more.

Sexual attraction, in particular, is dependent upon the power and free flow of the life force through you. It is not so much a thing of looks and clothes, but more a function of energy. Attraction is a magnetic activity. Some people seem to have it, while others do not. People who become successful film stars have it. It is something that is recognizable even on the screen, and it goes beyond beauty or handsomeness.

If you want it, then it is to your energy system that you must look. It is no coincidence that healthy, fit people, bubbling over with the energy of life, are more attractive than those who are weighed down with blubber or who have a low energy level. However, this doesn't mean that you have to look like a fitness instructor or body builder, for it has to do with the power of the life force. You can feel this attraction with some people who are not even fit. They are expressing this natural power.

Your Wild, Free Self

As our civilization progresses, we are becoming more cut off from nature and the wilderness. We find that many people are comfortable being couch potatoes, watching the TV with a drink in their hands. Or perhaps they are content to just spend their lives in an office, encased in cement and glass, never seeing the real, pristine wilderness in the forests and mountains. They are inevitably cut off from their own inner wilderness. This alienation from their wild, free nature is the cause of many of life's difficulties for many people. They feel that something is missing, that they just don't have the energy to put into making their lives really work. This is why sports men and women are often successful in life. They are still in touch with some part of their wild, free nature as a result of their physical activities.

Your natural self, your wild nature, by the way, is not an aggressive or ugly thing. It is just filled with the happiness of living and existing with a body. For living, itself, is a pretty amazing thing. Have you ever thought about how bizarre and extraordinary it is just to be alive, with a body and a mind, and that there is this thing called life out there to get involved with? This experience actually becomes euphoric as you open to it. Happiness starts to flood into you as you join in fully with life.

Our sense of natural self is often most easily experienced in the natural wilderness. This has been mentioned before, but it is so important that it needs reiterating. If you go and spend some time away from civilization, you will find that you have many other abilities and powers that have been lying dormant and unused. You will discover what it is to be fully alive, if only in a physical sense, which is an excellent foundation for understanding the complete meaning of this vital point. All of the greatest human beings, the founders of civilizations and great religions, communed with the wilderness. Wilderness is a vital part of life for humans: no wilderness, no real power, no aliveness. Society needs it for its health, and this is why we see the arising of the environmental movement. A society can starve to death for lack of food, but it can also starve to a different sort of death if there is a lack of wild, free, peaceful, and unpolluted places.

You need to tune in with the wilderness if you are to master your life in a complete way. Of course you can master some parts of your life without needing to access the wild, free part of yourself, but you will never experience total completeness without tuning in with the essence of nature.

To commune with the wilderness does not mean doing things like snow skiing and whitewater rafting, even though these sports are a lot of fun and derive much of their pleasure from the fact that they take place in a wilderness setting. To "commune" means to be there without any of the trappings of civilization, where you are just alive and with your essential self. This is where you can find a totally new experience of happiness. It is happiness without cause, just the sheer pleasure and joy of being alive. Happiness can be experienced in such places as a spontaneous natural high, appearing without the necessity for your mind to be doing anything at all.

Avoiding the Rut

Full aliveness has another qualification relevant to you. All living things are either growing or stagnating, decaying and dying. It is the same with humans. Negative feelings, lethargy, and boredom are a result of not continuing to grow and evolve. Check your life now. Are you growing, or have you stopped and are just marking time? Be careful, for *marking time* is another term for stagnation. It can creep up slowly, unnoticed and unseen into your life, like an insidious disease, and drive you into a rut of mediocrity and mundane trivia. The rut can eventually become so deep and the sides so high, and the effort required to motivate yourself to move on is so great, that it makes it almost impossible to get out.

You can be in a rut in many areas of your life: the way you relate, the amount of money you let in, your creativity and self-expression, and any other ability or activity. Remember that Oscar Wilde summed up that sort of life when he said: "The only difference between a rut and a grave is the depth."

Speed Up Your Evolution

All the greatest personal growth and human potential paths, as well as the secret teachings of the most ancient schools of learning, are aimed at speeding up the evolution of each student who practices the techniques. Evolution can be speeded up and, in fact, the ancient art-sciences are designed, not only to speed up the process of evolution, but to take it to its completion and fulfillment. This is possible for those who wish to master their mind completely. These superconscious realms of existence and experience will also be clarified for you later in this book. And, like everything else in life, they can be discovered by those who learn the laws of life. The realization that there are laws that can be understood and applied, frees you in the most wonderful way, because laws are the keys to an absolutely happy life.

Happiness is not a random thing. It is definable and repeatable. All you have to do is know the methods and laws that control it. Now let's look at those laws that most affect your enjoyment and success.

❖ ❖ ❖

CHAPTER 4

THE LAWS OF LIFE

The Unity of the Whole Universe

Whe live in a Universe governed by laws. It is often repeated that "God doesn't play dice with the Universe." Everything follows laws. This is all that science is, a rational and logical discovery of the laws of life. Each day the frontiers of our knowledge are being pushed back as science progresses. Superstition and delusion are dissolved daily, as are the concepts of luck, chance, and coincidence. Even the most seemingly unrelated events are being seen to be inextricably tied together. The new Chaos Theory is putting forward the proposition that all things are related, that the Universe is, in fact, one giant interacting entity that follows precise and discoverable laws. We just haven't yet built computers large enough to find out how all these laws work. This, of course, is no news to the sages of the ancient wisdom. They were quite aware of the unity of the whole Universe, and they used their knowledge of these laws for their own benefit and that of their pupils.

What is often forgotten is that there are scientific principles yet to be discovered, but just because they haven't been found doesn't mean they don't exist and work perfectly. Many of these principles exist in the realm of the mind and, at present, can only be proven by personal experience. You may be wondering why our education system has not included the information in the following pages in its curriculum. It is because science has no way of examining our minds. You can't take a piece of mind and put it in a test tube; there is nothing physical to be weighed or measured and no instrument that can observe a mind. Yet we all know we have a mind; no one doubts this because they use it every day of their lives. There is nothing external that we can agree on, because no two individuals can see the same mind at the same time. You need more than one witness or observer for scientific proof. Therefore, this information is not in our education system because it is not "scientific." Fortunately, the powers of the mind are provable and repeatable to oneself, and that's all that matters in the end.

Put Yourself in a Position of Power

We human beings are also governed by these mind, or nonphysical, laws and not just by the physical aspects of our lives. It is impossible to avoid this fact. You cannot contradict the laws of nature, and this includes the laws of the mind, without suffering the consequences. The mind and its capabilities obviously exist, so it is far more intelligent to discover and use them, rather than dismiss them because there is no scientific proof to give physical evidence of the mind's existence. There is no physical evidence of the content of a dream, but you certainly know when you have had one.

The ancient explorers of the inner realms of the mind, just like the explorers of the Earth centuries ago, brought back knowledge based on their own experiences. The wisdom of the discoveries of these great masters of inner exploration can be applied in your life to bring you the results you want. It is worth taking notice of them, as they can save you years. Only a fool ignores the advice of those who have been where they want to go, and have laid out the path for others to follow.

Are you aware of these laws of your mind and their effect on your daily experience? Have you the ability to create what you want, when you want, how you want? Can you alter your inner program to bring new experiences automatically into your life? Are you able to restructure the functioning of your mind so that you can become more creative, more loving, and more energized? Can you discipline your mind to bring you better health and increased vitality? If not, there is obviously a need for more knowledge in this area.

All of our experiences occur because something caused them to happen. They didn't just "appear." Nothing just "appears" or "happens." There are reasons for all things. There is no one playing dice with your life. It is wise to eliminate the words *luck, coincidence, chance*, and so on from your vocabulary. They are words that we use when we are unaware of the reasons for things happening. If you do dispense with these words and ideas, you will put yourself in a position of power and choice and will no longer be a victim to things or forces seemingly outside your control. What it was that caused the various events and circumstance to happen to you, that attracted them into your life, is within you and nowhere else.

As you shall see, there is nothing outside you that is making you dance to a tune like a puppet on a string. What has created your experiences is actually in your mind. Even if you are unaware of exactly what your mind is, you are using this faculty (and always have and always will) that is *already present* within you. The source of all exists there, and you will find it nowhere else. When you understand what mind truly is, what this thing is that we define as mind, then all this will be very apparent to you, and you will be able to become powerful and achieve your desires.

Change Your Life Script

The operating program of your life is already scripted. You can actually read your mind by learning to look deeply into it and so see what it has in store for you. It is not a particularly difficult thing to do. Like anything else, it only requires a strong enough desire. The program that controls your life is in there. After all, where else could it be? Flying around in the sky somewhere? Obviously not. The answers are always found within.

Most people are unaware that they are following a prewritten program; they believe they either have free will or are merely pawns in the game of life. This is an unfortunate misunderstanding of how a human being is structured. How this program went in and how to change it will be clearly explained. Regardless of whatever else you take from this book, realize that you have an operating mechanism, and it exists within you, even though you may be unconscious of when and how it is working.

Your life is not a series of unconnected events. On the contrary, you are playing out a script, a series of inner instructions, and, unless they are changed, you will continue to play them out for the rest of your life. The most wonderful thing about these instructions is that they can be changed. Even though you did not consciously put all of them into yourself, you are the only one who can now change them. Naturally, when you do this, you will find yourself discovering ever-deepening layers of happiness available for enjoyment.

To change anything at all in your life—internally, such as feelings and beliefs, or externally, in the opportunities available—you have to change the unseen program in your mind. This is unavoidable, and it requires a complete knowledge and understanding to be effective and produce the result you want. Your life experiences are created by the choices you make, and throughout this book you will become aware of the mechanism within you that is making those choices. You must begin here, with the choice process. From now on, cease to blame the outside world.

The only *real* power to change your life comes from yourself, from your own conscious abilities, and from the talents you awaken that are dormant within you. This is your key to freedom and to all the levels of happiness.

Keeping in mind that there are laws available for you to learn and master that will bring you absolute freedom and happiness, let's move to the first step that you must now take. The journey to absolute happiness begins with this first step, and now we will see exactly what it is.

❖ ❖ ❖

CHAPTER 5

ABSOLUTE RESPONSIBILITY

Living as the Creator

The first step to absolute happiness is to take full, total, and complete responsibility as the creator of every single aspect of your life. As we proceed, the reasons for this will become clear. This includes the good and the bad, the enjoyable and the unpleasant, the fortunate, and even the "unlucky" events of your life.

We are not talking here merely about ordinary responsibility, where you know yourself to be a responsible person—that is, you are reliable and you do what you say you are going to do. What is meant here, is taking the complete responsibility for everything that happens to you. This means that from now on you accept that you are the being who is the cause and source of all the events of your life. No one else is. You are no longer the victim, where life seems to "happen to you." You are now the creator, the driving force, the writer and director of your experiences.

You need to leave behind the belief that the cause of the circumstances and situations of your life is some outside factor. This is where you cease to blame, complain, whine, and feel powerless. You no longer choose to remain in victim consciousness where someone or something other than you is in control of what happens to you. You are the one who is doing it to yourself. No government, no other person or group. Just you and only you. *You* put yourself where you are today, *you* keep yourself where you are today, *only you* decide whether you are going to change or not.

If you are in a situation where you have unconsciously handed over the power of your life to someone else or to some institution, then realize you have done it to yourself. No one has done it to you. Naturally, you can take it back anytime you want and then cause your life to go in any direction whatsoever.

This is the most empowering and liberating concept to retain in your mind. Because if you are the creator of your life, you can then choose with absolute freedom what you are going to do. With this new attitude of complete responsibility, there is a feeling of exhilaration. No longer do you have to look beyond yourself for permission to create your life in any way that you want. You can remove the shackles of the things that bind you. Taking responsibility is the unavoidable and required first step on the path to full self-mastery.

Climbing Out of the Rut

This is a difficult concept for some to grasp. They would prefer to remain bound as slaves to something other than themselves. They feel it is easier to stay in the rut that has been dug over decades. These types of people can find a thousand excuses that are seemingly logical, rational, and obviously "true," to justify their remaining in victim consciousness.

How dull to have lost the spark of inquiry, to have absorbed a paltry nest of ideas from whoever was around, and defend these unexamined and unresearched concepts as the absolute truth. The unexamined life is an insignificant and insipid affair. You need a warrior's mentality to understand life and enjoy it to the full. This is not an aggressive attitude; it is one that involves awareness, strength, and determination to overcome obstacles. Don't fall into the trap of the victim, however comfortable and easy it may appear to be. Life has a strange habit of sneaking up on the misinformed and deluded and dragging them into reality.

As you continue through this book, you will discover that your deep mind knows everything; it is the "storehouse of all information." Later, we will look into just how deep it goes and how we can tap into this "Universal computer."

While it is obviously true that rarely will anyone consciously put themselves into life-threatening situations, this does not negate what is stored deep below the level of their conscious mind. If you are unaware of the script that is operating within you right now and throughout your life, then does it care? Does it change? Of course not. It just plays itself out, carrying you along with it.

You will also see just how incredible this organism is that we all are, that we call a human being. Even with our amazing technological society, we have hardly scratched the surface of this thing that we all call "me." When you practice personal growth techniques on a regular basis, you will increase the power of your intuition and your awareness, and you will see for yourself just how you are the creator of every experience. It becomes blatantly obvious, regardless of what you may have believed in the past and regardless of whom you may have blamed.

You will see that taking total responsibility is the only sane and logical course of action. Your unconscious mind knows the absolute truth. It knows everything. Your past and the future is stored in it to play out as the years roll by. There is only one problem with the unconscious mind: you are not conscious of it. We'll show how to change this predicament later on.

The point to grasp right now, for the proof will become apparent as we proceed, is that whatever situation you find yourself in, it is you who has put yourself there, by your actions or avoidance of taking actions. You made the choices. You are the one who is having the experiences, and it is your own mind that has created them. "Why?" or "How did this actually happen?" is the best response to events in your life, not "But it's not fair" or "I didn't bring this fate on myself," and so on. The squealings of the victim have never changed anything. Change is brought about only by responsibility and the taking up of the power that is available to you. It is just a matter of getting on with it.

The Response Ability

If you divide the word *responsibility* in half, it becomes the "response ability," or the ability to respond. This is the key to understanding it. How is it that you respond to the various experiences that come into your life? Is it with intelligence and positivity, enthusiasm and considered action; or with negative emotional outbursts, boredom and resignation, powerlessness and inaction? Do you look at things to find a positive and life-enhancing opportunity for yourself and others or, if the event requires extra energy to go in the way you would prefer it to, do you just roll over and take it, giving up at the first sign of difficulty? Do you have the ability to respond with the warrior's mindset and effect the changes you desire?

If you have a response ability that has caused you to fall into blame or negativity about something unpleasant that has happened to you or if things haven't gone in the way that you wanted them to, the only person suffering will be yourself and those around you, who have to live with a negative person.

Negativity is a self-indulgence that you cannot entertain in your life if you are to realize who you truly are and be able to create the life experiences you want. The past can never be altered. All you can do with the past is to accept it and let it go. Self-inflicted suffering about something you can do nothing about is a painful and unproductive activity. Some suggest that to be responsible is a bad concept, as it weakens people and makes them fall into guilt. If you fall into guilt and remain there, then that's what you *choose* to do. No one else is making you feel guilty, and if they are, then it is your choice to stay in their company and to react in that way.

If you can't help being negative, apply the techniques you will learn here later, or get some counseling or other assistance that will release the need for you to use your mind in that way. Release, or letting go, is the only solution to negativity. Some people need to feel negative, as it gives them a sense of identity in an otherwise desert of a life. This is always their choice, their decision. Let's hope you are not living with them.

Full Empowerment

To take full responsibility is the greatest and only opportunity for change and full empowerment. If you can grasp the fact that you have within yourself all powers and abilities, and that you can create whatever you want to experience, then you are a being who is responsible. Unfortunately, most people have a great fear of freedom, of being a loving, powerful, and successful person.

How is it for you? Are you behaving like someone who is totally free? Naturally, I am not suggesting that you go around breaking the law. The laws of society are the same as the laws of the mind. If you break these, you suffer the consequences.

Check your own life once again. Are you taking complete responsibility, or are you blaming someone or something for your situation? There are always solutions to problems. Usually they just require that you take specific action.

Life Becomes a Play

For people who take complete responsibility for their experiences and who learn the mechanisms of creation, life becomes a game, a play, an incredible journey. There is a whole smorgasbord of opportunities out there, and it is up to you what you take. So, know who and where you are at present, and agree with yourself to take complete responsibility from now on. Because if you don't take the complete responsibility for your life, who will? Those of a religious persuasion say "God." But a well-known saying states that "God helps those who help themselves." It is also well known among religious people that God has granted free will to humans.

This means that you are entirely in charge of your life. For those who are not particularly concerned with a concept of, or a belief in, God, they have only themselves to deal with. Whichever way you look at it, *you* are always left with *you*.

Your path to absolute happiness is well trodden by many who have gone before you. Just follow in their footsteps, and you will receive the same rewards. Paying careful attention to what is revealed here will give you a power that you have never imagined possible.

It is vital that you understand how it is that you have been conditioned to become the person that you are and why you have had all the experiences that you have had. You need to know how this life script is locked in place within your own mind, because only then can you change it. Your mind is a fantastic instrument, and it can deliver wonderful rewards once you are conscious of its mechanisms.

We will now see how this works, and by doing so, unlock the door to your freedom.

❖ ❖ ❖

❖

PART TWO

YOUR KEYS
TO FREEDOM

❖

HOW YOU WERE CONDITIONED
TO BECOME WHAT YOU ARE

To be able to become Absolutely Happy and create your life in the way you choose, it is necessary to understand perfectly what you are and the way your system works.

If you can grasp exactly what this entity that you call "me" is, then you have the opportunity to cause your life to progress as desired. If you do not know what you are and how "me" functions, then you are left only with hope, confusion, and uncertainty, rather than knowledge and personal power.

To actually know what it is to be a human being, particularly the one that you are, is the greatest release from the shackles of mediocrity. It is the only means to becoming the creator of your life and being truly happy.

CHAPTER 6

KNOW THYSELF

Discover the Secrets of Your Self

To master happiness, on all its levels, requires you to go back to the basics of how your life works and what you truly are. We are all so layered over with countless concepts and beliefs about what it is to be a human being and what the real reasons for living are, that it is easy to lose sight of the reality of what life is all about. Never forget that moving from beliefs to facts is the surest path to self-fulfillment.

In all the ancient schools of learning, of every culture and generation, there was always the primary requirement to understand. The sages and wise people, from time immemorial, whatever their creed, country, or the age they lived, consistently issued the same instruction. And anyone who travels the true path of discovering how life really works, has inevitably discovered that there is one unavoidable and vital command that must be obeyed before any real progress is made. This command, this instruction, this requirement, is identical for them all. It is to *"Know Thyself."* It was emblazoned above the entrances to the ancient schools. It was hammered into the minds of those who sought the truth.

The great secrets about life itself and what you are as a living being are not to be found in the outside world. For this type of knowledge, you must look within, you must know yourself. It is vital to know who and what you are and how your system works in delivering to you the events and circumstances of your life.

And yet, where do we hear this today? We are all taught to learn only about things outside ourselves, within the realm of the material world.

This is all well and good and necessary, but to only look externally will never give you the happiness you truly desire. Nor, of course, will you be able to gain the rewards you seek in the world if you do not understand or even have any knowledge of the mechanics of your own self.

What exactly does this mean: "Know thyself"? Many people wonder how you can know yourself. What is this "self" anyway? How do you define it? Is it possible to improve it or enhance its power so that you can bring into your life what you want in the easiest and most enjoyable way? And is the opportunity truly available to really change yourself and so change your life, or is that merely wishful thinking?

All these questions and more will be answered. And to answer them you need only turn to "you." There is no point in looking elsewhere. The great delusion and time-wasting misinformation is that happiness is somewhere outside your own self. You will find all you need to know if you look *within*. It exists there already.

So let us first of all look at what we know, what we can be sure of, and then explore the deeper and more hidden knowledge and discover the way to absolute happiness.

Your "Bodymind" Instrument

What do you really know for sure about "you"? Start with the most apparent. You have a body, mind, and feelings. Your identity is as that of a human being. You exist in this present day and age. You live in a world of nature and human-made objects. You can think, act and react, and create. The conscious powers that you have are limited to your physical body and personal mind. All these are for certain. For all intents and purposes, you experience yourself as a body with a mind. Therefore, it is obvious that you should attend to this human being that you are, if you want to find out how to bring yourself fulfillment. If the body and mind are happy, you are happy.

All human beings live with this body and mind as themselves. It is the factor in their lives that they are never without, because if you did not have a body and mind complex, you wouldn't exist as a human being. For the sake of ease, and to have a more accurate understanding and terminology, let's call this human system a "bodymind" because it is, in fact, an integrated, interacting entity.

Tuning the Instrument You Use

At present, you live in, as, and through this bodymind. A very useful way to understand this is to use the analogy of an instrument, such as a piano. You experience your life through this bodymind "instrument." Your mind "plays" your energy and physical body as you would play a piano. So, the bodymind is an instrument that you play to obtain your experiences in life. The tune you play on it can be boring and mundane or totally fulfilling and exhilarating, or anything in between. It's entirely up to you.

Everything in your life occurs because you are present in this bodymind. The bodymind is the only function you have and that you can be sure of having throughout your entire life. Yet, have you ever examined what it is or how it creates your life experiences? Can you see how vital it is to do so?

This bodymind instrument actually creates everything that happens in your life. Some people believe that life "just sort of happens" to them. This is not the case. There is an intelligence that brings the events and circumstances of your life into your life. Nothing is coincidental. You may be totally unaware of how this intelligence works and how it is working right now in your life. Even so, it is absolutely powerful and is the driving hand behind every single experience you have had, are having right now, and will ever have. Few people are using even the slightest amount of it, even though it is there, willing and able to function to a far greater degree, once you give the command.

The intelligence within your bodymind instrument is the key to your entire life and holds undreamed-of potentials. A little time spent here, discovering its hidden functions, will provide far greater benefits than years of effort in the material world trying to force things to happen with relationships, creativity, career, wealth creation, spiritual seeking, or any other area of life that you are interested in. This is the luxury, first-class path. You will find that this powerful mechanism is already running your life completely. All you need to do is gain the understanding of how it works, how it interacts with your bodymind, how to awaken more of its energy, and then all rewards will be available.

The key to understanding this bodymind intelligence is to realize that it has a *purpose* in your life. You are actually living for a reason. Let's now look at what that purpose is so you can use its power for your maximum benefit.

❖ ❖ ❖

CHAPTER 7

DISCOVER THE PURPOSE OF YOUR LIFE

Activate Your Hidden Powers

There is only one purpose in life, one single, solitary activity that all human beings and other living things undergo. It seems so simple and obvious, and yet it is usually only given halfhearted acknowledgment by the majority of people. And yet if they did give it their full attention, they would be able to follow that line of thought to its logical conclusion and so activate the hidden powers within them and achieve their goals with ease.

The purpose of life is to *fulfill* desires. There is no other purpose. This is why we have been born, and this is what we do all our lives. From the simplest to the most complex, all of life's creations are fulfilling desires. Animals desire to procreate and eat and enjoy their families and groupings. Plants desire to grow. People have their own wants, from the simplest to the most profound. The human bodymind instrument is nothing more than a *desire-fulfilling mechanism*. Desires can also be called experiences. And when we have finished with desires, or experiences, we have finished with our bodymind and so finished with life.

So all through our lives we do one thing and one thing only and that is this: we create desires/experiences and we live them out, from making a cup of tea or coffee, to the jobs we choose, the relationships we enter into, the holidays we take, the hobbies and sports we involve ourselves with. This is what life is: a continuous activity of chasing and fulfilling desires, whether we are successful at it or not.

It is in the nature of the mind to desire. It is an unavoidable and normal event. If one does not experience things in the world, then the mind creates fantasies and dreams internally. This happens in sleep, float tanks, isolation cells, and whenever you are not focused on the outside world. The mind is constantly creating, both internally and externally. Identifying this process allows us to move to the next step in the equation of happiness.

What Drives You?

The reason you choose and create the desire/experiences that you do, is not for the experiences themselves, but for the *effect* those experiences have on your bodymind instrument.

The external events and circumstances act as catalysts and stimulate your bodymind. They play a "tune" that you experience as feelings and emotions. Everything you do in the external world causes an emotional reaction internally. It is the desire for the internal reactions, the feelings and emotions, that control what you do in life.

Consider, for a moment, that you have the time and are free to do whatever you want. Usually you will go and do something to make you feel good, or whatever word you use for that inner experience—*satisfied, fulfilled, excited, stimulated, happy*, and so on. Let's take the word *happy* for the sake of this example. *Happy* covers all these and more in most people's minds. We all want ordinary happiness, let alone absolute happiness.

When you go and do something that makes you feel happy, you do not experience happiness six feet or two meters in front of your nose. Happiness is something that is experienced within you, *within your bodymind instrument.*

The reason you do all the things that you do is because of the *effect* that these experiences will have on your bodymind, because of the "tune" they will play on your "instrument," your inner system—in other words, because of the emotional reactions that will be produced within you.

Everything you do, you do for this reason. The external events are nothing more than catalysts that cause a *reaction* in your bodymind system. It doesn't matter what these catalysts, these experiences, are; it is the power that they have to stimulate your bodymind system that makes them important.

This is why we go for things in our lives. There are numerous varieties of catalysts in life. A catalyst can be anything that affects us: another person, a movie, a beautiful view, a sport, a holiday, a job, a book—in other words, any external experience in life whatsoever.

Many of these catalysts/experiences affect some people in the same way and others in different ways. It all depends on how their own bodymind instrument is "tuned." Sometimes, of course, you go and do things that you think will make you happy, but they have the opposite effect on your system. There are reasons for this, which will be explained as we proceed.

Stimulating Your Bodymind System

The next piece in this particular jigsaw is that these external things in your life, after a period of time, lose their power to affect you as strongly as they did in the beginning. No "thing" has the ability to totally stimulate you for every minute of every day for your entire life. And very few things have the ability to stimulate you for very long at all.

Let's say you buy a new car, perhaps your first one. It will undoubtedly make you feel very happy to have it. You may even feel exhilarated. For the first few days after you get it, you will be thrilled to sit in it and drive it. Maybe it's because you are now independent and don't have to rely on public transportation or borrowing your parents' vehicle. Or perhaps it's because it looks so good or drives in a way that gives you great pleasure. There can be many reasons why it turns on happiness for you.

Within a period of time, whether it's a few days, a month or a year, that car will lose its power to turn you on, to stimulate your bodymind system, with as much power as it did on the first day. You don't feel a charge of excitement go through you anymore. It will just become "the car," useful and so on, but really without any ability to affect you strongly.

This, of course, happens with everything. This is what our whole consumer society is based on. People like to constantly have new things and enjoy new experiences that stimulate their bodymind and make them feel happy.

So, once one of these things has lost its power to turn you on as much as it did in the beginning, you have to create another experience then another and another and another. Everyone is always doing this, day after day, year after year. It is the unavoidable activity of living as a human being.

Never forget that the majority of the experiences people create can be tiny or seemingly insignificant or of short duration, like reading a letter, watching TV, hoeing the garden, or going for a walk.

Our lives are a multi-layered series of experiences that constantly cause reactions in our bodymind system. Some are just beginning, like the brand new car; therefore, they stimulate us strongly; others are halfway through, and their power is waning; and still others are coming to an end, and their ability to affect our bodymind instrument has almost faded altogether.

The Source of all Experiences

So, all your experiences occur because something caused them to happen. There are reasons for all things. Sometimes we are consciously the motivating force: we think of something to do and then we do it. At other times, we are not conscious of what causes the events to occur.

The purpose of your life is to fulfill desires and, as will become even more apparent, it is always your choice which desires you create. The next step, therefore, is to become completely clear on how your choice mechanism operates to bring you your experiences in life. It is the primary faculty you will have to master in order to realize any improvements.

❖ ❖ ❖

CHAPTER 8

YOUR CHOICE MECHANISM

The Results of Your Choices

There are several sections of your mind that bring into your life everything that happens. The first to consider, because it is the result of, and arises from, all the others, is the mechanism of *choice*. This part of your mind works like a computer. A computer operates on a binary system, which is basically turning on or off millions of "switches." This is the basic, underlying activity of computers.

It is very much the same as the way that our personal mind functions. We are always either saying yes or no to every circumstance and situation that arises in our lives. We are even making choices about what to feel, think, and imagine. This is constantly going on, millions of times a second. Our whole system is being instructed by our intelligence on how to behave, react, and what to do as each event occurs. The results of these choices become your experiences, feelings, opportunities, and every single other occurrence that happens to you. Every factor of your life is a result of your choices.

Choices Manifest as Actions

This process of choice involves thoughts and the imagination. When presented with a situation requiring a response, your imagination runs both a visual replay of what is stored in your mind about that particular subject, and a verbal replay that consists of your thoughts about that subject. You then respond by taking an action. Your response, or action, therefore, is entirely dictated by the contents of this imagination replay and the conclusion of your thoughts.

An action can be any activity that a human being does. It can be either of mind or body. It can be a physical movement or the choice to remain still. It can be an emotional response, a behavior pattern, a series of thoughts, a decision, an expression, a deep breath. Anything whatsoever, which is included in the whole range of human experience and expression, is an action.

Here is a simple example: someone invites you to come see a film at the local movie theater. In that moment, you react to that offer. You either say yes or no, or you pause for consideration or for more information about the movie. Eventually you come down to a yes or no. You either take that action or you don't. There is no half way. "Maybe" equates to a "no decision" for a visit to the theater until you make the choice to go, which then becomes a yes.

Some things are considered and thought about for a while, but other choices are made immediately without any functioning of your mind seeming to take place. These choices are called spontaneous. But even though they seem to occur immediately, there has been an activity of your mind that, in a split second, makes a choice, and you then follow up with the required actions.

If someone says to you, "Would you like a cup of coffee?" and you are a coffee drinker, the experience of coffee will flash through your mind, and you will respond, "Yes, please." If someone asks you to go to a restaurant with them to eat a particular type of food, your response will be a result of what is in your mind about that food. If you are asked to go to China for a holiday, you will consider with your imagination all the things that you have heard or seen about China and again respond accordingly.

Your mind works faster than the speed of light and can consider countless options and make assessments in the blink of an eye, particularly if you are not interfering with its processing ability. This noninterference, or instant knowing, is called *intuition* and will be dealt with later on.

The contents of your mind feed into your awareness as the information to make decisions. The various structures in your mind act as filters to control whether or not you are going to take a particular action. Every possible action is assessed, mostly below the level of your consciousness, before you can respond with the yes or no that will either allow you to, or stop you from, taking the action. I will explain how these mind structures work shortly.

All this "searching through the file of the mind" can take only a fraction of a second. Your mind/brain is the fastest and most powerful computer on Earth. But there is still only the option to say yes or no to an action. There is no other choice in your life, only yes or no. You either take the action or you don't. Your life's experiences are controlled by this single activity of mind. Every event and circumstance of your life is dealt with in the same way. You either respond with a yes or a no, just like a computer, when there is an opportunity to do something in life.

Where Do Thoughts Come From?

The conscious choices you make are only the tip of the iceberg of your mind. All your thoughts, feelings, imaginings, choices, and decisions about what actions to take just appear in your conscious mind, like water spouting from a hot geyser. You may have seen geysers coming from deep below the surface of the Earth—they appear as a boiling fountain, shooting water several meters straight up into the air. No one doubts that the water comes from deep underground, even though all we see is the fountain at the top. It is exactly the same with our own thoughts and imaginings. They just "spout" into our conscious mind.

Your mind follows its own laws and uses its own information to come to its conclusions and, therefore, choices. You have only partial knowledge of this activity. The vast majority of it takes place in the part of your mind that you are not conscious of. This part of your mind is below the surface, like the water from deep underground that becomes the geyser. Every action, whether carefully considered and thought about or spontaneous, is still a function of whatever it is that is stored in your mind. Nothing bypasses your mind.

Some people believe that the thoughts and decisions that come into their minds, which they hear in their own heads, are presenting the most positive, life-enhancing and best course of action for them. This is not necessarily the case. The thoughts that you are aware of in your head, when thinking about and analyzing a decision, can only come from what is already recorded in your mind. In other words, they come from your conditioning, your past, what has gone in as you grow and live. You cannot use thoughts that are not there in the first place. It's like trying to think in German if you have never learned the German language, which is obviously an impossible task.

Choices Become Experiences

It is all of these choices, life-enhancing or otherwise, that become the experiences in your life, because you can only act upon and react to what comes into your mind. You cannot take any action, however small or large, without your mind being involved.

The choices that spontaneously arise in your consciousness, like the boiling water from the geyser, appear as either ready-made decisions or as the various considerations or options known as thoughts.

The unknown factor in this process is that the vast majority of the choices you make in your life, which then become your life's experiences, are entirely sourced from your subconscious. In other words, you are often totally unaware of how and why you make the choices you do, even though it often seems that you are totally rational and logical and are acting from free will. All the happiness or unhappiness resulting in your life can always be traced to the choices and actions you initially made. This is why, when on the road to absolute happiness and personal freedom, you need to take complete and total responsibility for your life.

Freedom from Limitations

There are many people who believe that they are purely and only conscious, rational beings, and that all the choices they make come solely from their rational faculties. What they forget is that these rational thoughts have only arisen from somewhere within the storehouse of their own mind. These prerecorded thought storehouses are the raw material of the rational processes. It needs to be remembered that there may be many other thoughts that could cause them to come to entirely different conclusions, if they had access to them.

In the same way that you cannot make steel without iron ore, you are limited in your rational processes by the raw materials of your own thoughts. You can only select what's there, just like a computer program cannot select a file that does not exist within its memory banks. This is why we find many aspects of science constantly progressing, and often some seemingly unchangeable physical laws being turned on their heads. Those that "discovered" these laws originally were making rational and logical decisions based on the thoughts that came into their minds. If they had had access to a different selection of thoughts, different raw materials, as, say, Einstein did, then they would have come to alternative conclusions and decisions.

So, if any of the store of thoughts preprogrammed into your mind are incomplete, incorrect, or untruthful, or even totally deluded, how can you possibly make decisions in your life that will benefit you? Maybe you're being led down a track that is identical to whoever impressed you the most as a child or who dominated you the most intensely. It is, therefore, vital to be really sure that what you are hearing inside your head is useful and accurate for your well-being. These structures comprise the controlling factors of your life. It is impossible to change your life without changing these. Later in this book, you will be given explanations and methods to assist you with changing the program. The methods are easy to apply once you have all the information, and you will discover that any effort you make will bring in results that far outweigh the effort you put in. Life is *longing* to give you what you want and will do so when you become clear on how it works.

Become Aware of Your Options

Your options in life are limited to what is stored within you right now, unless you apply what you learn in this book or change your program by some other method.

Have you ever really considered your options in life? Have you ever stopped to consider what life holds for you? Maybe you've thought that life is what it is, and there's nothing you can do about it. This is incorrect, for there is a great deal that you can do about it.

To discover the whole truth about yourself and to be able to access all the levels of happiness, it is necessary to discover and understand your own mind completely. You need to see what you can do to change anything and everything in your life. There is no greater adventure, no more perfect fulfillment for human beings, than the discovery of their own mind in all its aspects and in all its amazing and incredible potential. It is truly the greatest secret of success and happiness. The man who taught me the most, whom I will tell you about later in the book, would often say that your mind is an excellent servant, but a terrible master. If you don't master it, it will master you.

In our society, we tend to examine the mind in a very limited way. I was very fortunate to be able to study many of the ancient teachings about this most important part of a human being, with masters from the East. In these countries, they have examined very deeply what this structure actually is. In fact, in India, as in many of the Asian cultures, there are millions of scriptures and verses of varying lengths that hold tremendous secrets about the mind. There have been many highly intelligent people in those countries who have spent their lives examining it. We are very fortunate to be able to take advantage of what they have discovered.

This is one of the benefits of the "information explosion" that we live in. All of the cultures of the world are now contributing to the increase of our knowledge. And there is nothing so interesting as the most powerful faculty you have—your mind.

It is to this concept that we will now turn.

❖ ❖ ❖

CHAPTER 9

WHAT MIND REALLY IS

Mind Is More than Thoughts

Most people consider their mind to basically comprise a series of thoughts and images recorded onto the brain like a piece of videotape. This is a gross misunderstanding and the basis of all the problems in life. Mind, *in the terms that we shall use it,* is a far more awesome and powerful mechanism than you have probably ever imagined.

The word *mind* does not really sum up in any way exactly what this all-important mechanism is. You may have to put aside all your concepts of mind if you are to gain a complete benefit of the full force of what your mind actually has to offer. The normal meaning of the word *mind* is: the summation of all the conscious and unconscious processes. This is quite close to the truth, once you know what is hidden in the so-called unconscious. I'll make it very clear:

Mind is the creative intelligence that totally controls every aspect of your life, from the most basic to the most profound. There is nothing that is outside the realm of your mind. There is nothing that it does not control. There is nothing that it does not affect.

Mind is a substance, a definable, plastic medium that moves faster than the speed of light and can outpace the most giant supercomputer. It has the ability to mold itself into any shapes and patterns that it pleases and has abilities that will stun and inspire you. At present, we use and are aware of, far less than one percent of its capabilities and power.

It is your mind that holds the blueprint of your genetic structure; it is your mind that has guided and controlled the growth of your physical body from a single egg into a full adult human being. It controls all the chemical and biological activities of your body. It is the unseen hand behind the physical activities, whether microscopic or Universal in size.

On an individual level, it is your mind that knows how to heal you, how to keep all the organs of your body functioning normally, how to digest food, how to keep you alive when you are asleep, how to create thoughts, images, and feelings. Your body merely follows your mind's directions. These two, body and mind, are totally intertwined. But it is the body that is dependent on the mind, not the other way around.

Brain-Mind Clarification

Many people confuse mind with brain. There are numerous books that have the word *mind* in their title, but actually have to do with the physical brain. This is misleading and confusing to both the reader and, obviously, the authors of these books.

The simplest way to clarify this confusion is by using the analogy of a television. When you are watching your TV, you see the images of the program and hear its music, words, and other sounds. You know that the program is not actually occurring inside the box of the TV set itself; it comes from a studio elsewhere. The people and events on the screen are independent of the TV, they exist *whether or not* the TV is on.

Your brain is like the TV, the physical means through which the program can be seen and heard. Your mind is like the actual program that exists freely and independently. It requires the physical mechanism of the brain to translate its signals so that it can communicate through physical form.

Your mind, which is the intelligence that controls your life, exists *independently* of the physical matter of the "TV set" of your brain. Different parts of mind can be accessed by particular physical actions on the brain, such as surgery. During exploratory brain operations for epilepsy, a wire is inserted into the brain through a tiny hole in the skull. The patient remains conscious, as there is no pain felt in the brain, and can communicate with the surgeon. A small electrical charge is applied along the wire, searching for any problems. This stimulates parts of the brain and old, long-forgotten memories flash to the surface. It is as if the electrical charge "presses the buttons" on the brain and causes the old recordings to play back. This is similar to the TV, in that when you press one of the buttons, the channel changes and a new program appears.

Naturally, you don't always need to physically stimulate your brain with electrical charges to bring to the surface long-lost memories. The normal chemical activities of the brain do that for you when the intelligence of the mind is applied correctly.

Your mind also has the ability to cause the cells of the body to change in the direction required. People who can heal themselves through the use of the mind, give instructions to the cells through the correct application of mind techniques and use them, in unison, with the practical realities of the various physical healing methods. This is why placebos or sugar pills can sometimes work. It is the mind that actually does the healing. This might seem to be an amazing statement, but before the cells were discovered, the suggestion that they existed was also treated with ridicule. There is also the power the mind has on the genetic structure. I believe it has the ability to control genes and alter their functions. If mind can affect one aspect of the physical body, as in healing, then it must have the ability to affect all other aspects of the physical body. For science to discover the realm of pure intelligence and its effect on the genes, is only a matter of time. Mind, again, in the terms that we are using it here, is not limited to just thoughts and images. We are dealing with unknown powers of intelligence.

So, never forget that mind controls the activities of the brain. It is not the other way around. Brain is only a medium for mind. If you cannot accept this, then you will be unable to progress much beyond intellectual analysis. Your life will be lived in your head, and you will have to avoid the natural, wild, free, and loving part of your system. You will lead a limited life, bound by beliefs that restrict you. Later in the book, techniques will be given that can prove to you beyond all doubt, the power of your mind. If you follow the necessary procedures, you will be able to personally experience results in your own life. And let's face it, that's the only proof you can be certain of—direct, repeatable, personal experience.

The Computer Analogy

The mind is often divided into three categories: the conscious, subconscious, and unconscious. Each has its own distinct qualities and characteristics, even though they are made of exactly the same substance and are always interrelated.

Probably the simplest way to understand the mind is by studying how computers operate and are structured. This is not surprising, because those who invented and designed computers actually copied the way that the human mind works, for they were trying to create a machine that could duplicate the mind's activities.

However, mind is a far more organic and multidimensional mechanism than a computer, as we shall see later on. Even so, it is still very useful to use the analogy of a computer to give you a foundation of understanding.

A computer has three main parts:

The first is the screen that its functions are viewed upon. It is usually a monitor or a flat screen that you see on laptops and notebook computers. This is similar to the conscious mind.

The second is the memory in which the various software programs are held. It is these programs that allow the various calculations and operations to take place and which bring a result onto the screen in the form of images, letters, and numbers. This resembles the mind's subconscious activities.

The third part is the computer hardware itself, with its permanent operating program that allows it to function and supports all the other activities that are performed by the software that you put into it. This is analogous to the unconscious mind.

There is a fourth part of the computer that cannot be compared to any part of the mind. This part is the person sitting at the keyboard operating the computer. The person's role is very similar to the Self—that which is prior to and beyond mind. We will deal with it in depth in the latter part of the book.

By understanding how the mind's three functions—conscious, subconscious, and unconscious interrelate, you, the Self, will be able to change anything you want within them and so produce a result in your world. The first thing, though, is to be aware that you have a mind that you can do with as you please. If you spend time, like the ancient sages, looking within your mind, you will discover, as they did, that your mind is actually an object. It is something you have, not something you are. It is another faculty you can use—a personal tool, just like your hand. You can make your hand do all sorts of useful things, just by willing it to. It is exactly the same with your mind—the difference being that you have very little consciousness of the whole mind. Once you become conscious of it, you can do with it as you please. Until then, your life is a result of what is already conditioned into your memory.

Qualities of Mind

Mind itself is a jelly-like substance, like plasticine. You can shape it into anything, and it will retain that shape forever or, if you shape it again, it will obligingly hold that new form forever, without any complaint or negative response, apart from the release of any negativity that was held there in the first place prior to the change. It can reform itself as you please, or it will remain as it is for your entire lifetime. The shapes your mind takes are the actual structures that feed into your consciousness the thoughts and images that become your life choices and decisions and, therefore, your life experience.

Mind and its exploration make up the last frontier of anyone's life. For when you start to work with it, then, and only then, can you pierce through for the answers to all questions about your personal life and life itself. Knowing mind and its abilities will grant you the opportunity for absolute knowledge and absolute happiness.

Two aspects of it are relevant to your ordinary happiness, and it is these that we will first examine.

❖ ❖ ❖

CHAPTER 10

THE CONSCIOUS AND THE SUBCONSCIOUS

The Conscious Mind

When you press the keys on a computer keyboard, on the computer screen appear all the responses. You are able to create all sorts of different results, such as words, graphics, sounds, and calculations. You don't have to do anything else apart from pressing the keys or the mouse button. You are not concerned with what is going on inside the computer. The results appear automatically on the screen, and you are aware of them. You experience them as a result of your actions (pressing the keys) and the unseen functioning and calculations of the computer itself.

This is the same with your conscious mind. You "press the keyboard" of your mind through the ordinary faculties of thought, imagination, will power, analysis, and so on, causing all sorts of results "on the internal screen" of your conscious mind. You are able to think, plan, react, make decisions, relate, and perform all the other normal activities of being conscious. All these elements operate automatically within your conscious mind. You don't have to do anything about them, nor are you aware of what is happening below the surface of your consciousness. All you do is pay attention and "press the keys" of your mind, and it does its work automatically, just like a computer.

Your conscious mind is the place from where you make the decisions, or choices, in your life. Every day options arise, and you go with one or the other—for example, "Shall I go out with this person or not?," "Shall I take this job?," "Shall I go to see this film?," and so on. The conscious mind is where your *choices are revealed.*

The choices that appear in it become the experiences that you have in your life. For instance, you have the option to marry a particular person and your mind makes the choice, yes, and so you do. The resulting relationship is caused by the choice you made in the particular instant you make it. You then live the results, happily or unhappily, perhaps for the rest of your life.

This is a vital point to emphasize, and it will be repeated occasionally so that it will be retained in your memory. If you grasp it, you are totally free; if not, you are bound. *All the events and circumstances of your life come as a result of the choices and decisions you make.* There is no luck, chance, or coincidence. You always choose. No individual or organization "does it to you" unless you choose to let them. It is the thoughts that come into your mind as decisions and choices that cause you to take a particular path in life. It is your mind that causes your actions, even though you may be unaware of the processes by which your mind comes to those particular decisions and choices. Blaming, complaining, and becoming depressed about any aspect of your life is a sign that you have not realized that the mechanism that creates your life is within you. So what you need to know is this: where exactly do these specific thoughts and choices come from that create your life experiences by causing you to take particular actions? Because they really do come from somewhere.

Why Have You Made the Choices That You Have?

So, again, it is important to answer the following two questions: (1)"Why did I make the choices that I did in the past that have caused me to become the person I am today?," and (2) "Why did I make the decisions that I did in the past to give me the life experiences that I have had so far in my life?"

It is vital to know the answers to these questions. Why didn't you make other choices and decisions that would have given you better experiences? Why did those particular thoughts, choices, and decisions come into your head and not others? Imagine how different and perhaps happier your life would have been if you had made other choices. So why didn't those other choices come into your conscious mind? There must be a reason and, of course, there is. Discover the answer to this question, and you have cracked the code to your own life experience.

Like the computer, you are unable to think or imagine anything that is not in your personal program or memory. Your ability to make a choice or dream up a fantasy is dependent on the "raw material" that you have already stored within you. You cannot draw something that is not there from the well of your personal mind. Therefore, you cannot choose something that does not fit a pattern or has no references within the storehouse of your mind.

Your analytical skill is also dependent on what information you have within you at any given time. You cannot bring into your analysis of a problem, knowledge you do not have or information not present in your personal mind. In the same way, a computer cannot use a program or elements of a program that are not already stored in its memory to calculate a solution to a problem. If something is not there, it cannot be accessed.

Nor can you make choices about anything that is not present in your conscious mind. Events happen outside you, and your reaction to them is entirely dependent on what appears in your conscious mind as that reaction. You cannot have a reaction or experience anything if that action does not appear on the screen of your consciousness. However badly you want something, you have to have the mechanism in place, somewhere within your mind, in order to be able to take the necessary actions to bring it into your life. This is why it is so important to know the source of your choices. Your life is only what you choose. And why some things in life are not enjoyable or are not what you want is because what you choose from the subconscious and what you would consciously like are often two very different things.

In a computer, the source of its information and ability to calculate and perform its myriad actions comes from the program stored in its memory. In exactly the same way, the source of your thoughts, decisions, and choices is your own subconscious mind. Within you right now, as you read this, there is a storehouse of old memories that have filed themselves away below the level of consciousness. It is these "files" that are the source of what comes into your conscious mind. You are not aware of the activities and programming of your subconscious (just as you are not aware of the computer's activities away from the screen), but the subconscious still performs its functions perfectly.

The Subconscious Mind

The subconscious mind is essentially memory. In fact, the word *mind* came originally from the old English word *minde*, meaning *memory*. When you ask someone to remind you of something, you are actually saying "re-memory" me. Memory was the first identifiable component of mind.

The subconscious can be called the *personal* unconscious (we will deal with the Universal unconscious mind later). It is the part of your mind that contains and retains all the things that have happened to you in your entire life, even though you have lost touch with them. Your subconscious mind's storage capabilities closely parallel the programming functions of your computer. In the computer, nothing is forgotten unless it is deleted.

Nothing in your life is forgotten either. Every single thing is remembered and stored. From the moment that you were conceived, through your birth and infancy, early childhood and adolescence, right up until now, every insignificant item, minor event, minuscule and seemingly irrelevant detail, is stored within your memory.

This is often hard to believe for some people. Later in the book, you will be given methods that are easy to apply to activate past memories, and you will be able to discover for yourself that this does happen. One popular technique for this process, which requires a facilitator, is hypnotic regression. It is well known that the police in many countries use it to assist them in solving crimes. For instance, just after a bank robbery, the people present can hardly remember anything that happened. It all seems to be a blur, as it was so fast, usually taking only a couple of minutes. But once the police hypnotist is brought in, it is incredible to discover just how many details are retained. Hypnosis is used frequently in therapy to bring to the surface long-lost memories that are then resolved and integrated. In fact, all therapies are geared to bring the past to the surface and then deal with it. Everything is remembered, and the subconscious mind has an infallible memory.

Because of the way it is molded and shaped into patterns, it is this sub-conscious part of your mind, the program, that holds all the blockages to your full aliveness and empowerment. These patterns are the limitations and the saboteurs that hold down or restrict the real you from arising and expressing itself fully and freely in the world. Clearing your subconscious mind of unwanted patterns is the most important factor in becoming a totally free being, able to live your life to its fullest potential and expressing your whole self to your highest aspirations.

By changing what is in your subconscious, you will be able to change what happens to you in your life. This is because you will be altering the choices and decisions that come into your conscious mind, thereby choosing different events from those you did previously.

People often struggle to change their conscious thoughts by "positive thinking" and affirmations or any of the variety of popular "you can do it" modalities. This paddling around at the surface can sometimes have useful effects, even if only temporary. But to engage permanent change, you must go to the source of what comes into your conscious mind. And what comes into your conscious mind appears from the subconscious.

So, once these subconscious patterns are cleared and remolded in the way that you want, you are able to create what you desire in your life.

The next step is to comprehend exactly how this subconscious mind functions. Remember, that this is the only way to "crack the nut" of a successful and happy life. Happiness is your natural state, where the world seems to serve you and make your life easy and enjoyable. It longs for expression, and it is the easiest and most pleasurable way to live. Happiness brings love, generosity, kindness, consideration, joy, and a host of other excellent emotions and behaviors. Freeing yourself of the subconscious blocks and hindrances allows all these wonderful results to come into your life.

Let's see now how they went in. Once you have understood this, you will be able to apply the specific techniques and methods that I will give you to bring about the changes you want—first understanding, then conscious actions.

❖ ❖ ❖

CHAPTER 11

HOW YOU WERE CONDITIONED

The Two Functions of Mind

Mind itself has two clear functions, and you use both of them every moment of every day.

First, it *creates*, through the choice and decision mechanism, and other faculties we will discuss later, all the events and experiences of your life.

Second, it is the organism through which you actually experience life.

It can therefore be called an "Experiential Apparatus," something that brings into being the circumstances and content of your life and that is also required to feel, sense, and perceive these occurrences.

How the Information Goes In

Every moment of every day, our minds are absorbing *millions of units of information* about what is going on in our lives. It is being collected on many levels at once, and we are totally unaware of the vast mass of this input. Some authorities suggest that it could be up to 100 million bits of information per second. Whatever the amount actually is, it is more than we can consciously be aware of.

Each of these "bits of information" that are *bombarding our systems constantly,* we will call an "impression." An impression, once in your mind, is rather like a compact disc (CD), that records music or sounds and images. Every single moment, we are taking in impressions that are loaded with information, just like the CD.

Your mind, with the help of your senses, is taking in everything that is presented to you. Each impression contains all the factors that were in existence in your life at the split second they went in. They work, in a way, like photographic film. When you take a photograph, it captures on the film everything that was within the view of the lens at the time. A lot of things are not visible to the naked eye, yet when the photograph is enlarged, more and more details appear. You have probably seen pictures taken from a spy satellite in outer space. Nowadays, it is even possible to read a newspaper held in someone's hand in a street several kilometers below the camera as it orbits on the satellite in space.

The impressions that go into our minds are very similar to these photographs, in the sense that they are filled with information that is not noticed, or you are not aware of, at the time you are experiencing their input. With the help of the senses, the mind processes all the millions of bits of information that are coming into you every moment and sorts them into a form that you can comprehend. Each impression has several segments, and we are consciously aware of some of these.

These impressions are stored within your memory and are used as the "raw material" in the choice-making process that you undergo when a decision has to be made. It is these impressions that are the single, or individual, building blocks of your subconscious mind. And it is from their content that your level of happiness is dictated.

Let us look at it more closely, and see just how it works.

The Programming of Impressions

Figure 1: A Single Impression

Five Senses

All the senses are represented because they each collect the details that are appropriate to their functioning. Sometimes, consciously, you are unaware of, for example, any odor in the air. But your sense of smell is like the photo from the satellite; it can pick up the finest, infinitesimal odor that is around. It stores this in the memory as well, even though you are not conscious of this storage activity taking place. Each sense does exactly the same.

Other

There is a segment called "Other," because we always need to keep an open mind and allow the mystery of life to throw up additional information or keep its secrets until the whole truth is experienced. This whole truth is the truth beyond words and images. It is always important to acknowledge the mysteries of life and not pretend that we can define and rationalize everything. Some things are just too big to be held in a personal mind.

Vibration

You are aware, when you go into a room where there has been some terrible anger expressed or arguments raged, that something has happened. You can feel the atmosphere; you can cut it with a knife. Or, if you go into a place where there has been a lot of laughter, you can feel it immediately, and your spirits lift. If you go to a temple or church or any holy place where there has been prayer and meditation and the chanting of verses, you can feel the stillness and calm of the place. It literally affects you, and you fall into a respectful silence.

This atmosphere is called the vibration. It is a measurable effect and referred to in slang as the "vibes" of a place or situation. We are all familiar with this concept. This vibration is also stored on the "CD" information log of each impression that goes into your mind.

Perceived Reality

Let us take a simple example to explain how this works. We have a Mr. Jones, an employee of a large company, who has been called into the office of his superior, Mr. Brown, to be given some bad news. Mr. Brown tells Mr. Jones that due to economic difficulties, the company has to tighten its belt and retrench some of its staff and, unfortunately, Mr. Jones is one of those who is to be asked to leave.

The "Perceived Reality" that Mr. Jones experiences, which goes in as a series of impressions, is the *normal reality* of the situation. It is what is basic and obvious in any circumstance that we find ourselves in. Mr. Jones is sitting in Mr. Brown's office, it is daylight, he is on a chair, Mr. Brown is opposite him, and so on.

Rational Explanation

The rational explanation is that Mr. Jones is being told that his job is over. He accepts the story that the economic climate is such because people are losing their jobs all over the country. It seems *logical and reasonable*, even though it is unfortunate for him. He sees no reason to doubt the rationality and logic of what he is hearing.

Irrational Response

This is where Mr. Jones may have a paranoid or mistaken conclusion about what is happening. He may irrationally believe that the company doesn't like him because he is a troublemaker or a union member; or that his fellow employees have ganged up behind his back and want to get rid of him; or even that it is because he has a better car than the chief executive. There can be a variety of such responses that are utterly irrelevant and not based in reality or *have no evidence as fact*. These often occur when someone is under pressure, or emotional, or unbalanced in some way.

Unconscious Truth

This one is very interesting. When we are very young, our minds are still so open that we often have the ability to perceive the truth of any situation. You can still see this in some children. Their intuition is still operating perfectly—it hasn't yet been blocked by the education system or the conditioning process. They often blurt out what they perceive, much to the embarrassment of those around them. We tend to lose this ability with age. But it always remains, even though we are no longer conscious of it, and we all still know *directly, intuitively*, exactly what the truth is of any situation.

Let's take an example: a man is in a permanent relationship with a woman. Behind her back, he is having an affair. She is consciously unaware of it. Subconsciously, her intuitive ability to know the truth directly is still functioning, but it is buried very deeply. At some level, she knows that her partner is having an affair. She may be completely oblivious to it on the surface of her mind, but the knowledge will still be there in her subconscious. Most of the time it remains buried and hidden from view, but sometimes she may feel that something is going wrong in her relationship, although she can't put her finger on it. At other times, she may even become suspicious for no apparent external reason. Whatever the reaction, somewhere in her mind she is picking up the whole truth of every situation she finds herself in. This is why when people separate after such a relationship, they may suddenly remember all sorts of events and signs that obviously pointed to the unfaithfulness of their partner. Because of the distance of the separation, their mind becomes free from emotions that were present during the relationship, such as fear of being alone, and so is capable of perceiving the truth. For, fear is the great block to being able to know the truth.

The perception of truth is a latent ability. We all have it. You can reawaken it again at any time with the correct techniques and use it at your pleasure. In fact, people who apply in their lives the things they learn in this book will often find that this truth-knowing ability *awakens spontaneously*.

Now, back to our Mr. Brown, the manager who is telling Mr. Jones that he is fired. Mr. Brown actually has a secret. He has been told by his superior that his division of the company is not making the necessary profits and unless he gets his act together, *he* will be fired. Mr. Brown quite naturally freaks. He doesn't want to be out of a job, particularly if he is fired. It would make it very hard for him to get another job with a black mark like that to his name. So he considers his options carefully and decides to get rid of a couple of people below him and then tell his superior that he has identified the dead wood in his division and cleaned them out, and now the profits will reappear. He chooses Mr. Jones.

Mr. Jones is *consciously unaware* of Mr. Brown's hidden agenda and has no idea that this is what is really happening. But at some level of his being, he knows the truth, and even though he cannot access it, possibly ever, it is still stored in the depths of his memory.

There are many, many instances of this type of situation in life. People tell lies all the time, and rarely is anyone aware that they are telling them. Being able to know the truth, rather than have it hidden from you, is a very useful attribute indeed. You can choose, of course, whether you let everyone know you have that ability—often it is wiser to keep quiet about these things.

Emotional Reaction

This is the real key to mastering your subconscious, as it is the fuel of the belief structures that dominate your choices and actions. These emotional reactions, or loadings, are locked into each impression and also stored in the memory.

Emotion implies E-Motion, *Energy in Motion*. This is what an emotion is: a particular type of energy moving through your system. Whether it is happiness, laughter, anger, sadness, excitement, or whatever, it is a feeling that pulsates through you, and we define it as an emotion. There are also other, higher types of energies that move within us, but these come from a different process, and we will deal with them later on in the book.

Now, when this emotional energy is blocked or unexpressed, it has to go somewhere. It cannot just disappear. You can stop an emotion from forming, but once it has arisen, it has a life of its own and must find an outlet or, if unexpressed, somewhere to be contained.

An emotion that has arisen, but is not expressed in the normal way, is held and *stored within your system*. And this is one of the amazing things about your bodymind—that it can store and contain a staggering amount of this blocked emotional energy for a lifetime. But there is a price to pay for this natural function of suppression: it affects our entire lives.

The following example, about a little girl of four years old, will explain what this price is. She has a father who has always treated her with love and kindness. One day he returns from the office after a very difficult day. He is tired and cross. When he gets home, the little girl does something that normally wouldn't worry him, but today it makes him angry and he shouts at her, telling her off. This comes as a shock to the little girl, who has a basic core belief, based on experience, that her father loves her.

Her immediate reaction is one of anger and she feels like shouting back: "Don't be horrible, Daddy," or something similar. But the look of annoyance in her father's eyes brings up fear in her, and she suppresses that emotional reaction and buries it. Anger is the emotional reaction that comes up when you can't get what you want, or things don't happen in the way that suits you. So she just sulks and goes to her room, *holding down that unexpressed anger*.

Now, let's say, for the sake of this example, that this particular emotional reaction, the unexpressed anger, had an *energy power of one unit*. To keep it suppressed within her system, it is going to cost her at least another unit of energy. She is going to have to expend this in contracting her physical system to literally hold the suppressed anger in place. Later, I will tell you what happens when you want to release these blocked energies.

So now she has lost two units of energy from her system. This has denied her, perhaps for the rest of her life, some of her aliveness and energy, because nothing is forgotten, nothing just goes away. Imagine how many times this happens in an average person's upbringing. We are all constantly having to deny and hold down our power and keep it down. The ramifications of this blockage of emotional energy are profound and affect many, if not all, aspects of your life. We will examine the staggering effects these blockages have in the following chapters. They are certainly the most potent forces controlling your happiness, ordinary or absolute.

Mind Is Energy and Power

The filing and storage of memories continues unceasingly, day and night. Each impression, and these happen every split second, is automatically filed away in the appropriate section of the mind. As we have seen, all the sensory elements are contained in these files. They are like a movie film of life with all the tiniest details preserved for later playback. All of them are fodder for the sourcing of the decisions and choices into your conscious mind, which, of course, become your life experiences.

The mind molds itself multidimensionally into shapes, many of which are spherical and interlocked with each other. These can be viewed internally, in the same detached way that you can view a television program. When, through the correct practices, you glimpse into the workings of the mind in the subconscious, it is one of the most enthralling and awe-inspiring experiences you will ever have. The colors, shapes, images, feelings, and power are stunning and life transforming.

This function of memory totally controls your life, in the same way that your computer is controlled by what is held within its memory. Now we will look at it more closely, so that we can learn to use its power in life-enhancing ways.

❖ ❖ ❖

CHAPTER 12

WHAT WILL YOUR FUTURE BE?

How Memory Functions

Our next step is to understand exactly how memory functions. You will discover that it has abilities and control locks that can bind you into mediocrity or rocket you to exalted and totally fulfilling experiences. To do so, we need to concentrate on your subconscious mind. It is vital to realize how the whole mechanism of your subconscious works so that you can then use the simple tools that will be provided later in the book to create your preferred reality.

The reality you live in right now is made up of all the events and circumstances of your life: your career, wealth (or lack of it), relationships, leisure activities, and so on. Anything you would like to change in any, or even all, of these areas can be changed once you begin to master your mind. These changes you make, when they have come to fruition in the way you want them to, would then become your *preferred reality*—in other words, the way you would like to live.

Without understanding what your particular program is based on, you would be unable to use the tools offered later. It would be the same as someone who has no knowledge of how the mechanics of a car work, being given all the instruments and tools and told to fix it. They would first have to understand the mechanics of the car and then be shown exactly what happened when the tools were applied if they were to be successful. It is the same with your mind. Accumulate the necessary knowledge about the memory, and the rest is very straightforward. Ignore or gloss over it, and you take the risk of missing the whole thing.

Subconscious Memory

The subconscious, as we have discussed, is essentially all memory. It remembers everything from your conception through to this instant. Memory is not purely stored physically; it is a part of mind and therefore independent of the physical body, even though interlocked with it. This part of your mind has never forgotten anything and never will, even though you may be unable to bring your past to the surface of your consciousness whenever you please. Nor is it always necessary to bring to the surface of your consciousness your past experiences. It can be a great time-wasting event. There are reasons for this phenomenon, as we will soon see. *Going for results in life* is always the *only key* to growth.

Naturally, there are some people who endure profound traumas that have resulted from ugly incidents in their past. For these people, it can be very helpful to bring the traumatic memories to the surface and integrate and assimilate these experiences, if the traumas are holding them back. It is wise to seek out the help of professional therapists and, as long as the past experiences are not dwelled upon and turned over and relived for many years, this can be the most intelligent way to deal with them. Unfortunately, so many people spend decades "on the couch" of a therapist, for a very limited result, if any at all. The old methods of analysis are very weak and unreliable in gaining permanent results because they ignore the complete mind and only deal with a small part of it. The body-based therapies are more quick and powerful, but the ultimate method will always be to change your state of consciousness. The only real solution comes from this alteration or expansion of consciousness. Later in the book, we will be examining consciousness in detail and exactly what it means to alter your state, as well as giving you all the major methods of therapy and personal growth techniques.

Most people, who do not have great difficulties from the past to cope with, will be able to use the techniques detailed subsequently. These will move you in the direction you want to go by unloading any negative energy that may be associated with a particular aspect of your life. We will be dealing with all the major areas, such as sexuality, prosperity, relationships, higher states of consciousness and, of course, happiness. Each of these issues, interestingly enough, are sourced from within the same mechanism—memory. It is important to have a clear understanding of the structure of memory and how it totally controls your life experience.

What Memory Really Is

Everything that has ever happened to you is stored in your mind in a particular way and, if you wish, can be accessed. It is this particular way, coupled with the limitless qualities of the whole memory, that can dictate the quality of your life.

Your memory is the most complex filing system you will ever know. It operates via precise codes and in specific ways, similar to a computer memory. The difference between the two is that human memory is multidimensional and not dependent on physical materials. Your memory goes beyond the physical cellular structure into a realm where all experiences, both of your personal life and all other experiences of the *whole of life*, are recorded. It is similar to a hologram.

A hologram is a photographic methodology that can, by the use of laser beams, record a three-dimensional (3D) image onto a photographic plate. You may have seen holographic photographs in museums or even on key rings and other trinkets. When you look at them, there is an exact 3D image. You can, even in the more complex ones, see some movement in the image as you move your viewing position. Sometimes it is a ballet dancer turning, or a man winking at you. In others, the image can "hang" in space in front of the film.

The most interesting thing about holograms is that if you break off any tiny piece of the photographic plate and project light through it, the whole of the original image is contained within it. However small a piece you break off, it still contains every detail of the original image. In other words, the whole is contained in any one of its parts.

Many physicists now theorize that the Universe is, in fact, one giant hologram, and that if you had an instrument that could examine each part of it, you could discover the whole Universe in a tiny fragment. Imagine that! In one cell, you could find every single thing that exists.

Strange and unlikely as this may seem, this is the exact teaching of the great sages of all cultures and ages. Their single statement is that the Universe is within you in all its fullness. They say if you look within, you will find everything else.

This is exactly the same with your memory. It literally contains every single event and circumstance, not only of your own life, but of all life. From the Big Bang, the so-called beginning of the Universe onwards, everything has been remembered in the Universal memory, and the Universal memory is within you. Carl Jung, the great psychiatrist, termed this the "Collective Unconscious." How this can be is explained thoroughly later in the book.

The part of the memory that most people are familiar with is the personal memory, and really only a tiny portion of it. Even so, the deeper memory is within you at all times and has recorded on it all the aspects of creation and, most relevantly, every aspect of your own past from conception onwards.

Your memory's giant filing system has stored all the various bits of information in its own logical way. It may file under any of the senses, under an emotion, a feeling, an idea. and so on. Perhaps you have had the experience, when you were young, of smelling lavender at your grandmother's house and then 40 years later, when you smell some lavender again, all the memories come rushing back; or when you meet an old friend that you haven't seen for years, all the memories of the times you spent together return to the surface.

If your memory stores the lavender smell under a file that is labeled "pleasant experiences," then lavender will always be that for you. If it stores the accumulation of wealth under a file called "guilt," then you will find it extremely difficult to make any money. It is the label under which things are stored that can have a profound effect on your life.

It is well known that when people get older, they can remember details of their early life with great clarity. They can access things long forgotten that suddenly come back. This is because the memory is a filing system, and you can pull out any drawer you wish, whenever you want to, when you know how.

These memories are not powerless. Never underestimate them. They form themselves into particular patterns that totally control your life. What we need to examine next is how this happens. After all, if you are being controlled by some mechanism that you are not conscious of, then you are a victim to its whims and its functioning. It is far better to understand it and reform it in the way that delivers to you the results you want, rather than be bound into experiences that are unfulfilling.

To understand this concept, you need to start at the very beginning of your life.

❖ ❖ ❖

CHAPTER 13

HOW YOUR LIFESCRIPT BEGINS

In the Womb

From the moment you are conceived, you have the ability to store memory (many people are concerned with past lives, but we shall leave a discussion of that topic until later). So we will now progress from conception as the starting point of your physical existence.

It is now quite possible to regress yourself, usually with the help of a facilitator, back to not only your birth, but also to the time of conception and the following nine months. Everything is remembered and stored, even from those earliest times. Each cell has its own memory that is connected to the mind. Your mind exists, remember, prior to your birth, as the blueprint of your physical body. Your physical body grows into the shape that it does because of the pattern held in the mind. This is why people can remember things in the womb prior to having a brain formed. The brain is only the vehicle that your memory/mind occupies.

The growth of your body within the womb is a powerful—perhaps the most powerful—time for conditioning the subconscious. Your system is so sensitive, so aware, that it picks up on anything and everything. There are many examples of people who have been hypnotically regressed to a few months prior to being born and who have been able to report, while in a hypnotic state, their parents' actual conversation, word for word, which they could hear through the wall of the womb. Every mother knows that her baby is alive while in the womb and is communicating with her. The wiser mothers communicate with the infant by talking to it in loving and positive ways. As has been seen in many studies, the growing baby and the mother are one being, feeling the same things and experiencing the same experiences. If the mother eats spicy food, the baby suffers. When the mother is emotional, the baby feels the same feelings, be they positive or negative. What the mother thinks also passes through the baby's mind and is retained there by the baby for its entire life.

Not only do you take in memories and file them away, but you also *draw conclusions* about what is happening. This might seem extraordinary, but you only need to be regressed through one of the vast variety of methods available today to prove it to you. Some of these techniques will be revealed as we progress through the book.

You are literally coming to conclusions and forming beliefs about what is happening and what life is all about, even while growing as a fetus. These are pre-rational beliefs, in that you don't think them through; instead, they are immediately taken as facts. Everyone has them. In fact, it is impossible to live as a human being without them.

These conclusions about what is happening to you can even develop as complete beliefs prior to birth and influence your whole life. A man I know well, let's call him Bill, had the following experience: his mother was in a marriage that she did not like, in fact, she was constantly thinking about how she could get out of it. It was impossible for her because of financial problems and the fact that she had two other young children. She then got pregnant again (with Bill). She regretted the pregnancy, but because she was a Catholic, she could not obtain an abortion. Her beliefs wouldn't let her.

Seven months into the pregnancy, she was walking along the street and slipped and fell and landed heavily on her abdomen. The first thought that came into her mind was: "Thank God, the baby's dead." This thought was also experienced by the growing baby, Bill, and went into his memory bank. It was a very powerful input for him. The threat of death, coupled with the emotions felt by his mother and what he perceived as her desire to reject him, locked deeply into his mind. It stayed there in his memory banks and eventually contributed to him forming a belief about women. Later in life, he realized he had drawn the conclusion that if he allowed himself to become close to a woman, she would kill him. All this was at a subconscious level so, for a long time, he had no conscious knowledge of it. Bizarre as this may seem, the resultant events in his life were even more extraordinary.

He grew up, totally unaware that this belief was in his subconscious, motivating the way he entered into relationships. He would never involve himself with a woman who was likely to be available for a long-term relationship. He always found women who were either traveling and would be returning to their native countries soon, or were involved with other men whom they would then go back to, or were just short affairs—in other words, temporary relationships. This pattern continued until he was in his late thirties. At this time, he decided that he did want a permanent relationship, and soon a woman appeared in his life.

Now, this woman had her own issues to deal with, and it took them a year to commit to each other. Even so, Bill found that he was not able to get close to her, to surrender and open himself up completely. Something was blocking him. He then put into practice one of the techniques that I taught him to allow him to open to a deeper relationship with this woman. (The technique is called Vibrasonics, and it is detailed later on.) He had the following experience:

He was lying on the couch in his living room after having practiced the technique, and he fell into a dreamlike state. In this conscious dream, he saw himself get up off the couch (he actually stayed there physically), walk out of his front door, and cross the road. As he performed these actions, suddenly there was a car right in front of him that was about to hit him and probably kill him. He was able to jump clean over the top of the car. As soon as he landed, he felt relief, but then there was suddenly a huge bus bearing down on him that was going to crush him. He could not escape. In that split second, he had a dramatic realization: if he loved this woman, he would die. He awoke, startled by the arousal of this deep-seated memory. He then very clearly remembered the experience with his mother when she was seven months pregnant that had precipitated this belief. He later recounted that the realization suddenly flashed into his mind, like a jigsaw puzzle with all the pieces interlocking together at once. From that day on, he was able to open up to the woman in his life, and today they are one of the happiest couples I know.

In the womb, we also take on our mother's and father's attitude towards us. What they thought and felt when they learned that they were about to be parents had a profound effect on our minds. If our parents were happy, this thought enters your mind and makes you believe that you are welcome in life. If they were unhappy or disappointed about your upcoming arrival, or didn't care either way, then this thought process is recorded and will *influence the beliefs you have about yourself.* How your parents related to each other and what they talked about made a huge impact. Negative behaviors can do as much damage as a mother or father who smokes, drinks alcohol, or takes illegal drugs during conception and pregnancy. A conscious mother is the most wonderful and useful being you can have. She has so much power to create your life. If you are a mother, then this next story will be of great interest to you.

A woman got pregnant and decided to give her child the best opportunity that she could. She used mind techniques to create her baby in a way that would give the child the happiest and most fulfilling life that it could have. She wanted a baby girl with curly blond hair, who would be intelligent, loving, friendly, successful, and so on. She decided to fill herself with as great a variety of positive inputs into her mind that she could, so that it would give the baby a rich and varied experience of life while it was still growing in the womb. She would go to the best plays, listen to beautiful classical music, see the most inspiring films, visit art galleries, museums, heritage buildings, see wildlife, read the finest literature, and so on. She filled her bedroom with statues and pictures of the most beautiful women and would devour all the information that she could on the latest and most important discoveries in science and current affairs. She would talk to her growing baby, telling it how beautiful, intelligent, thoughtful, wise, strong, and healthy it was.

Every moment she could, she constantly fed positive energy into her growing child. Eventually, that baby was born. And do you know who that baby was? Shirley Temple, the child film star, now Shirley Temple Black, one of the finest ambassadors of the United States—an extraordinary woman who has provided immense pleasure to millions of people, and who has also developed into a highly intelligent human being, making a real contribution to society through her diplomatic work. She is also often mentioned as a possible President of the United States. Her mother must have done something right!

You can accomplish the same feat with your own children.

Memory remembers and acts on everything that comes into it. So, be certain that what you put in is useful and positively creative for your children. And, of course, it does not stop there, because the next stage can have a most profound effect on the baby and, therefore, the whole life of the individual. Be prepared, in the next chapter, for a revelation that will give you a tremendous understanding, not only about yourself, but about our whole society and why it has developed as it has and how we can change it to become a "Heaven on Earth," a place for continual absolute happiness, rather than the confused, violent, and war-torn place that it is at present.

CHAPTER 14
===

MOLDING YOUR DESTINY
===

Your Arrival on Planet Earth

Your attitude about life is something that is reinforced and sometimes totally created in the very first few hours during and after your birth. The treatment you receive upon arrival is so important, so vital, that it can totally control what happens in your life from then on. It can limit you or free you, make you dimwitted or intelligent, creative or dull, powerful or weak, rich or poor, sexually free, or blocked. If you understand and integrate your birth experience, then you will release many blockages that at present might be hindering you from creating for yourself a most excellent, successful, and enjoyable life.

Anyone considering having a baby should study very carefully the content of this chapter, as should anyone, professional or otherwise, who is involved in the process of birth. If the following material is not understood and applied where appropriate, if we continue to bring our children into the world in the way that we traditionally have, then we will only repeat the patterns of the past, programming the same old negative conditioning into our babies, which results in the turmoil and confusion that we currently have in much of the world.

In this present day, the human race is moving slowly towards a more fair and equitable life for everyone, even though we still have areas of ignorance and violence. Much of this progress is on a political level. But what is rarely considered when examining the "big picture" is that the individuals, rather than the organized groups, make up our society. Societies are only collections of individuals, and it is bizarre that this is so often forgotten. If we clear the problems from the individuals, upgrade their lives, and show them the way to happiness, society will quite naturally be transformed. Individual transformation is the solution to the vast majority of society's problems. If the process of birth could be corrected and given the attention it needs, then a giant percentage of human difficulties would disappear in the following generation, because you would be creating people who are not traumatized at the beginning of their lives.

The relevance that the process of birth has to you personally should not be underestimated. What happened to you in your own first few hours of life has, without any question, been a major contributing factor in molding you into what you are today, with the opportunities and talents you have. Your career prospects, wealth, relationship abilities, and creative skills are all tied in with those first formative hours. Fortunately, any bad experiences here can be changed, even if the events of birth were highly traumatic.

The Birth Process

Let's look at how the normal birth process has taken place in Western countries in the last 50 years, which would have affected most adults alive today. Nowadays, many mothers go to classes where they are often told about, or are even shown, the most horrific videos of the various types of delivery, including forceps births. This is a particularly ugly sight in which the baby's head is gripped by metal clamps.

The viewing of these blood-filled documentaries is a totally unexpected event for the pregnant women. It fills many of them with fear about the whole process. This is part of the mentality of disempowering the mother so that she becomes pliant to the needs of the medical staff, rather than her own intuition. For there is no better way to take control of people than by filling them with fear and then presenting yourself as the solution to that fear.

The birth normally takes place in a hospital. Greeting the baby's arrival is a group of people, mostly medical staff, who follow the accepted procedures that they have been taught at a hospital, college, or university. The mother is rarely made to feel that she is in charge of the process. She has become a *patient*, even though she is not sick, and has therefore handed over control of her life to the "professionals."

The great danger with the production-line approach to the birth of a new human being is that the baby is not treated—except in rare instances—as a person, but more as a "thing" or an "object." It is not respected as an individual with feelings and reactions identical to an adult's. Because it can't speak, it seems to have few reasons to be considered as a responsive and sensitive being. People who have regressed back to the time of their birth confirm that they are fully aware of what is going on, and they have all the feelings and emotions that a normal adult human being has. This is why it is vital to treat a newly born person with intelligence, and as someone who has yet to develop the ability to communicate rationally.

Unfortunately, the baby's arrival is rarely greeted with a feeling of warmth and love. It is more a "medical procedure." The arrival of an infant needs to be considered totally differently than the way a sick child or adult patient is treated. A baby's birth is not a problem, an illness, or a disease. It is an opportunity to greet another human being with respect, gentleness, and love.

This point needs to be impressed firmly into the heads of all those responsible for bringing new people onto the planet. Without a change at this level, we will be continuing to add to society's problems. The small percentage of problem births, where some medical action is needed, should not cause those necessary actions and attitudes to become the normal procedure for all births.

The First Journey

As the baby leaves the womb, it pushes its way down the birth canal and pops out into the world. Until it begins to exit from the mother, it has been living in a warm bath of fluid with all its needs taken care of. It had to do nothing for itself apart from grow, which is an automatic action not requiring conscious effort. Suddenly, it is taken from this liquid security and thrust out forcibly along the birth canal. This experience can be difficult, for it is a struggle to proceed along the birth canal. You are being squashed and squeezed and are, as always, drawing conclusions about what is happening. Many people actually come to decisions such as "Life is an unpleasant struggle," or "It is so difficult to live," or "I have to use all my strength to survive." You might find it hard to believe that newborn babies can come to conclusions. To prove it, you only have to try it out yourself, with the techniques I will explain later in the book.

Inside you right now are decisions you have made about this first journey, and these are at the foundation of your memory, often dictating your life experience. Because if you have at the base of your subconscious a belief that says "Life is an unpleasant struggle," then every time you are presented with an opportunity in life that would be easy, enjoyable, and might create lots of money or open doors to more creative self-expression, you would be forced to say, "No, thanks," by your choice mechanism, because such a positive experience would not correspond to your initial programmed belief. If, on the other hand, you were presented with an opportunity in life that offered struggle, unpleasantness, and difficulty, you would then say, "Yes please," because it would match your patterning. Further on, we will explain in more detail just how this works. First, let's get all the facts together.

The Birth Itself

After the journey down the birth canal, the baby emerges from its mother. Sometimes it is removed with the help of forceps. This means it has metal prongs, like big scissors, clamped to its head as it is dragged out of its mother. The delivery room is well lit, too bright for its young eyes, which have only known darkness. There are the medical instruments and strange (to the baby) smells. There are people doing all sorts of things and giving instructions to each other in loud (to the baby) voices. After emerging fully, the baby is picked up, held at odd angles, sometimes even upside down, the umbilical cord is cut, and it is wiped clean of blood. The fluid is coughed from its tiny lungs, and it is forced to gasp in the cold air, sometimes even slapped to cause this to happen. It is then weighed on a scale and wrapped tightly in cloth and then (sometimes) given to the mother (who is often drugged) for a look. If it is lucky, the baby is cuddled. After a short period of time, the baby is then picked up again, taken away from its mother, and placed on a cot on its own, usually totally freaked out. Welcome to planet Earth!

The above experience is one that is had by many people who have regressed themselves to their birth through hypnosis or a technique called rebirthing. It is also witnessed by those who are present at births.

This is considered normal and healthy. Normal birthing procedure is a very strange practice, almost perfectly designed to cause trauma in the newborn infant. It certainly locks into the infant's memory a series of very negative and fear-filled conclusions that can poison its life experience entirely.

Consider how you would react if this happened to you today. How would you feel if you were up to your neck in a thick swamp and someone took a giant pair of metal clamps and grabbed you by the head and dragged you out into the cold air. You were then hung upside down by a giant and slapped, coughing out the liquid that was in your lungs, grabbed and swung around a room filled with extremely bright strobe lights and people shouting at the tops of their voices. As you cried out in total fear and confusion, everyone ignored you and you were wiped with a rough cloth and wrapped tightly in another one, weighed on a giant dish that dropped suddenly and unexpectedly as you were put on it, and then left on your own in a completely strange, totally unfamiliar and scary environment. You would need years of therapy to recover from the trauma. You could probably sue everyone concerned and live for the rest of your life on the proceeds of the court case. But this is what an ordinary birth is like for the average person—let alone what happens when there are complications, such as a breech or problems with the umbilical cord. Babies, of course, can't sue for damages, as they can't speak and give testimony about mistreatment. If they could, it would be interesting to see how the birth process would change rather rapidly.

Imagine the conclusions you would draw about life if you went through an experience like the one detailed above. You would have "core" beliefs like "It is dangerous to be alive," "People here don't care about me," "My feelings and reactions are irrelevant," "What a horror, get me out of here," "I must keep still so they don't attack me again," and so on. These conclusions are lived out in so many people's lives because the choices that come into your conscious mind are sourced from your subconscious. So if, for example, you have within you the thought, "People don't care about me," you may very well create that in your life.

This is the mindset, the way that the majority of people's minds are formed, in our society. That planet Earth is not a safe and welcoming place, is the basic underlying belief system. And our lives are lived accordingly. We cover over this belief and hide it deeply from ourselves, behind the closed door of our subconscious minds. How did this happen? How did we darken and make dangerous the birth process, which is the most important event in our lives? How did something that could be so pleasant and enchanting become the psycho-emotional horror, with its ghastly life-long side effects, that it has?

The Ancient Logic

To understand why this is the case, all we need to do is look back to our ancestors. For there is always a practical or seemingly logical reason behind the most extreme social madness. The reason for making birth what it is today is based on a very sound and rational conclusion. Irrelevant now, of course, but still the start of the conceptual lineage that has brought us our present-day methods of infant delivery.

Thousands, even in some cases, hundreds of years ago, most people lived a tribal life. They were constantly under threat from other tribes and wild animals. For the tribe members to survive, there was a need for brave and aggressive warriors to fight and protect them and to hunt the animals they needed. The greatest warriors became the chiefs. So the question was, for the ancient tribespeople, "How do we make our men into strong and aggressive warriors?" This was a very obvious and wise survival mentality. Strong warriors offered the best chance for the tribe's survival.

In nearly all cultures and societies, remnants of this philosophy can be seen today. It was quickly discovered that the strongest warriors and fighters were those who were the most aggressive. It was this aggression that drove them to become fierce and cruel and to put fear into their enemies. Aggression is stored anger that longs for an outlet. This is what comes out in war when soldiers rape, torture, and kill.

The simplest way to make a person angry or, put in another way, not at peace with themselves, was by bringing anger into their lives as early as possible. The easiest way to permanently disturb someone's psyche was by separating them from their mother immediately at birth. Anger, remember, arises when you can't have what you want, and a newborn baby really wants and needs its mother. So, to create the warriors, the babies were separated from their mothers immediately after they were born. The tribespeople had learned from experience over generations, that it was these babies who became the most aggressive.

In many parts of the world, immediately after birth a baby was taken from its mother and denied the colostrum, the earliest secretion that comes from her breasts. Colostrum contains huge amounts of antibodies, so it is something very precious. In its place, the baby was given either honey or a mixture of herbs, and was denied the breast, for sometimes as much as two or three days. The belief was that this "cleansed" the baby. The ancient tribespeople had convinced themselves that colostrum was in some way bad for the baby. Why nature would have put poison in a mother's breast that would endanger a baby's life never occurred to them as being a ludicrous or absurd idea. The tribal traditions were simply followed.

What these processes of denial of the breast did was to disrupt the bond between mother and child. By disturbing this bond, the baby became frightened, angry, and, therefore, aggressive. This anger remained within the child's subconscious and could be expressed very effectively during the activities of fighting and hunting. Anything which is suppressed is always longing to come out, and will do so when the opportunity makes itself available. The aggression-loading in these ancient cases was expressed in a socially useful way, even though it lead to an unhappy, frustrated, and loveless life for all concerned.

This misguided act of separating the baby from the mother also had tremendous ramifications with respect to the way men treated women later in life. For, that initial anger was felt against the mother and, therefore, women in general. Even so, the mothers, sisters, and fathers of the greatest warriors were all made more important by being related to them and were probably unaware of the effect of the separation after birth, which they accepted as sensible and normal. Their own position in the social structure rose, so it was in their interests to contribute in whatever way they could to ensure that the boy became aggressive.

One of the few exceptions to this activity were the Pygmies. They believed that colostrum and contact with the mother immediately after birth was good. Interestingly enough, they survived by isolating themselves and lived in perfect harmony with nature. They had no need to conquer it. Like the Australian Aborigines, they saw the land as part of themselves, not something to be destroyed and mastered. Unfortunately, civilization has now driven them from their own forests, and they are falling into the traps of the so-called developed world.

The other major goal in early tribes was to dominate other species and other groups of humans, their own survival being the motivating factor. This attitude has lived on in our present-day culture, and it is why we are living in the horrendous environmental nightmare that we are. The feeling of being separate from nature arises primarily from the separation from our mothers during those vital first few days. (For, we are actually being separated from "mother nature" at the same time as being separated from our mother. And that which you are separated from is obviously *not you* and therefore needs to be controlled in case it controls you, and so, hurts you, and causes you to feel separate and alone once again.)

The Intelligent Approach

Look at the difference that the more enlightened doctors and midwives are now making with regard to delivering babies: the mother is placed in a special birthing center, which is more like a bedroom than a hospital. The lights are dim, the atmosphere friendly. Quiet, inspirational music or sounds of the ocean or nature are played softly. The staff is friendly and natural, rather than "playing" the role of being medically efficient. The mother is given the feeling that she is in charge of what happens, and it is the baby who is the center of attention, rather than the doctor or midwife. This empowering of the mother is very important. The baby, when born, is placed on the mother's chest before the umbilical cord is cut. It lies there and, in its own time, the fluid from its lungs pours out. The baby then takes its first breath and looks around to see where it is. It often finds the mother's nipples of its own accord. It is now the baby who is in charge of what goes on. The more intelligent and sensitive staff are in tune with the baby's needs and are able to see what it wants. It rests there on its mother's chest, and then the cord is cut. The skin contact is vital if the baby is to be able to live a totally healthy and happy life. The mother will know when the baby is ready to be washed and happy to be left on its own to sleep.

This is a much more sensible way to bring a baby into the world. How different from the way it normally happens. It is desperately important for our society and, in particular, the medical profession, which has the power to totally overhaul our method of bringing babies into this world, to change the birthing process. There are a few doctors who do employ this more caring approach, but they are still rare. Having made a series of educational videos on birth and infancy, it seemed to me that some of the doctors were more interested in making things more convenient for themselves. Their concern was a role they played. Others often induced—that is, brought on the birth early, because they didn't want to be disturbed in the evening, or they were going away for the weekend. Again, I emphasize that most doctors do take their responsibilities seriously, and perhaps the above-mentioned examples are the rarities. But many mothers feel that these are more prevalent than one would expect.

Water Birth

Another birth procedure gaining a lot of attention is the water birth. We have a neighbor who has given birth to four children while crouching in a warm bath. The baby slips out easily and painlessly into the water, and the mother brings it to the surface. Her children are all remarkably free of neuroses. A young woman recently had a child by this method, and her mother called and told me that the birth was easy and effortless, completed with a minimum of labor, and that the baby was extremely happy. The baby had not cried once, it slept soundly, and only gave a little whimper when it was hungry.

Water births are popular in Russia, where a lot of research has been accumulated on how successful and positive for both the mother and the baby this method is. We need much more research on this vital subject. The goal of birth should not only be that the baby arrives alive and physically healthy, but should also take into account the emotional and psychological state of the infant. For, physical problems can be seen and healed, but emotional scars can remain hidden for a lifetime, and so, limit people's happiness dramatically.

A Comfortable Position

Incidentally, there is an interesting story of how the present-day method of having the woman lying on her back to deliver her baby originated. In older times, and this is still seen today in Third World countries, the mother crouches, rather than lying on her back. The baby is then free to come out, following the laws of gravity. Many native women would literally keep a cloth tied under them, in case of the baby's unexpected arrival. It is so much easier and less painful for the woman to be able to crouch, rather than have to force the baby out while lying on her back.

It is said that this method of lying down, as well as the use of forceps, originates with one of the French kings. He wanted to observe the arrival of his child, but because he was a king, he could not lower himself by bending over to watch as his wife crouched. So the poor woman was laid on her back, with her feet in stirrups, and the doctors had the first forceps made so that they could use them to grab the child by the head and pull it out for the king to see easily. Neither the woman, nor the baby, was taken into consideration—only the comfort and position of the king!

Whether this story is true or not is unimportant. Obviously someone at some stage caused women to lie on their backs and introduced the concept of forced delivery.

If we want to de-brutalize society, then we must start at the beginning with the birth procedure. Many people are totally affected by their birth trauma for life. This mindset affects all parts of their lives. Self-expression, sporting and artistic skills, the ability to communicate effectively, personal power, and so on, can all be limited and sabotaged by the programming that is absorbed at this most vulnerable time. To become absolutely happy requires you to dissolve any fears associated with your birth.

This is why we often hear from the great teachers that you must be "born again." It is a literal statement. It means that you must re-experience your birth, dissolving anything that is hidden or held in your subconscious as a result of it. And let's face facts: we have all been born, so there is something there for everyone.

Next, we will look at the final major input into our subconscious mind, and then we will see how the whole structure dictates our life experiences.

❖ ❖ ❖

CHAPTER 15

BUILDING YOUR OPPORTUNITIES

The Earliest Years

B irth takes only hours to go through, whereas you are an infant for around two years. This is a time of great vulnerability and help-lessness; you require assistance for nearly every action. Food, cleanliness, moving around, amusement, and shelter all have to be taken care of for you. Without help, you would not survive. You cannot com-municate what you want, and if you are lying face down, you often need someone to help you onto your back. All sorts of things are happening to your body as you grow. There is pain from teething, and you have no power to stop this process. People can pick you up and do with you whatever they like, and you can do absolutely nothing about it. Even though there is tremendous pleasure and enjoyment associated with this time of your life, there is also much anxiety and even panic. This nega-tive conditioning is also stored deeply within your subconscious mind.

You may be wondering why it is necessary for us to focus on the negative aspects. It is because these are the patterns that block and inhibit you from achieving your full potential in life and enjoying all the levels of happiness. As you let go of these blocks and release your latent creative and personal power, you will feel as though you have truly woken up, or come alive, for the first time in *your life*. To allow this to happen, it is necessary to define the problem precisely—that is, define what it is that is stopping you from always experiencing absolute happi-ness. Once you have done so, the solution becomes apparent. If you do not define the problem accurately, then you will never be able to discover a solution.

Let's clarify infancy. Imagine how you would feel right now if you were totally helpless and needed people to take care of your every need. It would be frustrating, infuriating, and aggravating. You would fall into sadness and despair at your situation. Life might seem hopeless and not worth living. You would wonder why you were here, why you came to be part of this experience. This situation happens many times to an infant.

It only takes a few seconds for an emotionally loaded memory to be locked into your subconscious and stay there for life. When you are an infant, you can make intensely irrational decisions that motivate and control your experiences forever. You only have to see how some children change radically after a major event happens to them; how they go from being outgoing, bright, happy kids, to closed-off, sulky, and inhibited ones. This can occur even after a fairly minor event in the playground. The same thing is happening to infants, but even when we are around them, we are not as aware of the negative programming going in. And much of it is quickly buried because of the constant demands from other people for them to cheer up and appear happy. We have all learned to quickly put on a pleasant face when it is required.

The Power of the Mother

Your parents' attitude, particularly your mother's, is very important at this time. For the first few months of your life, you see yourself as being totally connected to her. You have not as yet developed the ability to experience yourself as an individual. Her reactions and her treatment of you impact your system very deeply. If your mother does not approve of you, or gives you that impression, it feels as though you are being totally rejected. Because you are so dependent on her for food and nurturing, if she rejects you it could literally mean death for you. This is a very real fear. Her behavior sends constant signals to you, and you interpret them at a very basic survival level, often completely irrationally. If she frowns while feeding you, even though it may be because of something totally unrelated to you (she might be worried about a bill she has to pay), your conclusion about what is happening may be life threatening. You do not have the power of rationality; it has not yet developed. You are reacting at a primal level and taking on board, into your subconscious, your interpretations of what is happening. Deep-rooted beliefs take hold at this time, which influence your decisions, even when you are 70 years old. As always, you are rarely conscious of these beliefs. They just sit there below the surface of your consciousness, influencing your choices in your everyday life.

To illustrate this point, here is a true story:

A woman came to see me who had the following problem. She was married to a wonderful man and had four children. She had come from a wealthy, aristocratic family in England, and she could not feel affection or closeness for her husband or children. There was a feeling of distance, even though there was no apparent reason for this feeling. She came to one of my seminars and practiced a particular technique, which caused her to flash back, in her mind, to when she was a small baby. The scene she suddenly and vividly remembered was one that she had no conscious knowledge or memory of. She remembered, with absolute clarity, being handed to her mother by her nanny. Her mother, who was a titled woman, merely held her for a moment, gave her a kiss on the cheek, and handed her back to the nanny.

In that instant, all the memories that she had buried came flooding back. The woman realized that all through her infancy, her mother had never been close and intimate with her. Her mother never gave her warmth and affection as a baby and always kept her at a distance. She realized that she had made the decision as an infant that she would never allow herself to get close to anyone else in her life. She could not bear the pain of rejection and alienation that she felt in the relationship with her mother. She so longed to be loved by her mother, but it never happened. Her closing down allowed her to protect herself from ever feeling that bad again. This decision remained with her all her life, until she realized what she had done and allowed herself to open up again. Imagine how many events along these lines have affected you and how they have affected your ability to enjoy happiness. By the way, if something has happened to you in your past, don't get into blaming your mother or whoever. It will really reinforce the negative pattern and entrench you in victim consciousness. As you will see later in the book, everything that happens to us is a result of our own desires and needs.

Surviving the School Jungle

Once you leave infancy, you are then thrust further into the world—you go to kindergarten and grammar school, your parents expect you to start doing things for yourself; you become aware that you are an individual, and you also become aware that you are very small and unable to defend yourself against bigger children. For some kids, the school playground is a war zone. It is survival of the fittest. Again, here at school, one interaction, one circumstance, can dictate your future. It could be a threat from another child or a fight. It could be a humiliating experience, where a group of other children laugh at you. It could be an experience of success that boosts your self-esteem and causes you to believe that you are a superior being in some way or another.

When this happens, you often continue with that particular area and make it your life. For instance, if you did well in sports, the praise you received could cause you to follow that path for life. Or, if you were successful in a singing competition or the school play, you could be drawn to an expressive and creative mode of life, such as the film or theater industry. Where you get your acknowledgment is a tremendous motivator for further action in that area. The deep belief that "If I do this, I am appreciated or loved (and so more likely to survive)" is very powerful for one's life choices and decisions, particularly when we are young children, and this belief is absorbed at a pre-rational level.

School teachers also have great control over your future, not so much by what they teach you, but more by how they treat you and react to you in response to what you do. We are all so sensitive, impressionable, and easily manipulated by what they say or do. Usually they are looked up to or feared. In either case, their input into our young minds is extremely powerful. Never forget that it takes only one event to influence you forever. You may have been in an art class, and the teacher, who was in a bad mood that day, tells you that your work is hopeless and that you'll never be an artist. This is a terrible blow to you. You have been humiliated in front of the whole class. You immediately make a decision to never put yourself in that vulnerable position again. You decide to bury forever any artistic or creative expression. That, for you, is the end of creativity for your whole life.

So many people, when they become aware (through the use of the techniques that will be described as we proceed), find that they made the major decision about their lives, which they are still living out, because of what happened in the classroom. Our lives are, in fact, lived out on about four or five major beliefs about ourselves and about what life has to offer. They are based on career, self-expression, relationships, standard of living, and one another, depending on our particular cultural background. Our life decisions are subconsciously run by these check-points before we go in any direction. It is these few primary beliefs that dictate our destiny.

Sexual Confusion

Another area that is only now coming to the surface and being dis-cussed is the subject of child abuse. If you have been abused sexually or physically, it can also send you down a life path, that on later reflec-tion, you would rather not have proceeded upon. Most child abusers have been abused themselves as children, and all they can do is repeat the pattern that was laid down in their own lives. Children are extremely vulnerable to adults, or older, bigger adolescents. If they are unfortunate enough to have suffered from abuse, and apparently a large number of children have, then it is vital to clear it in order to be sexually free. There was an interesting article written by a woman in a newspaper that shows the power of this sort of experience and its effects on a per-son's life.

This woman told the story of how all her life (she was now almost 40), she had been a radical feminist and man hater. Her conscious reasoning for this attitude was intellectual. She had analyzed the male/female power structure and was able to accurately identify the areas where women were underprivileged and taken advantage of. She had joined various groups and had been involved in political organizations trying to force change in society. Her work had contributed to the excellent changes that we now see with respect to the equality of women.

As the years went by, her friends had become interested in personal growth, and she also started attending regular therapy sessions in order to access her own self on a deeper level. To her total surprise and shock, she accessed a memory that had been completely buried when she was seven years old. Her father had come home one night drunk and had raped her. It was a one-time event, never repeated. Nothing was said about it between her and her father. The shock, horror, fear, hate, and pain that that experience provoked was completely buried and forgotten by the girl, but its ability to cause her to make the life choices and decisions that she did, later in life, remained with her until it was brought to consciousness once again. She realized that this horrific experience had been underlying much of her motivation and intellectual analysis about male power. She had been trying to deal with and express an internal problem by projecting it onto the outside world.

Once she had integrated this experience and resolved it, she found that her hatred of men gradually and spontaneously dissolved, and she found that she wanted to enter into a relationship with a man. Her radical feminist drive fell away, and even though she still worked for women's causes, the negative side of her personality with respect to men in general, disappeared. She discovered that not all men were ugly, violent chauvinists. And, of course, she now realized that by holding that negative belief, those were the types of men she had attracted into her life, until she consciously integrated what had happened. In life, you only find what you believe you'll find, whether that belief is conscious or subconscious.

This woman ended up becoming far more effective in her work for women's liberation. She had made a decision at seven years old as a result of that horrible experience, which had translated into her work, attitudes, and life choices for the next three decades. Obviously, this is not to say that all women who apply their energy to women's issues were abused. What it does say is that if there is an extreme motivation for your actions, then you had better look within yourself for the causes. The sexual act holds the possibility of being a nightmare or the most enjoyable physical and emotional experience known to human beings. We will look at it in depth in a later chapter.

How Experiences Become Beliefs

As we have seen, all the various experiences you have been through have been loaded into your subconscious "biocomputer" (a good word for the personal mind), and have been feeding the signals into your consciousness that have caused you to become who and what you are. Your experiences on the screen of your life are nothing more than a result of what is stored within you. They can come from nowhere else. Why what has happened to you has occurred, is a totally logical and explainable and, therefore, understandable process. The really useful question to ask yourself is, "What can I do about it?" Look around at your own life right now and see if you can identify any recurring patterns manifesting in your life. Or, think about whether you hold any beliefs that are hindering you in fulfilling your potential. What beliefs do you hold about life in general and your own opportunities in particular? And what are the beliefs that you hold about the possibility of having a permanently and ecstatically happy life? Our next chapter will clarify for you the way that the whole belief structure works, because it is beliefs that are the cause and the source of your life experiences.

❖ ❖ ❖

CHAPTER 16

BELIEF PATTERNS

The Filing of Impressions

As each of the impressions and events are absorbed by your memory, they are automatically filed away in a precise and totally logical fashion. As mentioned previously, the mind works in a very similar way to a computer filing system. On a computer you can bring up any file you like, just by holding an arrow cursor on the file name on the screen and pressing the button. It automatically activates that part of the computer's memory, and your desired file appears immediately on the screen. The file can then be read and more information inserted into it. It is very similar with your mind.

The impressions and events that appear in your life, as they enter your mind, can be stored under an enormous variety of "file names" in your memory bank. It depends entirely on what the strongest part of that impression was, as to which "file" it is stored under. The mind will also store individual bits of information under a variety of file names, as it is a multidimensional structure. It is constantly working in parallel with a number of aspects of itself. But there is always the main file "name," from which all the stored information can be quickly accessed.

For example, the mind can store impressions under any of the senses, such as taste, smell, (remember Grandma's lavender?) or touch. Or, it can store impressions under a particular person who had a strong impact on you, such as a parent or teacher; or under an emotion such as anger; or under a particular location—perhaps the school you grew up in. It can store impressions under colors, laughter, the ocean, or a sport—in other words, anything at all. And the contents of each of these files has a contributing effect on your choices and decisions.

For instance, let's say that when you were young, there was a back alley behind a house you were visiting and when you went out to it, a large black dog suddenly and unexpectedly appeared and barked loudly at you, giving you a severe shock. From that day on, you will have filed into your memory, "Back alleys are dangerous." Decades later, when you are running late for an appointment and there is a shortcut down a back alley, you will hesitate or even decide to go the longer way along the road, rather than take the shorter route.

You won't know why you do this; it will just arise as a feeling of concern or slight anxiety and cause you to make the decision not to go down the lane. You will probably not even remember the black dog, but in the future, you could even find yourself in the situation of looking at a house to buy 30 years after the dog barked at you. The house could be perfect in every way, but when you go into the garden, you see that there is a back alley. Even though the original incident has long been consciously forgotten, it is still there in your subconscious memory as a belief. It feeds into your conscious mind as "Back alleys are dangerous," not perhaps as an actual concept, but more as a feeling. If it does come up as an actual concept, you may still not be aware of the original experience, but you may justify the concept by thinking that back alleys are dangerous because they can allow burglars an easy entry and exit point. The conscious mind is very clever at justifying an irrational subconscious belief. Whatever way it appears, it will still influence you not to buy the perfect house you are looking at. For an irrational reason, your present life experience has been inhibited and sabotaged. And you are entirely unaware of the cause. The subconscious mind is all-powerful, and if you are not aware of what is stored in there, *it* controls *you*. If you were aware, it would no longer be subconscious, but conscious.

The Chain of Memories

Many impressions, such as the fearful black dog incident, have a charge of blocked emotional energy tied in with them. What you also find is that all events that involved anger can often be reactivated when you feel and express anger about something totally unrelated.

For instance, you have probably had the experience where you are expressing anger, and a whole lot of other things that have made you angry and which you haven't expressed before flash before your mind. You might be raging at someone at work who has let you down, and after you have finished, or even during the outburst, you will remember events from the past that angered you. You may even express the anger that you felt about them, as well, and phone the person involved and blast them down the phone, while you are all fired up.

This is because when you "open the file" marked "anger," it plays out, or makes available to your conscious mind, all the other contents of that file. Blocked emotions are always longing for release. This will happen with any emotion. If sadness arises in a situation, the file of sadness will reveal its contents, even of long-forgotten memories. When you are having a really great laugh about something, then many of those other very funny things that have happened in your life will rise to the surface as you explore and express the file marked "laughter."

This happens because each impression, as it goes into its particular file, is tied to previous impressions that have the same qualities, or at least one of the same qualities. And other impressions, as they enter in the future, are automatically slotted into the file that is relevant to their content. So, they are all available at any time you open the particular file in your mind.

This is exactly how belief structures originate. We experience an event, the impression goes into our mind, we form a conclusion about it, and sometimes an attitude develops immediately. We then experience several other events that fit the same criteria (even though a single powerful one can be enough), and these also become stored in the same memory bank, with their emotional loadings.

It is these groups of similar memories and impressions, which form patterns based on their content, that become what we call "beliefs." The content has, at its base, conclusions and decisions about life you made at the actual time the original experience happened or that developed after a few incidents occurred. Unfortunately, these conclusions may sometimes be completely incorrect and even ludicrous, such as "Back alleys are dangerous."

Beliefs Are Assumptions About Reality

Never forget that the beliefs you hold are only assumptions about reality. Test them carefully in the clear light of rationality and evidence. Be willing to bring to the surface of your mind your belief structures about who and what you are. (Techniques to help you with this process will be given later on.) Many people hold strong convictions about what life is and what they know, even when these convictions are based on misinformation, erroneous conclusions, and negative emotions.

To hold on to a belief or conviction and behave in a way that is not delivering the results you want in life can never lead to happiness. The beliefs will have to be changed, or you will have to let them go. It is our beliefs that motivate and dictate our entire lives, by sending to our conscious minds the decisions and choices that then become our life experiences. An unexamined belief structure, the attitude of believing that whatever is heard in one's own mind is "the truth," is a sad and sorry way to live. Belief patterns will be played out forever, whether they are accurate or deluded. The best way to examine them is to check your outside world. Is it working? Are you successful? Can you achieve your goals? Are you expressing and receiving love and respect? If not, why not? There must obviously be something wrong with your beliefs. After all, they run your life.

What is also important to remember about this process of accumulating beliefs is that it is not so much *what happens* to us that affects us, but more *our reaction* to the experience and the *conclusion that we then draw* from what has happened. It is the conclusion that holds the power, particularly when it is associated with a blocked emotion.

An example of this is the following: two children are playing in a football game at their school one afternoon. They both make an identical mistake in passing the ball during the first half. At halftime, the coach chastises them both in exactly the same way. He says to each of them: "What a hopeless player you are; that was the worst pass I've ever seen. You'd better forget about getting anywhere in football if you're going to play like that!"

The first child is crushed and concludes that he does not have any athletic ability. He begins to form a belief that prevents him from playing any sort of sport or doing any physical activity because of fear of humiliation. This one experience sends him "into his head" as his means of expressing himself. He might become a bookworm and stay away from any physical activity whatsoever when he grows up.

The other boy, however, comes to a different conclusion. He knows he is a good player, and just because he makes one mistake he is not going to change his opinion of himself. His conclusion is that the coach is a fool; so, the boy's life continues in a physically expressive way. He, unlike the first boy, is unaffected by the coach's insensitive outburst.

It is the *conclusion*, not the event, that is important. What conclusions have you made about your abilities in the various areas of your life? If you are uncertain what is in your memory, look around and check out your life. This will quite clearly show you what you have stored in your subconscious mind.

All your actions are always checked subconsciously against the beliefs appropriate to them before you take any action. You are bound hand and foot by your beliefs. Your destiny is controlled by them.

So many of our beliefs are formed around our attitude to sexuality. People's beliefs about this subject are myriad and varied. There is no more powerful block to free-flowing sexuality than the beliefs we hold about it. This is because the content of our mind controls our sexual activities, and the controlling factors of our minds are our beliefs. But before we get to that, there are some other important pieces in the jigsaw puzzle of our mind that we will look at first, which can also block our happiness. You need to understand these thoroughly before you are able to grasp the essence of sexual freedom and the way to lead a completely successful life.

❖ ❖ ❖

CHAPTER 17

OVERCOMING EMOTIONAL ADDICTIONS

The Power of Feelings

The motivating factors in many, if not all, people's lives are their feelings and emotions. Humans are essentially beings who are entirely motivated by these two factors. We do things because of how they make us feel. Whatever the feeling, be it happiness, fulfillment, excitement, passion, love, personal power, tranquility, and so on, it is always feelings and emotions that drive us.

Sometimes there is a distortion in our mindset that causes us to subconsciously seek negative emotions. We may unknowingly create events, circumstances, and relationships that cause negative emotions to arise within us. The reason for this is very straightforward, even though the effects have unpleasant ramifications for our entire lives. This is an unavoidable result of the way the mind works. To find the cause of it, we first have to look to the home we grew up in.

The Foundations Are Laid at Home

When you are young, home is the entire focus of your life. It is the place where you receive nurturing, food, shelter, company, security, and so on. In essence, it is the place that *ensures your survival*. Survival is, of course, the *primary drive* in life. It pushes your choices and actions from the deepest level of your bodymind. Rarely do we feel the strength of this drive in our everyday life.

For example, some people say they are not frightened of death. This misplaced confidence comes from the fact that they have never been in a situation where death is staring them in the face. They only have to be trapped underwater in a big wave and feel that drowning is imminent, or be in any other situation where they are about to die, such as hanging off the edge of a cliff, to suddenly feel the fear and the power of the survival instinct rise to the surface and overcome their intellectual fantasies of being free of the fear of death. The terror that arises enforces, in no uncertain terms, that the survival instinct will overpower any intellectual concepts. In healthy people, the need to survive rules the psyche, and it is even more profound and powerful in children, who have not yet developed the intellect to overlay this basic instinct.

Home represents survival. Even if the atmosphere is unpleasant, it is still the symbol of survival. Each home has its own atmosphere, or vibrations, which are a result of the interactions and energies of the people living there. This is recognized as the *feeling* of home. If you were brought up in the calm of a country life on a farm or in a plant nursery, with quiet, warm parents, then the feelings of peace, stillness, and the regularity of the seasons will be instilled in your memory. If your experience was that of living in a bland family, where nothing much happened, where very few emotions were expressed, this will be lodged into you as the most familiar vibration. If your family was lively, with constant excitement and a busy, frantic social life, this will be the vibration you identify with home. If the experience was negative, with emotional or even physical abuse, then you will find that this unfortunate emotional base has also been recorded into your mind.

In a difficult home environment, it is not until children are older that they realize what is happening and leave. At a young age, they tend to accept what is happening, bad or good. When you are young, you have *not yet developed* your rational and logical faculties enough to be able to assess what is actually going on in your life. You take everything for granted and presume that this is the way life is.

It is this energy/atmosphere that becomes familiar to us, and we will always feel the safest and most secure around these vibrations regardless of what they are. This is because you get used to the energies of home. They become infused into your system; they become a part of you. Every time you enter your home, the atmosphere becomes reinforced as the atmosphere of survival. It goes in at a pre-rational level and continues to go in subtly even when you have developed your rational faculties. Whatever the experience of your home life, it is embedded within your psyche, and you will have it there, stored in your subconscious memory banks under a file that is labeled "Survival."

The Primary Motivation

Once you have grown up, you will be addicted to these particular feelings, energies, and emotions. Subconsciously, a pattern has been implanted that tells you that your best chance of survival is by *recreating the atmosphere and vibrations* of your original home, whatever the quality of that experience. You will literally find that you are driven subconsciously by those emotional patterns even though you may not express them in your own behavior.

This drive, in some people, is often so strong and so attached to the base of their psyche, that in some cases this addiction is the actual foundation of the individual's personality. When this is the case, the person will do everything in their power to create a scenario in their lives that will be identical in atmosphere and vibration to that of their original home.

They will subconsciously be drawn to a person or people who also have the desire (consciously or subconsciously), to live with similar energy and emotional patterns. They will be absolutely addicted to these vibrations that appear to them to be safe and secure. The hook is very deep in their mindset. They may even tend to have an air of desperation about them, as they drive themselves to find the external stimulus and security that these energies give them.

Different people become addicted to *different emotions*. Some are addicted to life being a series of problems, because this is what their parents lived out. Others may have a parent who was a tyrant and miser. They will very likely, unless they take absolute responsibility for their lives, find themselves in the company of a tyrant and miser forever, as their marriage partner. These emotional addictions are the *fuel of our beliefs*. They are an integral part of our choices, and all our choices come from our beliefs.

The addictions can be of any variety; they are not only negative or life denying. If we were brought up with peace, calm, and many enjoyable and pleasant energies, then we will feel happiest and most secure in a similar environment and home atmosphere. If we came from a family where the vibrations were full of encouragement, creativity, and laughter, then this is what we will attempt to recreate in our own adult homes.

Whether the vibrations were pleasant or unpleasant, boring or mundane, or filled with exciting events, is irrelevant. Our addictions will match the reality of the circumstances of our own early lives, unless we have consciously made a decision to change them and applied ourselves correctly to that end. To dissolve them requires, first of all, consciousness that they exist, and then the application of the necessary methods and techniques to supplant them with other energies.

The Effect on Your Life

These powerful feelings are like a drug addiction that must be satisfied. In extreme cases, the person seems to crave the emotionally stimulating experiences to such a degree that their life is entirely controlled by this desire.

You probably know people who are always having a drama of one sort or another in their lives. It happens at work or home. There is always something going on that keeps them "hyped up." Or, perhaps you have heard of people whose lives seem to be a continuing series of unhappy events. They have always got a sob story to tell, about how life seems to always give them experiences that aren't enjoyable. They, of course, are never to blame and would be shocked if you suggested that the cause of their unhappiness may be within themselves. The reason for this sort of mentality always begins in early childhood.

Many people also put all their power into playing out the necessary behavior patterns to create the vibrations they are addicted to. This means they will behave in an angry or sad way if that was the atmosphere they were brought up in. This particular addiction pattern will create a life of unpleasantness for themselves and for their own family where they are now the parent. There is an old saying: "The sins of the parents will be visited upon the children." It could also be phrased as: "The emotions of the parents are also played out by their children."

To many people, the home is the most powerful representation, or symbol, of their personal survival. This goes far beyond the "roof over my head" idea. Anything that brings the possibility of losing the home locks straight into the subconscious and becomes a death threat to these types of people.

The breakup of the home, represented by a divorce or separation, can be subconsciously life threatening to some people, and this is why they will even go to the point of violence to hold their relationship together. The threat of the breakup of their family plugs straight into their own need to survive. When something symbolizes life, such as the family, and it is taken away, for a few tortured souls the threat and actuality of their own death arises from the deep recesses of the mind, and a horrible fear overpowers them. Rather than face the fear and deal with it internally, they project it outside onto the world and try to force the circumstances to change so that they do not have to confront their own fear of death.

For most people, though, the addiction is not all-consuming. They have developed their rational minds and are able to control themselves even in extremely disturbing situations, such as the breakup of a family.

Even so, most people are totally unaware of the emotional addiction mechanism that causes them to do what they do. They are not conscious of these addictions even though they have such power over their lives. It all "runs on automatic" for those who are not aware of what is going on. They believe that their feelings and emotions are somehow fixed in cement, and they say to themselves and others, "Well, that's just the way life is," or "That's what I am like; that's the sort of person I am." They accept life at face value, never digging deeper into themselves to see if change is possible. Their fate is also to attract partners who match their parents' patterns and moods, so they can assist with the re-creation of the same atmosphere of their childhood home, be it horrific or wonderful or anything in between.

If it is impossible, for whatever reason, to recreate the required atmosphere at home, then the work environment can be used to fulfill this addiction requirement. People will choose jobs and behave in ways that will satisfy their needs and allow them to play out their addictions, so that these patterns within them still get the attention they require.

Many people find that when they leave home, they rebel and travel and explore life, swearing that they will never live as their parents did. Then a decade later, having settled down, they look around and find that they have *recreated their own upbringing almost perfectly*. It feels secure, and they just accept it. Their early addictions have been played out. It is the emotions that really rule most people's lives, and these early emotions, if left in the subconscious, will draw us powerfully to recreate them later in life.

Most people are *totally unaware* of this addiction factor and spend their lives in some sort of frustration that life isn't turning out in the way they would consciously like. They don't realize that they need to look to their own addictions to discover why they have taken the actions that they have, which have resulted in their present frustrating life experience. *You cannot contradict, with the conscious mind, a powerful drive that is in the subconscious.* You are not conscious of the contents of the subconscious, and anything that you are not conscious of, or aware of, controls you. Anything that you are conscious of, you have the opportunity to control, purely because you are aware that it exists and you can see it and define it and therefore choose not to play it out.

Getting Off the Addictions

Most people *feel fear* if you suggest to them that they examine and let go of their present emotional addictions. This is because these are tied in so deeply with the survival mechanism developed in childhood. Anything that undermines this structure could be equated to death, so quite naturally fear is a normal response. Even though the fear is irrational and even though their life experience is unpleasant or mediocre, they will hang on to these addictions for dear life and avoid leaving the past behind, as it feels secure and safe.

This is why you see people who are physically abused by their partner staying with that person. Even with the horror of such a life, confronting the emotional addiction that keeps them there is too much to bear. It is better, so their subconscious calculates, to be abused and survive, rather than risk death.

Naturally, there are a *variety of other causes* integrated with these decisions; emotional addictions are not the sole reason. But you can be sure that the emotional addictions are a root cause. You must look deeply into your life and see if you are living out an experience that is not as good as it could be, on an emotional level, purely because you are repeating a past pattern that was programmed into you as a very young child.

Nowadays, with the opportunities that our present world offers, many people can get off these addictions while they are relatively young. They can reject the family home and atmosphere if it is life-negating and unfulfilling. The world is their oyster. International travel is easily available, and there are many options on the smorgasbord of life that can give them a taste of other experiences. They can consciously make a decision never to recreate the family home atmosphere again in their lives. Those who are committed to personal growth can always leave behind any negativities and not pass these same experiences on to their own children.

But those who do not work on freeing their own subconscious mind and altering the initial patterns that run their lives, will revert to their past addictions once they settle down, have their own children, and grow older. For the human biocomputer, this mind-body mechanism that we are, can and will only play out what is programmed into it.

Addictions to emotions and feelings are just like any other addiction. A drug addict who wants to get off white powders or smoking has no option but to stop feeding the habit. The primary step is to stop ingesting the drugs. Addicts have to control themselves. In the same way, with negative emotional addictions, you have to stop living them out so you no longer feed them. *You stop "feeding" them by no longer playing them out in your life.* Your own choices and behaviors are brought under conscious control and, coupled with various mind-clearing techniques, you create a different series of programs that will allow you to express your own power and creativity in the most pleasurable and enjoyable way possible.

This is the most intelligent way to live. It results in more and more happiness and also, as we shall see in the next chapter, the freeing of your intuition.

❖ ❖ ❖

CHAPTER 18

FREEING INTUITION

Why We Suppress Intuition

Now let's put the whole thing together so you can see the effect in your own life. Blocked emotions, as explained earlier, require your bodymind system to contract, to hold on tightly, in order to keep the suppressed energies in place. To recapitulate, these unexpressed emotional loadings have an energy value that we measure in units. We spoke of a young girl whose father came home from work one evening and, for the first time in her life, shouted at her. She was unable to express her anger at him because she was frightened, so she suppressed her anger on top of the thought: "Don't be horrible, Daddy"; and underlying this, the other thought: "Why won't you just love me, Daddy." Instead of expressing these feelings, she sulked and went to her room.

This repression of anger has cost her in energy expression. She has to retain the actual value of the anger energy—say, one unit, and she also needs to have a matching amount of energy, another single unit, to hold it in place in her subconscious.

Each suppressed emotion follows the same pattern of energy retention and contraction. Our whole bodymind system has numerous contractions that are required to hold blocked emotions in place, and which we are totally unaware of until we decide to release them. How many times have you suppressed emotions in the past, such as stifled anger or sadness, from infancy to today? Probably countless times. All of them contribute to your lack of personal power, as they are costing you a lot of energy to keep in place.

This holding down and contraction of emotional energy causes you to become a *semi conscious being*. This is where you are unable to retain concentration continuously, or even for an extended period of time. What happens is as follows:

The Digestion of Impressions

As we have discussed earlier, your bodymind system is constantly taking in millions of impressions, some of which have emotional loadings. It processes or "digests" these individual bits of information by storing or filing them into the appropriate memory banks.

A useful *analogy* for understanding this activity is to look at the way you digest food. Normally when you eat, once the food has left your mouth and is on the way to your stomach, you are completely unaware of it. The intelligence within you is taking care of all the processes of digestion and assimilation, without your conscious awareness being involved. You just eat up, and the bodymind does the rest.

If, for whatever reason, your digestion is upset, *your attention is drawn to it*, and you feel a pain in the stomach or intestines. You can no longer ignore the digestive function, as it is impaired. You then take the necessary action, such as taking a medication or fasting, to release the pain so that everything can get back to normal. Once healed, you can then again forget all about the digestive process and enjoy your meals.

It is very much the *same with your mind* and the "digestion" of the millions of impressions that are constantly bombarding you. Here the reality is that you have a problem with the digestion of emotional blockages. The pressure of holding them down, and the energy cost in "units lost" for action and self-expression in the world, combine to drag your attention from the outer world to the inner one, in exactly the same way that your attention is dragged to your digestive system if there is a problem with food.

If you imagine that all these emotional blocks are like beach balls, and you have to hold them below the surface of the sea (that is, your bodymind), you can get an idea about what is going on within you. A beach ball held under water is longing to bob to the surface. So each of the emotional "beach balls" requires the "cap" of equal energy to hold it down. They are constantly trying to push themselves to the surface and so be released. But then you sense temper tantrums or other excessive emotions trying to come up, and you realize that they are not acceptable in the adult world. Therefore, to keep everything in place, you have had to armor yourself with a *powerful personality structure* that can hold everything down and present an acceptable face to the world.

It requires energy to remain conscious, or aware. Normally when you lack energy, you fall asleep until you have built up your resources once again, and then you wake up, ready for action. Because of the constant requirement to store suppressed emotions, you require so much of your energy/attention to hold these "beach balls" in place, that you *slip into a semi-conscious state* even when you are awake. You slip in and out of full consciousness. Your mind is constantly wandering and daydreaming and fantasizing, and you are drawn into its activities. You recognize this, as I mentioned earlier, when you find that you've been reading a book and have gotten to the bottom of a page without having retained anything written there. You have to go back and start again at the top of the page. There is not enough energy available for you to maintain the necessary concentration.

Figure 2: How Emotions Are Held in the Subconscious By the "Caps"

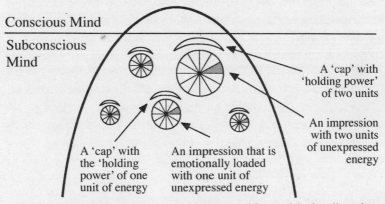

Conscious Mind

Subconscious Mind

A 'cap' with 'holding power' of two units

An impression with two units of unexpressed energy

A 'cap' with the 'holding power' of one unit of energy

An impression that is emotionally loaded with one unit of unexpressed energy

This is the same as when you have a problem with the digestion of food. Your attention is dragged to your stomach, and you are unable to pay as much attention to the outside world as you would if your digestion was functioning normally.

The energy required to hold down the "beach balls" of the blocked emotions within your subconscious mind stops you from having the required energy to retain your concentration fully in the present and to be aware of what is going on 100 percent of the time.

Release Gives More Consciousness

If you are able to release the blockages, the "holding ons" of suppressed emotions, you will have more energy available to remain fully conscious. This is why I always say to people that *"life is a consciousness game."* Becoming more and more conscious is a required activity for anyone who wishes to attain any degree of mastery over their lives. It is all a matter of "waking up."

Much of the chatter you hear in your head, the normal day-to-day thoughts you are familiar with, is the filing away of the constant bombardment of the millions of impressions that you are taking in, which are being processed and filed away by your mind. You are forced into paying attention to this activity, of the normal workings of your mind, because of the lack of energy that results from suppressing unexpressed emotions. You do not have enough energy to stay fully conscious and alert to the outside world, and so you are constantly slipping in and out of full attention in the present and into the workings of your mind. Your awareness is being continually and forcibly dragged to this "impression-digestion process."

When you are completely clear and free of all blockages within your system, there is a tremendous release of energy. You no longer have to expend your energy resources in holding down the emotional beach balls. Your attention ceases to be dragged into the observation of the digestion of impressions. So you quite naturally fall into a permanent state of *full consciousness and intuition.* Your system becomes "in tune with" life.

What Is Intuition?

Intuition is the state where your consciousness is no longer involved with having to pay attention to the digestion of impressions and the actual workings of your mind. In the same way that you are totally uninvolved with the digestion of food when you are healthy, when you are completely free within from any emotional blockages, you are no longer involved with the mechanical workings of the mind. Your mind can then perform its functions without your interference and work at its maximum efficiency and speed. When you are in this state, your mind immediately presents you with the exact information or knowledge you require, without you having to go through or follow the thinking processes. This is called *intuition*. The mind works like a high-powered computer, giving the correct answers instantly. You've "gotten out of the way" by removing the contractions in your system. You have released your energies and so freed up the engine of your mind so that it can operate like the supersonic jet it was designed to be. This "supersonic" mind speed is intuition. It is an absolutely happy state to be in. It is yours for the asking if you clear yourself of all the blockages and delusions that have been conditioned into you and that you, subconsciously, hold in place.

An added benefit of becoming intuitive is that synchronicity also appears in your life. Synchronicity is a wonderful faculty to have. It basically means that you are in the right place at the right time. You tune into life and find that the things you desire seem to appear almost spontaneously. You have probably seen on TV when an interview is "out of sync." The person's lips mouth the words, but the voice is a few beats behind. When the technicians correct the fault, the words and the mouth movements come back into synchronicity. It is very much the same with your life. The buildup of contraction and negativity has, for most people, put them "out of sync" with life. By applying what you are learning here, you will be able to come back into synchronicity. When you do, you will be thrilled by just how easily life works for you. Everything seems to be at your beck and call. It is a very pleasurable way to live.

The Power of Healing

The life force operates in your system with the primary purpose, after survival, of *evolving you*. This manifests in your daily life as your own personal growth and self-expression, and at a microscopic level, as changes to your physical being as a result of the environment you are living in. This can be seen in the long-term time frame, as the difference between Neanderthal Man and present-day human beings. The evolutionary force is very apparent on this physical level. It is almost impossible to see this within the span of a single life, but it can be apparent over a few generations in specific areas. Nijinsky, who was a world-famous ballet dancer, came from five generations of professional dancers, and it was said that the bones of his feet had evolved into something quite different from other people's due to the changes that had taken place in his ancestors' feet over the generations and which had been passed on to him. Because of the power that this new bone structure gave him, he was able to perform the most marvelous dancing the world had seen.

With evolution as its major mode of expression, as its constant desire, life has to bring in another aspect of itself to allow the evolution to take place. Any member of any species that is sick, diseased, blocked to the life force, or out of harmony with itself needs to be cleared and brought into balance and harmony, so that the process of evolution can continue.

The life force always continues to send its energy into each human system to attempt to clear it of its blockages. This is the force known as healing. We are all familiar with it. It is the part of you that will heal you if you cut your skin or have any other experience where healing is required. This healing force does not only focus on physical disease, but also on emotional and psychological blocks, for these have to be cleared out as well.

Life Wants to Clear You

Most therapy is designed to perform the same task: to flush out the past blockages by creating a space where they can be released in a socially acceptable manner. One of the most well-known methods is called Psychodrama, where a group of people play the characters in a group member's past. This creates an opportunity for the person to say to the others in the group all the things he or she had repressed as a child.

For instance, a person may ask the others in the group to play the roles of his or her parents and siblings. The person then expresses to the others, who are playing family members (they refer to them as Mom and Dad and so on), what they are feeling.

By getting into such a psychodramatic situation, the files in the mind are activated, and the old memories are stimulated in the person, and a lot of hidden emotions spontaneously come to the surface. The person is able to say and express emotionally all those things that he or she was unable to express as children and which had been locked in their sub-conscious minds for decades and, of course, which had cost the person in energy to hold these repressions in place. People often feel exhilarated by such a release experience, saying things such as, "I feel that a weight has been lifted off my shoulders."

The evolutionary force works in much the same way. As the healing energy of life pushes into a person's psyche, attempting to clear it, it causes the person to be *attracted to a situation* that closely resembles, or has many elements from, the past experience they have blocked within them. A person who has been attacked by a shark knows that the only way to release the fear is to go back to the sea again. In the same way, Life knows that the easiest method to bring a suppressed memory to the surface is to recreate the experience as identically as possible. The memory itself is then *quite naturally* drawn to the surface. Just like lavender brings all memories of Grandma to the surface, so too does this faculty of memory work in any other situation. It is exactly the same methodology used in Psychodrama.

To give you clarification of how this *whole system controls your life*, let us continue with the example of the little girl whose father came home and shouted at her:

Let's say that this girl, who is harboring an anger block (probably quite a few of them by now) has reached the age of 23. She is, like most others, in a semi-conscious state. This, remember, is the *normal state of consciousness* for human beings; normal in the sense that most people are in it, not normal in the sense of being balanced and in harmony with life.

In her mind, there is this block. Now, remembering that the life force has only one intention: to clear the blocks so that evolution can continue, it therefore brings in its force of healing to try to flush the blocks to the surface.

So, the girl has the life force pushing at the anger blocks, which originally developed from the relationship with her father. She will be attracted to a man who has *similar qualities* to her father, because this will be the *easiest way* to bring the memories to the surface. Maybe he will look like Dad did, or have the same job or hobbies. Maybe he will have the same pronounced accent or have mannerisms and body language similar to her father. He can be young or old. It doesn't matter what the reminder connection is; if there is something strong enough that matches the suppressed memory, the push of the life force will cause that young woman to make a conscious choice to enter into a relationship with such a man, even if she is totally unconscious of the real cause.

Though the drive and attraction come from the subconscious mind, the surface mind is normally *totally oblivious* to this fact and can only justify at a conscious level why she is attracted to this man. The expertise of the surface mind is that it can justify anything it wants to. She will consciously find all sorts of reasons why this man is attractive.

Let us say that she has now found this man who matches her patterns, who has some of the qualities of her father. What will happen is that, after a period of time, perhaps as much as a year or two, she will begin to *feel safe with this man*. This is because of the security of the honeymoon period where lust has been pulsating away, and the two people tend to treat each other as figures of love. This kind and caring treatment will allow her defenses to drop. Remember, the surface personality has been built to hold down and control the subconscious repressed energies. Because the relationship is now a "safe space" where love and caring are the regular behaviors, the structure of her surface personality, which holds down the "beach balls," feels safe to stand aside. This, then, is the signal to her subconscious that it is okay to release the anger held within her.

What the little girl in her wants to say is something such as, "Don't be horrible, Daddy!," and on a deeper level, "Why won't you just love me, Daddy?" But what *comes to the surface first* is not the original concept that went in, but the surrounding anger that has built up and stayed there for years. All the woman feels is the anger; she has no consciousness of the concept during the first arising of the old, repressed pattern. The anger or emotion is "wrapped around" the concept, and it is always experienced first.

If she is not aware of what is going on, she will have no option but to *project that anger* onto something in her life, usually the man in question. She will find some fault in him or his behavior that has never worried her before and "have a go at him" about it. She might even say that he is being "horrible" to her. He will not be expecting this for it has been all love and kisses until now. The honeymoon, being so rudely brought to a conclusion, will probably cause him to react defensively, and he may even get angry with her. This could develop into a full-scale argument.

When this happens—that is, when the two people start arguing with each other and both express negative emotions, the original cause, which in this case is her anger against her father, is avoided. This is because the two people will be projecting their anger onto *something in the present* rather than allowing the past to be released. As soon as you take the attention away from the original cause and project it elsewhere, you can no longer access it.

Even so, the original memory of anger with Dad has been hooked into, and the new mode of expression of anger between her and her partner has *created the opportunity* for her to get to the bottom of her repressed emotion, by expressing it out in full. It has been boiling there for decades and, having opened, the channel is unwilling to close again. The scene has been set for anger to now be an acceptable part of her relationship, one that was previously all love and kisses.

The life force is interested only in removing the blocks to evolution. Now that an initial breakthrough has been made, it *continues to push for* release of the pattern. She is now primed and ready for any opportunity to express anger and lets this man have it whenever he slips up in any way whatsoever. Naturally, he also has patterns that match hers and is playing things out subconsciously as well.

Unless they enter into a conscious relationship, gradually their relationship will deteriorate until they either resuppress the original emotions totally without resolving them, which will reduce the energy available for them in their life, or they will leave each other. Of course, if they do part without having resolved the original block, they will merely remarry or get involved with someone else who has matching patterns, and the whole process will start again. We have all heard of people who have married and divorced and married again, only to discover that they have married more or less the same person. Patterns will repeat themselves until resolved. Most people never resolve them; they just play them out for their entire lives. Think of the patterns in your life. Are there any that repeat? Not just in relationships, but in every area. If there are, then you can be sure that there is a subconscious cause.

Conscious Relationship

What could have happened, in a *conscious relationship*, is that as the anger arose in the young woman, she could have been aware enough to "detach herself" from it and not project it onto her partner. She would not have suppressed it, but would have let it come out without avoiding responsibility for it. Or, the partner might not have taken it personally and not reacted to it defensively and allowed her to release her ire by asking her what is truly going on and drawing her out, letting her express herself angrily so that the underlying cause could come to the surface. She, in the right situation, would have reached the root of the concept that precipitated the emotion and been able to let it out. She would have literally heard her own voice saying, "Why won't you love me, Daddy?" as the child in her finally was able to release the suppressed emotion that was initially locked in at the age of three.

Unfortunately, rarely does this happen. The patterns are difficult to catch. The knowledge of what is happening is hard to come by, and the ability to remain aware, and therefore centered, needs *concentrated development.*

You will experience an *increasing of your consciousness* as you practice the methods taught here, which will help you tremendously in remaining centered and alert to your patterns. It will require dedication in the beginning, but the rewards are richer experiences of happiness and the arising of permanent intuition and, as a bonus, great relationships.

The following chapter explains the primary structure of personality and what you must do to become conscious and dissolve what it is that binds you to the semi-conscious state.

❖ ❖ ❖

CHAPTER 19

BREAKING THROUGH NARCISSISM

Narcissus

Narcissus was a young man in a famous Greek myth. His story is very useful for assisting you in understanding your own mindset.

Briefly, one day Narcissus saw his likeness reflected in a still pond of water, clear as a mirror. He became so fascinated by his image that he became obsessed with it and refused to move. He couldn't take his eyes off himself and eventually starved to death.

What most people do, as a result of holding on to the contraction, is to become obsessed with their own self-image. They also then "starve to death," in the sense that so much of their energy is required to hold the whole mechanism of personality in place that they are unable to be fully alive.

Their attention is constantly being drawn back to their inner life to be sure that the structure of personality remains solid. If too much of their attention, or energy, is called to the outside world, the structure of their inner life is drained of energy and then starts to break down, *allowing the release of negative emotions*. As soon as this happens, their attention/energy is quickly dragged back to their inner life to re-energize the structure, and so, rebury the emotions.

Why it is necessary to be drawn back to the inner life is because the source of energy is within you. When you sleep, you normally awaken refreshed. So, when you have expended too much energy by paying attention to the outside world when awake, you are also drawn within to replenish your energy supplies. This whole attitude of constantly bringing or turning your attention to yourself is what is known as the *Narcissus mindset.*

This whole mechanism becomes a very powerful structure that holds together the person you are. You have the beach balls of suppressed emotion held in the mind. The muscles, ligaments, organs, and all the cells of the physical body are also involved in containing these energies. They literally "grip" and "hold on" to these blockages to keep them in place. They are in a state of permanent contraction, but at a subconscious level. You can feel this if you have a deep tissue massage. The contraction and holding on is absolute; there is no part of the body or mind that is not involved.

On the surface of all this is the armored personality, which layers over the contraction mechanism and presents to the world an acceptable "face." This surface personality is usually totally unaware of what is underneath it. We have become so strongly identified with it as "me" that we consider it to be our self. The personality is the image we create, feed, and require, to keep the whole system integrated and functioning smoothly. It is what is commonly referred to as "ego."

How this manifests in ordinary life is a very familiar, albeit unconscious, reaction. This is truly what the Narcissus mindset is really about. It is this *constant drawing back of attention to oneself.* When you watch and listen to people talking, you can quickly see this happening. Most people are unable to truly listen. They can hear what is going on, but their attention is often inside their own mind, considering what they are going to say next.

You can experience this quite clearly when someone says something, and then the person he or she is speaking to merely responds with something in their own minds, rather than responding to the first person's conversation. Here is an example:

Lunch with the Narcissus Triplets

I was at a luncheon once, which was attended by about 12 people. A man was there who had recently returned from Chile. My wife comes from Chile, and so I was quite interested in what he had to say. Unfortunately, there were some women there who had also been to Chile, who were totally locked into a deep Narcissus mindset. The conversation went as follows:

Man: I visited the mountains and went to try the snow skiing there.

Me: Really, what is it like?

Man: Well, it is really beautiful, and... [He is cut off rudely.]

Woman One: I know, isn't it great? When I was there I did...[She went on to describe her own experiences, interspersed generously with the words *me, me, me*, and *I, I, I*. Eventually, she shut up, and so I asked the man another question.]

Me: Did you go anywhere else in Chile?

Man: Yes, I did. I went down to the capital, Santiago.

Me: What was that like?

Man: It's a wonderful city, but very smoggy; in fact, when... [Once again he is cut off, this time by another woman.]

Woman Two: I know, I know, isn't it so smoggy, that's because it's ringed by mountains. When I was there I went... [She went on and on with another dull tirade about what she had done, also using *me* and *I* over and over. Again, once she stopped, I asked the man another question.]

Me: Did you go anywhere else?

Man: Well, actually, I went to the South; they have the best seafood in the world there. You should see the size of... [Before he could finish, he was interrupted by yet another woman.]

Woman Three: Yes, Yes, Yes, isn't it fabulous? When I was there, I could do nothing else but eat the seafood. Usually what I did was... [And again, we were all presented with another symphony of *I's* and *me's*.]

I never actually heard a single story from the man! All that happened was that these people jabbered on and on about themselves, foghorning their own stories. It was vital for them to do this so they could keep the whole structure of their personality in place.

Learning to Truly Relate

This is quite a common, if not normal, method of relating. Very few people know how to relate in the sense of "bringing out" the other person. To draw someone out and encourage them to speak by your questions and relevant comments on the subject they are talking about is a rare skill.

Talking about trivia does not fall into the category of true conversation. Any fool can discuss what was on TV the night before or what the stories were in the latest gossip magazine. To really relate, which is the only method of connecting with another person, is a skill that requires concentrated development.

Why people are unable to really listen and focus their attention on someone else is because they need their energy to hold their own personality mechanism in place. They have so much negative emotion to hold down. Once they give too much of their attention to someone else by concentrating on them, the call is made to re-energize their own system as they begin to subconsciously feel that the whole structure is disturbed by the lack of energy. By focusing on themselves and talking about themselves or telling their own stories, they are able to save their energy. So, they have no option but to continually draw the attention back to themselves by talking about something to do with them. This is the "me, me, me" or "I, I, I" dialogue.

What someone can do who wants to become more conscious and resist the dragging back of their own attention/energy to themselves and so leave it focused on the person they are talking to is this: breathe consciously and regularly as you listen. Keep the breath going at a normal pace. Don't stop breathing. As the desire comes up to tell your own story or to bring the attention back to you, breathe a little more deeply and remain focused on the other person.

What this does is let the emotions, or blocked energy, slowly steam off" as you continue to give your attention to the other person. This is not a major event, where you start to feel overpowering emotions. On the contrary, the emotions release themselves very easily. As long as you continue to breathe regularly from the diaphragm, you will be able to comfortably control what is going on. If not, then all that will happen is that your automatic reactions will again come into play, and you will find that you have drawn the attention back to yourself in some way or another.

How to Really Listen

Many people actually believe that they are good listeners because they can keep quiet and let the other person "hold the floor" without responding very much. But all that is happening in this situation is that they are *playing* "good listener." It is a role they use to hold everything in place. They are not really giving their attention to the other person. They may be quiet and appear to be doing so, but in reality they are not. Their energy/attention is still on themselves. To truly be attentive means that you respond appropriately to what the other person is saying and draw them deeper into their own expression. Many people who are so-called good listeners actually feel resentful that they have not had a turn, or they feel angry that they are being used as a sounding board.

Another good example of misunderstanding what is happening when people believe that they are really listening is when they are interested in the subject that is being discussed. Because it is of interest to them, it allows their personality structure to be undisturbed. Their mind is constantly flashing back and forth to its own memory banks to contribute to the conversation so that they are continually receiving a boost of energy/attention.

To truly listen means to give of yourself and, therefore, your energy, to someone else, *whether or not you are interested in* what they are saying. If there is no "feed" in it for you, but you continue to pay attention to the other person, you will soon feel the unlocking of the blocks to your own system. This is very useful, as it eventually frees you. After all, a loving person is someone who can give entirely of their energy to someone else, without thought of themselves.

Many people say, when they hear this suggestion of giving completely of your energy/attention to someone else, "But I may end up just listening to someone raving on for hours or being boring." Again, intelligence is required. If you are stuck with a bore who is, basically, a radio without an "off" button, then you can easily move away. In fact, what happens is that if you are truly giving your attention, asking appropriate questions, and are fully conscious, people find it difficult to remain in trivia and want to express themselves at a deeper level. And the deeper level is always interesting. You'll find that you will be able to draw them out by truly listening and concentrating on them.

So this practice of continually drawing attention to yourself by discussing things that are only of interest to you and not being able to truly share a conversation 50-50 with another, is known as the Narcissus *mindset*. It is poison for relationships and a hideous mistake in any field that involves other people, such as creativity and business. Narcissism denies you life and full self-expression. It turns you into a bore.

This is particularly relevant for people who are victims or followers of some charismatic figure, dead or alive. They believe that by denying their own power, they are well adjusted. It is very easy for a Narcissist to hide from their own blocked emotions by transferring the responsibility for their own growth onto someone else. You find a lot of these people in cults and religions. They avoid dealing with their own issues by avoiding responsibility. They focus on themselves as being sinners or not worthy or some other delusion. It is still Narcissism in another of its guises.

The opposite to Narcissism is full consciousness and awareness of what is happening on the highest level of life. This is the realm of intuition and synchronicity.

People who are locked into the various degrees of Narcissism cannot bear criticism. This includes nearly everybody, of course. Why is this? It is, again, very simple to understand.

Why Is Criticism So Hard to Take?

Remember how I explained that when you are young, you see your mother as the source of life: food, nurturing, companionship, shelter, love, and so on. If she gives you a negative vibe (she may scowl or be cross for some reason), even if it is nothing to do with you, it will feel like death because you identify totally with your mother in the first few months of life. If she rejects you, you literally believe that you are dead. And the survival instinct is extremely strong, so you learn quickly, as you grow, to stay on her good side and try to please her.

The step back from rejection is humiliation. We are all aware that if we are being humiliated, then we are also being rejected by whoever is doing the humiliating. Criticism feels like a humiliating experience. If you criticize someone, you are rejecting their behavior or something about them. This can be very threatening.

The whole structure of your personality requires acceptance to be able to remain intact. If you are criticized, this structure starts to break down or, at the very least, become disturbed. This is why many people cannot bear even the slightest criticism. Their foundations immediately begin to wobble.

A Narcissist is affected the worst. The more Narcissistic you are, the more of your attention/energy is required to keep the whole structure in place, because the more emotions you are holding down. Therefore, the more you feel threatened by someone criticizing you, the more strongly you react. You might still control yourself, but you will feel a great deal of anger or fear or some other blocked emotion arising. This is why you find the advice of the wisest masters to always be along the lines of "turn the other cheek." This attitude allows you to become conscious of your patterns, thereby releasing the blockages within you, rather than just reacting negatively to whoever it is that is pushing your buttons.

If you are locked into Narcissism, you are wallowing in stagnation. Because you cannot grow if you constantly have to hold on to everything. Narcissism causes people to contract and recoil from life, from total self-expression. We recoil into ourselves, and so, cut off from the free flow of the life force; we inhibit our nervous system, reduce our personal power and abilities, and often invite disease.

This whole structure of recoil and contraction from life causes us to avoid relationships on some level. We withdraw into ourselves in varying degrees, depending on our particular mindset.

Reactivating Personal Power

The way to reactivate your personal power and free your energy is through relationships—that is, the way that you relate. What this means is that you have to do everything in your power to actually listen to and draw out the person you are relating with. You need to be interested in them and be in empathy with them.

To really be there with the other person causes them to decontract. By really giving them your energy, without having a hidden agenda, allows them to open to you. The more you are there, in the now, with the other person, the more you can grow within yourself.

In fact, your growth is entirely dependent on the amount that you are willing and able to relate to others—to genuinely relate. And the amount that you are willing and able to relate to others is directly intertwined with the amount that you are willing and able to relate with yourself. This is the same as saying that your growth depends on how honest, truthful, and perceptive you are about yourself and your own act in the world and all the games you play in relationships. These are reflected in the particular behavior pattern addictions you have, like "being right" all the time, domineering the people you relate with, or resisting being loving.

One of the worst things of all is not letting your partners express themselves truthfully without them fearing your reactions to that free expression. This means that they are imprisoned by the lines you draw in the relationship. They know that they dare not say what they really want for fear of your reaction. This is a hopeless way to live and only results in a slow stagnation and contraction of the relationship.

There is a far deeper understanding that you will need to develop about yourself and the mechanism that you relate through. This is the next stage: you are more than what you seem to be. We need to peel another layer of the onion and reveal to you the hidden structure of your personality or, to be more correct, the myriad of selves that you have living within the awesome instrument of your mind. These selves have so much power over you; yet they also have the potential to awaken you to a brilliant new experience of life.

❖ ❖ ❖

CHAPTER 20

UNDERSTANDING YOUR PERSONALITY

Subpersonalities

We will now consider the structure of personality, the next piece in the jigsaw of what it is to be a human being.

Personality comes from the word *persona*, used in ancient times to denote a mask worn by actors. It also includes the word *person*. One of the problems with identifying yourself as a person is that you are unconsciously stating to yourself that you are a mask.

This is, in fact, very close to the truth. Our personality is a mask that the Self wears. The accepted procedures of our society dictate that we all have to have a personality, a series of behavior patterns, which are needed to relate and function in the civilized world. If you are unable to function in this way, if your personality doesn't function normally, or you do not have one at all, then you are considered to be unbalanced, mentally ill, or utterly insane. It is, therefore, important to realize exactly what your personality and its structures are.

The Self, *your self*, is not a person. It wears a personality, in the same way that an actor wears a mask. Acting is, in fact, a useful discipline for understanding ordinary human life. A good actor can create a character and totally absorb him- or herself in the role. This person literally builds up the characteristics and behavior patterns through the application of techniques that are very similar to the way you created characteristics during your childhood. The actor can act and react as if he or she is actually the person being portrayed on the stage or screen.

In the same way, all people act and react as if they were truly the person or personality they are playing in life. However, anything that can be formed and dissolved, created and discreated, while it is being observed by something else within you, cannot be what you truly are. The behavior patterns and characteristics that make up the "personness" that you believe yourself to be, obviously fall into this category. You cannot be something that has been layered onto you. To believe that you are your behavior patterns is as silly as believing you are the clothes you wear. Personality is something you adopt or build as you react to the environment you find yourself in.

A *Multiplicity of Selves*

Each personality is a structure of beliefs, characteristics, ideas, talents, abilities, prejudices, certainties, and delusions. We are beings who actually have myriads of individual personalities. There is not just one single integrated personality in our mind. We are constantly creating new ones and discarding the old, from the moment we are born, right through to our adult years. What is interesting is that the ones we discard do not disappear; they are stored in the subconscious mind. They are still "alive," and can, if loaded with negative emotion or not allowed to express themselves, sabotage our lives. You must consider each of them as a living, individual person with its own needs and desires.

Consider the ones you used in the past, but no longer have use for. The infant and young child ways of relating are no longer practical or appropriate in your adult life, nor are the ones that you used on the school playground.

There are many ways of relating in your present life as well. Consider the different personalities you have now, such as the behavior you use for your parents, lovers, friends, enemies, and work associates. You wouldn't relate to your boss in the way you relate to your lover—unless, of course, you wanted a raise!

Also look at yourself when you are being critical or aggressive, and contrast that energy or behavior pattern to when you are being kind and loving. It is as if there is more than one person within you—which, in fact, is absolutely true. Each mode of expression is actually a subpersonality, an entirely unique "person." What we call a *personality* is nothing more than a collection of subpersonalities. Some of these are stronger than others, and these tend to dominate your life, causing you to believe that your identity is represented by these more powerful subpersonalities.

The childhood ones you have are no longer in use, even though they still live below the level of your consciousness. From there, they can and do still motivate your life and are often the cause of success or failure in your various experiences.

All human beings long for full self-expression. To be unable to do so is a frustrating experience. Most people also want to be able to fulfill their desires. Anger is nothing more than being unable to get what you want or have life work in the way you want. These two needs, to express oneself and to get what you want, are present in the individual subpersonalities that live within your mind.

Each subpersonality has these two needs in varying measures. Consider the child ones that are hidden in the subconscious. In many people, these are able to be satisfied and given expression in normal ways, such as playing with children, games, sports, and leisure activities. As long as they are happy, they continue to live as an integrated part of your system. If they are not, they can sabotage your life experiences.

How Subpersonalities Are Formed

The beginnings of your personality and, therefore, subpersonalities start the moment you are born. There is some suggestion that they can also start while still in the womb but, for ease of understanding, we will presume that they begin in infancy.

When you are a very little baby, your mother represents life to you. She is the source of food, nurturing, love, and so on, as we have discussed previously. For you to be alienated from her in any way causes you to feel dangerously threatened. Survival is your primary concern, and she represents survival to you. It is in your interests to keep her as happy as possible because if she sends any negative signals to you, you feel very insecure. Remember, rejection by the mother can equal death in the mind of an infant.

You quickly learn that it is painful not to have positive vibes from Mom or whoever the mother figure is in your life. You develop behavior patterns and modes of expression that cause her to behave pleasantly and happily toward you, such as your acting like a playful child or clown. These are the first subpersonalities developing in your mind.

Your first means of expression, and therefore, *core subpersonality*, is as a vulnerable child. This initial "self" is not only vulnerable, but also extremely sensitive. It reacts to everything. It picks up every single impression sent to it, and any that are not loving are felt as painful and dangerous. It only wants to be loved. Nothing else feels right to it. It is easily confused and can become fearful from the most minor things. This is one of the reasons babies cry so much.

What happens is that this vulnerable child quickly has to adjust to the environment it finds itself in. It has no option but to form psychological defenses and emotional armoring to protect itself from the behavior patterns of other people who come into its life. Even well-meaning people are perceived as possibly life threatening if their behaviors are loud or perceived as false. This includes many behaviors that seem normal to other people. Remember, the baby is extremely sensitive, so it automatically starts to armor its vulnerability and sensitivity with other subpersonalities who, together, can act as a defensive shield to the original vulnerable child core subpersonality. This next layer of subpersonalities contains the "protector-controllers." Their job is to protect the vulnerable child and control the baby's own behavior so that it does not attract into its life any unwanted experiences that could hurt it. The protector-controllers continue to grow throughout the childhood years and remain with us for life.

The Protector-Controllers

The protector-controllers are subpersonalities that include the analyst, the pusher, the critic, and the clown. Each of these, and there are many more, has the function of discovering the rules in the baby's environment and keeping the world at bay so that pain and hurt can be avoided. These subpersonalities have a "thicker skin" than the vulnerable child and are less sensitive. In some people's cases, they can become very thick indeed and lose all sensitivity to other human beings' feelings and needs.

The analyst intellectualizes and analyzes all the circumstances people are confronted with in everyday life so that they can make a decision that is conducive to being stable and protected. It thinks things through and comes to conclusions.

The pusher causes people to take actions in the world that bring in things like finances and that create security. It might push people to work hard, makes sure they arrive on time, and are reliable, and so on, so that they are accepted. Remember that the step back from not being accepted is to be humiliated. Prior to humiliation, that is, at a more intense level, the nonacceptance becomes rejection, and the step back from rejection is actually life threatening. This feeling originated from the earliest conclusions about the relationship with the mother. If she rejects you, you believe/feel you may die. So every protector or controller subpersonality does everything in its power to ensure that you are accepted and so not threatened.

The other subpersonalities that try to guarantee acceptance are the clown (your performance as a humorous, friendly type of person) and the critic. The critic is the voice you hear in your head that criticizes you when you make a mistake. Its function is to tell you off before you make any mistakes in the world that could cause you to be humiliated and rejected. It is the same voice that criticizes other people in your life.

You have probably had the experience of hearing voices in your head arguing with each other about whether or not you should take a particular action. These are the subpersonalities, each individuals in themselves, going through their processes of protecting the vulnerable child by negotiating with each other on the best way to keep you safe and accepted.

There are a large number of different subpersonalities existing within the mind, and each one is potent and can have a dramatic effect on your life, particularly if they are suppressed. They all feel they are relevant and important, just as individual people do. They are all mini-egos, with their own ideas, beliefs, reasons for existing, and quirks. To ignore them is a dangerous practice, as they can literally kill you and are often the cause of death. Actions such as suicide are obviously a result of a voice in someone's head telling him or her to commit such an act and pushing them through to the end. They can also kill by causing psychosomatic diseases.

In primitive cultures, pointing the bone at someone was enough to kill them. They had no injuries that would cause death; it was only their minds that had the power to stop their body functioning. We can see clearly that the mind has the power to take away life in this way. It would be foolish to ignore the power of the mind to create diseases. If it can kill, it can certainly make you sick. And why did these people die when the bone was pointed at them? Because they believed that the bone had that power. Beliefs are very strong, and all subpersonalities are based on beliefs.

A way of discovering how beliefs act and how you can access them directly has been invented. Let's look at how this can happen, because if you can communicate with them, you can free them from creating negative effects on your life, as well as bring to the surface much, if not all, of your suppressed power. You will be quite amazed at just how many hidden talents and abilities you have living within your mind that can be brought to the surface for use in any way you please.

❖ ❖ ❖

C H A P T E R   2 1

DISCOVER YOUR HIDDEN SELVES

Voice Dialogue

This brilliant system, created by Drs. Hal and Sidra Stone, can
access all the hidden and disowned "selves" or subpersonalities.
It is elegant and simple, yet a most powerfully effective way of
accessing the buried subpersonalities. To really understand it, you will
have to go to a facilitator or a training workshop, but it is such an excellent technique that I want to alert you to it so that you can take advantage of any opportunity that arises to try it for yourself.

To explain briefly, a client sits opposite a facilitator in a comfortable
and normal setting, such as a living room or other pleasant space. The
client usually has some issues to resolve. Voice Dialogue can actually be
used in many ways, such as:

a) resolving an emotional difficulty;
b) finding the cause of a physical ailment;
c) discovering the meaning of a dream;
d) delving into a more powerful or successful part of yourself;
e) unlocking or enhancing a creative talent;
f) finding the subpersonality that knows how to make money;
g) discovering the spiritual aspect of one's nature;
h) accessing the "self" that is a great lover; and
i) discovering the part of you that wants to become fit and filled
    with vitality.

The possibilities are endless. All aspects of your behavior and self-
expression are governed by a particular subpersonality.

Once you have decided what part of yourself you wish to explore, the
facilitator invites you to move your position to a place in the room you

◆ 135

feel drawn to. This is remarkably easy, as you usually feel immediately attracted to a spot and move to it. Once there, to your initial surprise, a part of yourself, an individual subpersonality, comes to the surface and begins to express itself. It is totally spontaneous.

Now, this part can be ordinary and familiar or totally unknown and forgotten by you. What can also come out are subpersonalities that can behave and speak in a way you had no idea was within you.

This is, by the way, nothing to do with any clinical condition, such as split personalities or multiple personalities. It is the normal way a healthy human being functions.

To help in understanding what Voice Dialogue is, here is an example of what actually happened to a man attending one of our Voice Dialogue training seminars:

Example: This man had suffered with back pain for as long as he could remember. He believed that it had been there all his life. He had tried all the normal therapies, as well as alternative ones, to no avail. He decided to try to access the cause of it by using the Voice Dialogue technique. His wife was facilitating him, and he chose to speak straight to the pain itself.

He moved his chair to the first position he felt drawn to, and the "voice" or subpersonality that came out identified itself as "control" (voices will often identify themselves as who they are). His wife asked whether this was the cause of his back pain and was told, "No," that to find out what was the cause he would have to go to "guilt." (Voices will also often advise us where to go next for the cause of a problem.)

When he moved his chair again and accessed the "guilt" subpersonality, "guilt" told him that it was formed at about three or four years old (interestingly enough in this case, "guilt" had no memory or knowledge of "control"; they had been buried at different depths of his mind). "Guilt" then told him that he had had the following experience in a kindergarten (he had no conscious knowledge or memory of this event):

He had been playing with all the other kids. There was a tree in the garden with a low branch on which a bird's nest rested. The teacher had told all the kids not to climb the tree and touch the nest, as there were two eggs in it which would eventually become birds. He did not heed the teacher's instructions and climbed the tree when the opportunity arose. Unfortunately, he knocked down the nest, and the two eggs smashed. As it happened, when the nest hit the ground, everyone turned and looked at him. He felt horribly guilty.

He was then asked if this was the experience causing his back pain and was told by "guilt" that it wasn't, that he would have to speak to "shock-horror." This was, for his wife who was facilitating him, an extraordinary experience, to say nothing of his own amazement as he unfolded and revealed the patterns of his mind.

He moved his chair and got to "shock-horror." This subpersonality was about nine months old and admitted that it was the cause of the back pain. His wife asked how it happened.

"Shock-horror" said that at this early age, he was being taken out on a float board into some water, either a lake or a river. His father, who he did not know very well at all, as he was at work most of the time, was pushing the board out next to him. He peered over the side and could see he was out of his depth. He freaked and started crying and screaming. He was not able to speak yet, so had no way of saying what was happening. His father just laughed and kept pushing the board out. He became very frightened that he was going to fall off and drown. At that point, he made the decision never to put himself in a position where he was out of control again. To make sure he never forgot this point, he deliberately locked up a muscle in his back so that it would become painful whenever he found himself in a position of being out of control. This pain would remind him to take control immediately. Obviously, there are many experiences in life when you do not have full control of what is going on. This realization caused him to have continual back pain throughout his life.

When he heard this story, the man was amazed that such a thing could happen and immediately felt a release of the back pain that had resisted all other treatments over three decades. He was stunned at the simplicity of it.

Here is another example: My own first experience experimenting with Voice Dialogue was to attempt to go back to my childhood. I was sitting opposite the facilitator and, after discussing this goal, I moved my position. I felt drawn to a particular spot on the floor and sat there. Immediately, literally within a matter of a few seconds, I suddenly felt as if I were seven years old. Even my body seemed smaller, and I felt the embarrassment that a seven-year-old can feel in the company of someone he doesn't know. I was able to remember clearly things I had no conscious knowledge of, which were happening in my family at that time. My awareness was the same, but I felt and literally experienced myself as a seven-year-old again. Even my voice took on the rhythm and modulation that it had when I was seven. This is a common experience for many people who undergo such a session.

When you talk to the facilitator during Voice Dialogue, you can directly experience any subpersonalities that are willing to come out. It is a remarkable way to explore your own mind and see just how powerful these parts of yourself are. It is also a most interesting experience to be a facilitator. To really grasp what Voice Dialogue is, direct experience in a training seminar or with an experienced Voice Dialogue facilitator is required. If you are interested, contact the office of Drs. Stone by looking in the back of one of their books, such as *Embracing Ourselves* (distributed by Hay House).

The accessing of subpersonalities is also a secret to discovering the Higher or True Self. Never forget that personality is something you have, and is not something you are. It is only a collection of responses, reactions, and beliefs. Spiritual Realization is awareness of the fact that you are not an individual person, but something that observes the personality. We will deal with this later on in greater detail.

Expand the Boundaries of Your Expression

Everyone is bound within the confines of the subpersonality they are playing in the particular areas of life. You set parameters that you are unable to go beyond within each subpersonality. For instance, if the subpersonality you use to make money is limited by beliefs and concepts, such as "Money is evil," or "I don't need money," and so on, then however hard you try, no matter how many hours you work, and whatever you tell yourself, you will be unable to take the actions necessary to allow you to generate the cash you want. If you try something in the money field and your subpersonality feels that there is something unpleasant about behaving in a particular way that will get you money and is, in fact, necessary to get you money, then you will have no chance of being able to create it.

Or, if you have a series of concepts and beliefs stating that a relationship is tough, difficult to keep together, or a hotbed of arguments within the subpersonality that comes out in personal relationships, then this is what you will experience. The parameters of this particular subpersonality are limited to those negative experiences and cannot be stretched to involve closeness, love, caring, ease, pleasure, and so on. You are bound by the blinkers of the subpersonality, and usually these blinkers are in the subconscious mind, so you are not even aware that these problems are sourced from within yourself.

A useful adage to keep in mind is this: "Whatever you hear in your head is not necessarily true." Subpersonalities, just like anyone, can be misinformed and deluded. Only the reality of direct experience will give you the truth. The way to check if you are deluding yourself or not is to look into your life and see if it is working perfectly. If not, then something is amiss, and quite often that something is one of your own subpersonalities.

Self Image—The Key to Personal Freedom

Personality is also identical with self-image, and it is important to realize that conscious self-creation is the key to personal freedom. For example, it is no coincidence that every single culture with a religious tradition follows identical practices when taking people into religious orders. If you are an individual who wants to be a monk or a nun, when you first arrive at the monastery, your head is shaved, you are given an entirely new name, your clothes and belongings are taken away, and you are given a robe to wear. Your identity is changed absolutely, and you may even go through a variety of ceremonies that cause you to totally leave behind the past personality and all the other life experiences you have lived.

Over the centuries, the people who have run monasteries have seen that it is necessary to create an entirely new subpersonality that can function in the religious environment. The old ones are inappropriate, and they can rarely cope with the requirements of a monastic life. So they have to be totally let go of, and something new has to be created in their place. It is also necessary to let the past go completely. This is a fairly drastic approach and, even though it seems to work on the surface, it is rarely successful. You only need to consider what happens to all those other subpersonalities that are still in the subconscious. Nothing disappears. They just lay there waiting for a chance to come out or perhaps become mischievous. Certainly you find that in a monastic life, "no sex" is the rule. There must be countless frustrated sexual subpersonalities in the subconscious mind of myriads of religious people. Perhaps this explains the sexual confusion of so many of them.

Integrating Your Disowned Selves

What has happened to the vast majority of people is that they have become identified with a tiny percentage of the subpersonalities, and all the others have been buried. This burial into the depths of the mind is called "disowning the selves." Each subpersonality is, in a sense, a "self." It has its own life and qualities. It has its own memory and desires. And, like anything else in life, the more time you spend with it, the more familiar it becomes. The subpersonalities you are identified with are the "primary selves," and they become who you are. People will often defend this collection of subpersonalities with their memories and beliefs to the death, even though they may be deluded. And people often die for their beliefs because a voice in their head tells them that it is noble or honorable to do so.

The buried or disowned selves are some of the most valuable selves you can have. In a civilized society like ours, inevitably the natural, wild free ones are the first to go. Babies have to be tamed and civilized. In the male, the wild subpersonality is known as the Warrior, in the female, the Amazon. These two are very strong and free. They are the animal nature, not in the sense of aggressive or violent, but in the sense of energy and power. You only have to go to the zoo and look into the eyes of a gorilla or lion and get a sense of the wildness that exists within them, to feel what is available. Humans have this quality, but it is rarely seen and usually comes out with a flood of ugly, aggressive behavior. This is because the life force wants to clear out blockages, and when a situation arises where more expression of energy is required or allowed, there tends to be a release of blocked anger and rage along with that extra energy expression.

This happens in sports. The emotions of both the players and the spectators run freely, as the energy is released in the game. An interesting thing happens in a society that becomes civilized: the more civilized it becomes, the more important sports are. This is why you see such a huge industry around athletic endeavors nowadays. People, when they are civilized, become alienated from nature and their own wild, free aspects. Sports allows them to either participate and express these aspects or, if spectating, project those disowned selves onto the people playing, thereby gaining some identification and satisfaction from the game.

People who have not completely buried their Warrior or Amazon natures are often attracted to careers or activities where there is an opportunity for physical action. Apart from sports, the military and police hold attraction for these types. Things like rescue services, fire fighters, paramedics, and similar occupations require the participation of people who are in touch with this subpersonality.

As I mentioned previously, one of the easiest ways to get back in touch with the natural parts of yourself is to go and spend a couple of weeks in the peace and silence of the wilderness. Do not take anything from civilization with you: no radio or other electronic device or instrument that makes music or plays recordings, nothing to read, no phone (except perhaps for emergencies), and no games. In other words, take nothing with you made by human beings. Just take the bare essentials, and live and be in the wilderness environment. Don't make a holiday of it, with enormous amounts of camping gear. Go for walks and swim, but do nothing more.

In the beginning, your mind will speed up, and you will want to do this and that. Let it wind down—it can take a few days—and then you will notice a completely different energy arise from within yourself. You will feel it as a very deep and essential part of your nature. You will feel in tune with the environment. Something new and powerful will arise. You will see just how important it is to maintain large and pristine areas of wilderness in every country in the world and what a terrible crime it is to clear the existing wilderness. Wilderness is the soul of a people. Without it, there can be only a materialistic and contracted experience of life. Everyone should be in touch with nature in this way, for at least a few weeks each year, if they want to remain healthy and centered.

You Are Always Able to Change

Each subpersonality has a particular energy, and you can become very aware of the subtle and, in some cases, quite distinct difference between each one. Start to become sensitive to the different energies and feelings of the primary selves that you are most familiar with. When you get the chance, go along to experience Voice Dialogue, as it will give you the opportunity to differentiate between these energies within the first couple of sessions.

Everyone is capable of changing and growing, and all growth and change comes from consciousness. Consciousness, in this sense, means to be able to be aware of where you are right now with a full and complete understanding of yourself and your present circumstances. It means to be able to not identify yourself as a particular subpersonality or group of subpersonalities, but rather as the faculty that is aware they exist and are operating in your life. (Again, we'll examine exactly what this consciousness is in Part Four.)

Change is the only constant in life apart from your own awareness. Everything that can be experienced is always undergoing change of some sort. Nothing remains the same, including you. It is possible to hold on to something, some aspect of oneself and keep it in check, but this will cause stagnation. You can grow or you can stagnate. The choice is always yours.

The primary step, and unavoidable starting place in your passage to growth, is to realize that you have a personality, and that you also have the ability to release the blockages within it and bring forth any expression you want.

What is also vitally important to remember is that all these effects do not take place only in the mind. There is very much a physical result and reality to them. When you go through the processes of releasing the contractions and old negative beliefs permanently from your system, there are often some physical effects. For, the body and energy system are, in fact, totally integrated with the mind. Therefore, you can expect to start to feel and experience some change on a physical level. This is one of the most amazing and inspiring results on the journey of personal growth. The release from these blockages is a thrilling and exhilarating experience. There is a physical release and a physical euphoria. So now we will focus precisely on your energy system, because it is here that you will find answers to some of your most interesting questions.

❖ ❖ ❖

AWAKENING ENERGY

The Storage of Blocked Energy

The majority of people live in a semi-aware state due to the repression of blocked energies. The reason, as described earlier in the book, is due to the loading of unexpressed emotions, mainly from childhood, and the resultant armoring of the whole bodymind structure. The semi-aware state is one where the person's mind is always fantasizing, daydreaming, imagining, or thinking; and it is difficult or impossible to retain attention for any period of time without the interference of the workings of the surface mind.

This state, which is the normal and average experience for nearly all human beings, is held in place because of the holding down or holding onto the blocked emotions. Emotions are just energies expressed in a variety of ways. The holding on causes a permanent contraction of the whole system. The mind holds the program that instructs the body to literally contract itself to hold down the energy (emotions) and keep them in place.

This blocks the free flow of the life force and is felt as pressure and stress. Much of this has been buried in the subconscious, and few people are aware of it. It can come to the surface when there is an increase of demands in the outside world, but normally people tend to operate without awareness of this inner tension.

The Physical Effects of Energy Blockages

Unexpressed emotions are held in particular areas of the physical body. For instance, the neck and shoulders retain a lot of anger, and the jaw and throat tend to hold down suppressed emotions. It is as though you have had to swallow what you wanted to say—which is often the case when growing up. The inability to express yourself can make you feel angry, sad, vengeful, and many other emotive reactions. There are many people who hold tightly onto their pelvis. You can recognize them by the way their bottoms stick out. It is as if they are trying to drag upwards and backwards away from their genitals. Often this is tied up with sexual guilt and frustration, or a fear of surrendering to the physical experience. They may associate the sexual act with the possibility of "losing control," and therefore being overpowered and dominated by another person.

All parts of the body are affected in one way or another, and it is these muscular and physical contractions that give a person their own particular body language. If you start to observe people carefully in the way they hold themselves, their facial expression, and the way they walk, you can quite easily begin to learn the language of the body. An easy tip for understanding this is to exaggerate a person's posture and see how you feel when you imitate it. Start with the jaw. Clench it up and notice what emotions arise and how you feel. Also try puffing out your chest, and feel the sense of self-importance that arises. Underlying this action is, of course, a feeling of inadequacy that this posture is trying to overlay. This technique is a fascinating way of seeing just where each person is coming from.

If you want to understand yourself more, check out the way in which people hold themselves physically, with tightly held jaws, protruding chins, rounded shoulders, locked pelvises, and all the other variations. Each muscle and ligament that has been brought into play to hold onto a psycho-emotional contraction, also holds the emotion and impressions that went in originally. This is why 20, or even 40, years later, when people undergo some release methods, detailed shortly, they can bring up deeply suppressed emotions and memories that have been held within their system for all those years and which have inhibited them from enjoying the fully alive state that is every human being's birthright. After releasing these blocks, their physical bodies actually change shape, and they can feel an enormous flow of energy—the life force—through their system.

The ramifications of these blocked emotions are intense and profoundly relevant to everybody because they reduce the flow of the life force, the basic energy, through your system. You can imagine just how many of these blockages there are and how much of your basic energy is required to keep them down. If you find this hard to believe, then again just go to your local zoo, and see how powerful the chimpanzees, gorillas, and lions are. Even these zoo creatures, who are totally inhibited compared to their free, wild cousins, still have an awesome power and speed that we civilized humans have lost. The de-energizing blockage of emotions is one of the primary reasons why we have lost our basic, primal, wild, free, and natural power.

Releasing Blocked Energy

Personal empowerment is the result of unblocking your energy system. You will always be filled with energy if it is allowed to flow freely. There are several energy release techniques, both ancient and modern, that can assist you with opening up your system. Some tend to focus on the body, particularly the muscles, others on regressing through activating emotions. Another school goes straight for the energy system itself, and there are some that deal with observation in the moment on what is in the mind and chasing that down to a release point.

One of the things to be wary of if you decide to look into any of these methods is that you don't fall into the "therapy trap." This is where you spend several years going over and over an old emotional wound, never letting go of it. It can be very expensive and may result in very little growth for you. The key to using these techniques successfully, and some of them are brilliant, is to go for a clearing, a freeing of the system. Don't get too tied up with what comes up. Accept it, integrate it, and move on to more and more life pulsating through you. Letting go of the past is the key. If someone has abused you, consider very carefully whether revenge is the best course of action. It can be very time-consuming and can hold you back, locked in the past, blocking your ability to move ahead to a new experience of life. Forgiveness can often be a more productive approach and provide greater benefits for you.

Working on yourself is a very wise and intelligent practice. By beginning with the body itself, you can bypass years of analysis and therapy "on the couch." These conversational methodologies can also be very time-consuming and often yield few results. You have a body, and its health and vitality are of primary importance. Many people who do go straight for the bodywork systems find that they can have such an immediate and energetic effect that they heal themselves remarkably quickly.

The Primary Physical Requirement

Breath is life; life is breathing. If you stop breathing for more than a few minutes, you are dead. If this is not a significant and obvious sign that breathing is the primary requirement for life for human beings, then what is? You can exist for weeks without food and days without drinking, but only minutes without breathing. Our society has spent countless billions of dollars examining the intricacies of food and drink, but hardly a cent on the breathing process. By accessing the breath, you can regain a far more conscious state than you live in at present.

If we consciously begin to breathe fully, using the whole of the lung capacity, then we feel the arising of old fears that were implanted during birth. As the fear arises, we stop breathing fully, without realizing that we are doing it, so that the fear can be reburied. We forget that we are breathing, and our mind wanders. This temporary lapse is enough to "redownload" the old fear. We then revert to the normal shallow breathing.

Bringing yourself back to the natural and correct full breathing process requires the complete release of any old contractions and their associated negative emotional/energy blockages. This must be done slowly and carefully. Yoga has excellent techniques for reactivating breathing. It is best to learn them from a qualified teacher. It is no coincidence that the most ancient of all personal growth technologies, such as Yoga and the Eastern Martial Arts, always emphasize the correction of breathing as the unavoidable and earliest step in their methods.

Interestingly, one of the most significant aspects of the birth process is the constriction that it puts on our breathing processes. The sudden release of the fluid from the lungs and the resulting intake of cold air, causes the breathing system to go into contraction and even shock, especially if the slap is added to being held upside down.

The message loaded into the subconscious memory from such an experience is that full breathing is a dangerous and even life-threatening event. The experience of being forced to breathe before we are ready causes us to block our natural, full breathing, and unless we consciously free up our breathing processes through specialized activities, we never regain this lost ability. And when we do start to rebreathe fully, then often there is a rerun of the birth experience with all the associated fear emotions that were felt at the time. If you were birthed intelligently, then the experience would be a far less unpleasant one. However, most births are usually dramatic affairs for babies, not to mention mothers.

There are several excellent methods of reawakening your blocked energy, so freeing you to re-experience your own inner happiness. It is well worth exploring one or more of them so that you can have a direct experience of this. Theory is all very well, but nothing beats experience.

We'll look at the main methods in the next two chapters. First, we will examine two excellent techniques that will help you greatly in clearing your mind and bringing into your life the experiences you want.

❖ ❖ ❖

TWO GREAT TECHNIQUES

Twenty-Two Times Eleven

Twenty-two times eleven (22 x 11) is a brilliant technique that works on many levels when practiced as detailed below. It helps you bring to awareness your core concepts and beliefs (your mindset) and will assist you in becoming aware of, and breaking, your emotional addictions, as you reprogram very clearly the experiences and feelings you want to live out. It is so simple and yet so powerful that its effects will surprise you.

Here is what you do.

1. Choose a goal you'd like to achieve or a desire that you'd like to fulfill, and write it out as a statement. Here is an example just to give you the idea: "Money now comes to me abundantly in perfect ways." The statement should be a clear and definite desire you would like to see fulfilled. It is *not* an affirmation; it is a statement. It is important to differentiate between these two. You will see why as we proceed.

2. Every day for *11* days, write out 22 times the statement that you wish to see fulfilled. To be effective, your statement must *strongly* contradict your present circumstances. A *weak* or *general* statement is unlikely to bring you a result. There should also be no *futures*, such as, "Money *will* come to me," because your mind will follow your instructions precisely, and it might bring money to you when you are 90 years old! You want it sooner than that. Nor do you want any

negatives in the statement, such as "I am not poor anymore." The mind tends to hear "poor" and creates this for you. Also keep the statement short and precise.

3. After each statement, write down underneath it (not on a separate page), whatever the response is that comes into your consciousness. There should be, therefore, 22 responses each *day*. A response can be in *words, feelings, emotions*, or even a *blank* or *sense of nothing* coming up. In this last case, always write: *"No response."*

Whatever thoughts come up, however irrelevant, always write them down. Feelings or emotions can be *identified* by writing them down, such as *anger, sadness*, or *excitement*. It is vital to record every single response (or no response). This is the *key* to opening to a *deeper level* of your mind. You are learning to communicate with more of your mind. If there is no immediate response, verbally repeat the statement silently in your mind again, even close your eyes and listen deeply. Wait only *ten seconds* or so and continue, writing *"No response"* if this has not brought anything up. Concentrate effortlessly and be open. Do not try to *force* an answer. Many of the responses will just be the normal monkey chatter of the mind. *Record these also as a response.* So if your mind comes up with "I wonder if I should give Bill a call," or "Wouldn't it be nice to have a cup of tea," or "I mustn't forget to take the car in for a tune-up," then these thoughts should be written down.

In other words, everything that pops into your mind is a response, however irrelevant it might seem. What you are doing is allowing your mind to open up, and it will only open up if it is allowed to flow freely, which means whatever comes up is acceptable and not judged. You are not looking for a particular response; you are just allowing your mind to reveal to you how it is structured and release anything stopping you.

You are also—and this is very important—focusing on the statement, *no*t the response. Some people misunderstand this and focus on the responses to see what is in their subconscious. Doing so tends to block the flow of responses from the subconscious, as you are not focusing on the positive statement. You need to just be the interested observer of whatever appears. What you are actually doing is implanting the positive statement. Whatever comes up is being dislodged by this process, and it is necessary to let it go. Just be aware of whatever comes out. Sometimes there will be positive responses and sometimes negative. It doesn't matter; you just keep writing and responding. Writing out the negative responses actually clears them out of your system. Avoiding doing so leaves them in there.

4. The 22 times must be completed in *one sitting*, and the eleven days must be completed *consecutively*. There must be no break from the writing during the sitting, and no day left out in the 11 days. If there is any break at all, then the 11 days must commence again from day one. So if you miss a day, then you start again at day one. The reason you might miss a day is because you have reached a block, and it makes you forget to do it. If you can't even spend 20 minutes a day writing a statement to bring you, say, money, then you will have no hope of developing the power to actually bring that desired abundance of money into your life.

If there is a break during the writing of the 22 statements on a particular day (for example, you get up for a cup of tea) then this session too must be commenced from the start. Beware of any overpowering or trivial reasons that may occur to *draw you away* from the process. These are the very things that hinder you in life when attempting to achieve a goal. Don't take a break for tea or coffee. Prepare yourself so that you can ignore all interruptions. Make sure that the phone is unplugged, or turn on an answering machine. If necessary, put a "Do Not Disturb" note on your door. Also, you can't write 11 statements in the morning and 11 in the evening. They must be done in one continuous and unbroken sitting. Therefore, make sure you set yourself up correctly.

5. The statement should not be *altered* within the writing period of the 22 times, or the 11 days, except to polish, clarify, or improve it. And this should only be done *at the end* of one of the sessions of 22 times, not during it. As long as the content and the main aim and thrust of the statement is the same, then this is allowed. So you might have started with "Money comes to me abundantly," and you realize that it could be stronger, so you add "now and in perfect ways," so that it becomes "Money now comes to me in abundance in perfect ways.

Sometimes a response will appear that will feel really important, such as, "If I am rich, I will not be respected." This might have come from some input in childhood. Someone might have told you that the rich are crooks and that no one really respects them. As you now want to become rich, this re-arises to the surface. If something like this does come up, then your next 22 x 11 would hone in on this response, as this will be a major cause of limited money in your life. So you would write a contradictory statement such as: "In perfect ways I am now rich and respected."

6. Do not analyze the responses *during* the writing period, for this interrupts the flow. The responses can be examined at the end of each session, at the end of the 11 days, or not at all.

7. During the process, you may feel lethargic, tired, or emotional. Even so, continue, as these are *normal reactions* that are often expressions of sabotage patterns. Whatever comes up is the correct response. The time it takes to become clear is dependent upon the amount of material you have to process.

8. The 22 x 11 should be periodically repeated until you achieve the result you are requiring, or *until you lose interest* in having that desire fulfilled. Also, be alert to Life itself sending you messages that inform you about actions you need to take with regard to your desire. These appear as so called coincidences or unusual events that seem meaningful. Be certain that you respond to these signals correctly.

9. *Always let 11 full days elapse* between each 22 x 11 treatment about a particular subject, such as health, relationships or money. You can do as many different 22 x 11's as you like each day, about different subjects, but always leave the 11-day minimum period between each identical subject. You can leave as long a period in between each one as you wish, so you might do one, say, every four, six, or eight weeks on a particular subject.

10. You can hand write or use a typewriter or word processor—but don't use the copy function! You have to write or type each one of the 22 statements. Make sure that you *do not rush through* it just to complete it in a short period of time. Use it for what it is designed to be—a means of exploring your own mind. Also, be alert to the results in the outside world once you begin a 22 x 11. Learn to

recognize and respond appropriately to them. Take any actions necessary that may be required to speed you to your goal.

11. Persist. If you have the desire and you want it fulfilled, keep going. The *only struggle* is with your own mind. Life grants abundance if you truly want it and are clear enough to let it into your life.

Keep the process to yourself. It is easy to disempower your ability to be successful by telling others what you are doing. There are always people who will be threatened by your growth and may try to hold you back. They can often do this unconsciously. *Succeed first,* then tell later, from your own experience.

<u>*Examples of 22 x 11*</u>: A young man who is living in a house with a number of different roommates finds one of them very attractive. Her name is Sophie. She is totally disinterested in him and has let him know this by her behavior and actions. However, this has not put him off, and so he decides to use the 22 x 11 to win her affections. He decides on a statement that sums up his desire perfectly: *"Sophie now loves me passionately."*

You can see that this statement is short and precise. It is to the point and encompasses the desires of the young man perfectly. This is important to remember when composing your statements. Do not make them too long, and do not be general. And do not have more than one subject in a statement, such as, "Sophie loves me passionately, and I am fit and healthy." Keep everything clean and succinct.

What happens when the young man writes is that his conscious mind throws up its answers:

1. Sophie now loves me passionately.
   No, she doesn't; she thinks you're a twit.

2. Sophie now loves me passionately.
   Why would she want you?

3. Sophie now loves me passionately.
   She doesn't even find you attractive.

4. Sophie now loves me passionately.
   Why can't you stop doing this stupid process?

5. Sophie now loves me passionately.
I want a cup of tea.

And so on. His mind will keep generating all sorts of responses. He may actually "dry up" a few times and feel that nothing more is going to come out. This is only a sign of a deep block being contacted. He needs to continue. Sometimes the responses will be positive, sometimes negative. He might even write half a page of responses or more, as things rush to the surface. Whatever they are, merely continue until you have fulfilled your goal or lost interest in it.

Eventually, he might come up with a deeper response such as:

Sophie now loves me passionately.
You're not worthy of being loved.

This statement may hit him very deeply, and he will feel the strength of it and its power over his life. Imagine having a belief like this in your subconscious mind. If you are not worthy of being loved, you will make yourself unlovable so that no one will love you and so you will live out the belief. This is what happens, and there is nothing you can do about it apart from dissolving the original belief, which is what the 22 x 11 assists you with.

You may also feel the negativity leaving your system as an energy rather than a realization on a conceptual basis. It doesn't matter, just so long as you are achieving the result.

The main point is that our young man is not changing Sophie; he is *changing himself* so that he can become lovable and attractive to Sophie, thus bringing into his life the experience he wants.

What is likely to happen to someone in this situation is that he may find, after, say, the fourth day, that Sophie sticks her head around his door and asks him to accompany her to the theater, as she has been given two free tickets. Or one evening, Sophie, who is still totally disinterested in him, brings home her friend Jane. Our young man sees Jane, and his eyes nearly pop out of his head. He finds Jane far more ravishing than Sophie. Jane is also instantly attracted to him. Sophie is removed from his mind in a flash and replaced by Jane.

What has happened here is that your higher intelligence knows perfectly what the feeling or emotional experience is that you want. In the case of our young man, it was the "passion" that was important to him—not specifically Sophie! Your mind will always give you the internal experience you are looking for. This is why many people who do these techniques find that they have a far better external experience than they could have imagined.

Here are some other examples of 22 x 11 statements:

MONEY NOW COMES TO ME IN ABUNDANCE IN PERFECT WAYS.
I NOW FEEL LOVE AND JOY THROUGHOUT MY WHOLE BEING.
I VALUE MYSELF HIGHLY.
I LOVE AND ACCEPT MYSELF AS DO ALL THOSE AROUND ME.
I AM NOW IN PERFECT HEALTH AND FILLED WITH VITALITY.
MY WORK NOW FULFILLS, EXCITES, AND ENRICHES ME.
I AM NOW IN AN IDEAL RELATIONSHIP WITH MY PERFECT PARTNER.

(You will find more in the following section headed "Declarations.")

One of the purposes of this technique is to bring into your life the information and opportunities, the people and the signs, that will cause you to take appropriate actions and forge you towards your goal.

Don't forget that you must *take the necessary actions* to effect these results. It is not merely a matter of sitting down and writing. It is vital to do what is necessary in the world. We'll deal with this more thoroughly later on.

Technique: Declarations

In addition to, and in concert with, the 22 times 11, there is the technique known as *Declarations*. These are also very useful and can be extremely effective in bringing you what you want.

The function of Declarations is to bring to yourself an event or circumstance, or to attract to yourself information that will assist you in making the necessary changes to allow you to live out the experience, by a particular date.

A Declaration gives your mind clear and precise instructions about the desire you want fulfilled. You may find that a Declaration can be quite long, even as much as a page or more, as it is necessary to detail the conditions of the desire so that there is no confusion or lack of information for your mind.

Once it is detailed in a way that satisfies all your requirements, you can use a short and precise 22 x 11 to assist you in bringing it to fruition.

Write out your Declaration once (obviously you can rewrite it as many times as you require in order to become happy with it), and when you have written it out to your satisfaction, read it three times each morning and night for the first two weeks, then drop it back to three times a week until it is fulfilled.

Some examples:

a) I declare that by the (date—include month and year) I have acquired the ideal business for myself, and it has come to me in a perfect way. It fulfills the following... (list your requirements).

(22 x 11 suggestion: "I now own a highly successful (type of) business.")

b) I declare that by the (date) I am working in my ideal career/job that fulfills the following conditions: for example, "I work with friendly, interesting people; have flexible hours, travel opportunities, work in a beautiful office with an ocean view, have promotional opportunities, am able to be creative, am highly paid (name the salary you would like)," and so on.

(22 x 11 suggestion: "I am now employed in my ideal job/career.")

Be sensible with your dates. Don't write that by tomorrow morning you will be a millionaire if you have always been broke and have a severe money problem. The same applies with relationships: if you have little to offer, or have never been able to commit yourself, or are a bore or smelly, don't think that you will find Mr. or Ms. Right in ten minutes. It is you who has to change by taking the necessary actions to improve your mindset with regard to the subject you wish to work on.

Three to six months is a good starting point for bringing something new into your life. To become a millionaire from a zero-money mindset usually takes three to five years depending on the line of work you choose and the amount you are prepared to put into it. But the information of how to do it can come almost immediately. It is all a reflection of the amount of personal growth you are committed to.

If the desire does not appear by the stated date, it can mean there are still more saboteurs to clear. You will have received signals from life as to what is necessary to get your act together in this department, but you may have missed them. Keep going with the declaration, as it will eventually come to fruition even if you have to adjust the date to a later time. This is because once you have set a declaration in motion, circumstances that you were unaware of, within your subconscious, may require more time to sort out.

Practice both of these techniques before you go on to the next module in the course. Reread the instructions, and really make sure you "get it." It is very easy to be a wimp about your own growth and just make this information merely pleasant reading. But to get the results, and that is what this book is all about, you will have to do the work.

And finally, the absolutely vital point that needs constant re-emphasizing is that the work you do within your mind, even though absolutely unavoidable and necessary, is only part of the job. It is your actions in the world that will bring you the rewards. You need to clear your mind of the sabotage patterns and limitations, but without actions in the world there can be no fruits to your labor. Now we will move on to the techniques that deal directly with your energy and power.

❖ ❖ ❖

CHAPTER 24

FREEING YOUR POWER

The Science of Freedom

Yoga does not just refer to the physical exercises that have been popularized in the West. The word *yoga* means union with your essential self, and its function is to totally free the individual who practices it, on all levels of his or her being. The familiar physical exercises are called postures and are a part of the system of Hatha yoga. They are excellent for clearing the physical and emotional system. But there is far, far more to yoga than meets the eye, far more than just the postures. The beauty of the yoga system is that it is thousands of years old and has been used by millions of people for centuries, and so has stood the test of time. In other words, it works very well. For some reason, there are some deluded people who believe that it is a religious belief system. Nothing could be further from the truth. It is purely a science—a rational, logical exploration of the capabilities of the human being, based on detoxification of the body, emotions, and psyche, and the strengthening of the powers of concentration to increase and expand consciousness to the maximum.

As you explore yoga, you quickly realize just how brilliant and thorough it is. In fact, all the so-called new discoveries of psychology and the methods and processes of personal growth and release, have their roots in yoga.

What follows in this chapter is a selection of the most popular and easily accessible of these modern psychological and emotional release methods "discovered" in the recent past by Western psychologists and psychiatrists to free up your energy system in the quickest and most efficient way. They are all fast-track methods that will speed your progress and release energy and power that you didn't realize you had.

Rebirthing

Rebirthing is a modern derivation of one of the ancient yoga practices of *pranayama*. *Prana* means the *life force*, or natural energy, and *yama* means *control of*. So, pranayama is the control of the natural energies. Many of the techniques involve the use of the breath. Rebirthing, or rebreathing, as it is sometimes known, involves the use of the breath in a particular way to regress your consciousness back to your birth to clear any negativities that may have remained there.

The technique involves what is known as "connected breathing." This simply means that there is *no pause* between the in breath and the out breath. You lie down on a mattress, with the assistant or facilitator, who is called a rebirther, sitting close by. One of their functions is to remind you to continue to breathe in the correct way because you will sometimes quickly fall into a semi-conscious or even unconscious state. This is perfectly normal because when you start to explore your unconscious, you usually go unconscious! You need the rebirther to continually remind you to breathe fully and connectedly, and remain conscious.

Once you have settled on the mattress, a full conscious breath is deliberately taken in through the nose or mouth, and then the out breath is completely let go. There is no pause between the in breath and the out breath, and the next in breath. It is continuous. This can seem like quite a big effort in the beginning, but it will eventually become manageable. There is no controlling of the out breath; it is merely a release. If you try to control the out breath, you may cause your system to contract temporarily, rather than let go. You just let the breath out. The rebirther will remind you to do so.

If you fall into a sleepy state, which is a very common occurrence, don't worry. This is to be expected. I remember once rebirthing a woman who could not remain conscious for more than a few minutes, even when standing up. It is quite remarkable that a person can, by just breathing connectedly, lose consciousness in a matter of minutes. This particular woman could not even wake up and breathe properly, even though I raised my voice very loudly within an arm's length of her ear. It is incredible to see this happening. The depths of unconsciousness people fall into can take them into a space within themselves in which they are totally oblivious to the outside world. They become far more unconscious than when in the deepest sleep. This is because the blockages are so deeply buried and perhaps so traumatic that they cannot yet be processed and integrated. They, of course, wake up immediately once the session is over.

Some people have difficulty remaining conscious, so it can be helpful for them to sit up or even stand, as they practice the connected breathing technique. There are also rebirthing methods where you use a warm-water tub to respark your memory of being in the womb.

What occurs during rebirthing is a steady series of reactivations of the memory, particularly events that have blocked you in the past and have been buried. It is very common to regress to your actual birth and relive the whole experience. It is also common to remember a variety of circumstances that have been very powerful decision points in your past. You can actually relive the thought process that caused you to make a particular choice about yourself, your abilities, and your opportunities in the world. Seeing these with the more mature intelligence and understanding of the present day, gives you the opportunity to change those decisions and so change your life—completely and radically if you want.

It is also extremely important to make changes slowly and surely. Don't be tempted to try to release all the emotional blocks within a short period of time. Twelve months is the absolute minimum for permanent, radical change. This is because the physiology of the body needs to change. The cells, nervous system, and the organs of the body move at their own speed. You can only damage them by trying to rush. It is the same as running a marathon on a hot day when you have been a couch potato all your life—not a wise move unless you want to finish the race on a stretcher.

Body Release Methods

There are several techniques that use the physical body as a means of accessing the blocks of the past. As the memories, with their full content of blocked emotion, are held in the muscles, ligaments, and skin, the body-based techniques go for deep muscular tissue massage to release and free up the system. By pressing very firmly, the masseur, using his knuckles, elbows, and feet, works out the tension in the deeper tissues and massages it away. As this is done, it is normal to remember all sorts of events from the past that have hindered or sabotaged you. Probably the best known of these techniques is Rolfing, created by Dr. Ida Rolf. This original technique has spawned off several other styles that basically follow the same idea.

Another well-known method is Bioenergetics, developed under the auspices of Dr. W. Reich by Dr. Alexander Lowen and Dr. John Pierrakos. Dr. Pierrakos went on to create Core Energetics. Bioenergetics is based on the idea that by having a person perform certain physical movements, coupled with breathing and vocal actions, they can access the past blocks very quickly. It is, when in the hands of a great facilitator, an excellent technique. Much of it is based on the postures of yoga, with some variations to activate emotion more quickly. It is actually unknown to most Hatha yoga teachers that the purpose of the postures is to release blocked emotions, as well as to make the body become flexible and strong. Bioenergetics fills this gap. In a Hatha yoga class, everyone keeps quiet; in Bioenergetics, the idea is to express sounds and words, for they assist with releasing emotions.

All modern release methodologies are based on three factors. The first is accessing the subconscious through verbal expression. The best of these is Voice Dialogue, which was described earlier in the book. The second is accessing it through the breath, and the third is through freeing the energies within the body, as in deep tissue massage and techniques like Bioenergetics.

In contrast, the ancient processes work directly on the energy flows themselves, and we will examine these shortly. They are the real jewels in the crown and give the highest rewards. Even so, it is very useful, and sometimes necessary, to experience some of the above body-based techniques, as they speed up the attainment of results of the more ancient methods.

Professional Facilitators

When looking for a facilitator for one of the above techniques, it is vital to go to someone who is intelligent, experienced, and who has qualifications. Get recommendations from other people, read a few books on the subject, and have some discussions before you dive into it. They can be brilliant and powerful experiences and really shift you along, helping you to release a huge amount of negativity, if you have set up the situation as ideally as possible.

I would always be wary of people who have attended a weekend course and who have appointed themselves as professionals. With any of these techniques, you are opening yourself up and revealing parts of yourself that are vulnerable and loaded with negative emotions. With a great facilitator, you can make terrific steps forward and inward to becoming completely clear and energized. With one who is well meaning but not completely qualified, you are risking either wasting time or remaining in a too-vulnerable state after the session is over.

No one of these systems is enough, even though their practitioners usually swear by them. You can't repair a car with one screwdriver, nor can you repair decades of conditioning with one technique.

Personal empowerment and absolute happiness are a result of unblocking your energy system through whatever means are necessary. You will always be filled with energy, positivity, and a joy of living if your energies are allowed to operate without hindrances. By exploring any of the methods detailed above, you will, at the very least, relearn how to express yourself without inhibitions, as you did when you were a child. This, in itself, is very empowering.

The enjoyment of sexuality, and the key to becoming attractive, are interlocked within your energy system. Sexual expression is very important to master, because it is here that you can discover just how much emotion is blocked and locked away. There are reasons for this, and we will now look at how sex has become the issue that it has and how you can find sexual freedom.

❖ ❖ ❖

C H A P T E R   2 5

SEXUALITY

Sexual Freedom

The ability to enjoy ever-increasing happiness requires a clarity and freedom about sexuality. This does not mean that you have to become a sexual explorer, trying out a variety of sexual opportunities. Freeing and directing your sexual energy is the same as freeing your own life force. The two are not only intertwined, they are identical. People who undergo an energy release technique with their partner, such as Rebirthing or Bioenergetics, and then go directly into a sexual encounter, discover that the sexual experience is deepened and enriched to a tremendous degree. Sexual ecstasy is often the result.

Many people think they have a good sex life, but when they start to release the contraction and armoring in their bodymind, they quickly realize what they have been missing. The extension of the duration and deepening of the orgasm, the ease of control of ejaculation, the ever-deepening surrender, the whole body release into waves of pulsating ecstasy, put the ordinary "genital sneeze" sexual experience into the realms of the mundane and mediocre.

Sexual freedom is truly only personal freedom expressed in this way. The freer you are sexually, the freer you are creatively. Your attitudes to life in general become more tolerant and easygoing. You are also much more enjoyable company.

Once you begin to clear yourself sexually, you gain the ability to become deeply intimate with your partner. It is the closeness, surrender, and openness that grants the merging of the couple into one totally ecstatic experience of lovemaking. This can occur once the subconscious of each person begins to be freed of negative conditioning. Interestingly enough, sexuality can also be used as a method of clearing the subconscious so that the experience becomes more and more pleasurable with each encounter. This is called *conscious lovemaking*. It is where you do not delve into fantasy, nor remain "in the head" in any way, but instead you surrender to your own euphoric energies as they release and flood through your body. The experience of sexual surrender and merging is one of the states of absolute happiness.

The Awakening

The most potent time of our life (after early childhood), for our subconscious conditioning, is puberty and the awakening of our sexuality. This is the age when our sexual energies really start to fire, and we find other people sexually attractive. Sexual awakening actually occurs at a much younger age. In fact, some believe that our sexual interests are not something that actually "awakens," but are always present from birth. It is the rules of civilization that keep our sexuality under wraps in early life.

During childhood, the whole genital area is made into something to be guilty about or, at the very least, hide. This has gone on since infancy and has been impressed in the subconscious. We are taught that there is a part of the body that is very different from all the other parts. It becomes a part to be sensitive about, that requires covering when in the company of others and something that needs a special quality or ability if you are to be able to have an enjoyable relationship. This is the result of the input of society.

Unfortunately, for both young and old, because of this and other factors detailed later, sex is a most confused and misunderstood activity. At best, all the negativity about it has been layered over, resulting in a method of sexual activity that gives a partial release in the genital area. This is what is called "good sex," and people who perform in this way consider themselves sexually well adjusted and become quite heated or insulted if a suggestion is made that there is a far more enjoyable way— the implication being, in their minds, that they are inadequate.

The handful of people in the world who are freeing themselves have an entirely different experience of sex to the average person. They can enter into an altered state of consciousness during the sexual act, where their individuality dissolves, and they merge with their partner. The mind ceases its constant chattering, and exquisite energies run up and down the spine and through the body. Their whole system unlocks and opens up, and they are plunged into a highly charged, almost electrical state. Coupled with this there is a complete opening of the heart, and they feel ecstatic pulsations of love throbbing them into bliss. The act itself, which can take several hours, leaves both people with feelings of heightened awareness and establishes them in a state of absolute happiness that lasts for hours and even days afterwards. This is not the experience for most people because there are still issues about the body and sexuality that they need to deal with.

The Problem with Sex

You may be wondering why it is that the above description is such a rare experience for most of the population. Why is it that such a natural act has been hidden from view and layered over with guilt and suspicion for so long? It is really the single most important issue to clear up in society, because once people become conscious and open about the subject, then so much garbage can be dumped from their lives. The way to this result, quite obviously, is intelligent education and correct information.

Once again, we need to identify the problem precisely before the solution becomes apparent. And sex, as can be seen easily in any market-based society, is a real problem and a confusing issue for countless millions of people.

The primary drive is to find a partner, and then the requirement is to be a successful and appreciated lover. If anyone is unable to fulfill either of these two, then they may feel insecure or even humiliated. At best, there will be a frustration that will occupy much of the thinking and feeling time of that person. This is certainly not the formula for happiness. Who has not experienced the driving need to find a partner with whom you can be intimate? This need can become all-consuming, particularly in youth when the hormones are throbbing.

Sexual confusion is a result of negative conditioning that remains in the subconscious mind. The restriction and control of the sexual impulse is an unavoidable part of living in a civilized society. If it was not done, there would be no civilization. We would still be savages. Civilization means to "bring out of a savage state." Savages are not noted for their sexual sensitivity, particularly in the way men treat women. So, in the attempt to live in peace and harmony, sexual control is unavoidable and necessary. How it is done, therefore, becomes the issue.

In the past, society dictated that the subject of sex be hidden and not discussed. In the last few years, censorship has been lifted, and what do we see? Not a flood of positive films, magazines, and books about the art of love, but a torrent of the most extreme pornography, much of it tied in with violence, abuse, and degradation of both women and men and the perversion of children.

This is an inevitable outburst because of the conditioning that the mass of humanity has gone through. You cannot fill someone's head with guilt and fear about something, as well as making it something that should be hidden, without it coagulating as poison and negativity in their minds. When that same subject is fed by that most powerful physical urge of procreation, then you have a recipe for disaster. It is like turning up the gas on a sealed pressure cooker. When you lift the lid, what is in the cooker bursts all over the ceiling. When you release the centuries of negativity about sexual matters, of course it bursts to the surface and can often be an ugly sight, splattering over society as pornography and perversion. This is what has happened in the present time as the subconscious minds of many people explode with regard to sex.

There is hardly anyone alive who has not been influenced negatively about sex in one way or another. This is why the pornography industry is far greater in size than the mainstream film industry. What we are seeing in this late 20th century is the pressure cooker of centuries being released.

Your Own Sexual Conditioning

It is wise to examine your own conditioning with regard to sexuality. Sexuality and the sexual experience, if they are free from negative conditioning, are easy, fulfilling, and euphorically pleasurable. If you were not told this fact or did not have clear examples of this mentality when you were growing up, imagine what might have gone into your subconscious mind and be hidden there, causing you to make the choices that you do now with regard to sex.

Think back and remember, what were the examples that you had? How did your parents behave towards each other? Was sex hidden or considered dirty or naughty? What was the attitude about sex of the person you admired most? Were you told, or did you believe, that not having sex was in some way holy or superior? Is sex something that is rushed or has to be done in the dark? Is it something that you feel you have to do in order to fulfill your marital duties? And so on. Sexual conditioning can have a myriad of delusions.

The easiest way to check what is stored in your subconscious mind with regard to sex is to examine your own present sex life. Then you will know what is in there. Remember, even if you believe that you are sexually well adjusted, the easy check to whether you are truly free or not is to see how deeply you can open yourself to your partner in a one-to-one, intimate, personal relationship. It is not anything to do with athletic ability or needing the requirement of alcohol or drugs to make it exciting. It depends on whether you can truly relate with all parts of your being.

The best sex is a natural progression from openness of the whole mind and the freeing of personal blockages to allow the life force to flow within you. It is never something to do with technique or performance.

Free Flow from the Heart

What happens when your subconscious is negatively conditioned about sex is that you block off the free flow of the life force. You inhibit or limit its natural functioning. Real love is experienced as an outpouring of energy from the heart. The heart center, unfortunately, is one of the first places to be closed down in growing children. It can become as tight as a walnut, blocking the flow of any emotion whatsoever. The life force is like electricity in the way that it functions to activate our systems.

The inhibiting and limiting pressures that are put onto us by our conditioning, that cause us to behave in the "civilized" ways that we do, that lock up and armor our muscles, slowly build up until they substantially reduce the flow of our energy. You can see this contraction in the body language of most people.

The solution to enjoying ordinary sex to the fullest is to release the muscular contractions, the nervous system blockages, and the negative conditioning and concepts about sex that have been put into your mind. Then, or at the same time, enter into a relationship in which both of you are committed to unblocking all the hindrances to true intimacy. You will find that by entering into a true and full relationship, you can develop the ability to become a great lover, even if previously you felt you were utterly hopeless and inadequate in the sexual act. Sex can then become a wonderful experience.

It is the relationship that is the key, that is what is all important. After all, you cannot enjoy sexual congress without a partner. It is obviously vital, therefore, to really understand and be successful at relating if you are going to be able to enjoy great sex on any level.

Great sex can make you absolutely happy. It is, of course, not necessary for becoming absolutely happy. Naturally, though, if there are confusions, negativities, or unhealthy attitudes towards sexuality, then it is very difficult to enjoy the various pleasurable states of happiness that are available. Blockages of any type inhibit happiness.

The other requirement for great sex is the state of your physical body. Not only is it important to be clear of physical blocks, but it is also vital to have a lot of energy available. There are ways to do this, regardless of age and past experiences. We'll look at what these are in the next chapter.

❖ ❖ ❖

C H A P T E R   2 6

HEALTH AND VITALITY

Three Steps to More Vitality

There is nothing that makes you unhappy more easily than being in bad health or having low vitality. It is very hard to be cheerful when you don't feel well or are de-energized. When you are filled with energy and vitality, you often feel on top of the world. It is a terrific thing to be healthy, and it is worth really concentrating on the subject and mastering it.

To become and remain a healthy person requires the consideration of three things—first, the environment you are living in. If you are in a place where there is physical danger, or extremes of pollution, then get out. It is very hard to deal with these types of problems, and you risk your health.

Presuming you are in reasonable health, living in an environment that is not harmful to your health, and you are not ingesting any pills or potions, the side effects of which you are yet to discover, then you need only concern yourself with points two and three.

The second is having a body free of toxins, and the third is that you are supplied with good and complete nutrition.

Even though you must concentrate on these ideals, never forget that what is in your mind can also have a total and complete effect on your health. Psychosomatic diseases are very real, and their symptoms just as life threatening as those caused by toxins, viruses, and bacteria.

Psychosomatic diseases can be affected by the application of the various techniques given in this book. Interestingly enough, many illnesses considered psychosomatic, and also believed to be beyond the ability of the medical profession to heal, can be traced back to diet.

I will detail for you the way in which I believe it is possible to bring yourself to a very healthy state. It is the system that my wife and I use, and we have both found it to be remarkably effective and easy.

The first thing to do if you are not well or just simply unhealthy is to go to a couple of different medical doctors and have a thorough check-up. These days, there are some excellent advances in diagnostics that can give you immediate answers to problems. Again, if you can identify the problem precisely, then you know what needs to be done. Always research widely the possible causes and solutions. Don't just accept the first explanation presented to you.

If you are not satisfied with traditional medical results, and even if you are, it is also a good idea to go to a couple of different qualified people in the natural or alternative healing professions and see what they say. If there is a common denominator in them all, then you know you are on to something. As well, you can try my method of achieving excellent health. If you are already fit and healthy, then you may find, by using the following suggested diet, that your energy levels increase to an amazing degree. Mine certainly have, and I know many people who have enjoyed the same experience. It is a great feeling to be filled with vibrant energy.

Clearing Toxins in the System

The ability to feel energy pulsating through you to the maximum extent is a result of your system being free of any obstructions. Anything at all that blocks energy flow needs to be removed. If you have taken into your body, through eating, anything that cannot be digested easily or is a substance that requires the body to accumulate fat or fluid around it to protect itself from irritation, then you will be reducing the flow of energy through you. Any blockages such as these must be eliminated.

The food you eat is filled with additives and chemicals. Apples have 18 different chemicals applied to them during their growth. Peaches have chemicals that go right through the flesh and into the seed in the middle. Cows are injected with various medications to protect them from diseases and are also given hormones and other substances that will cause them to grow larger. Chickens, pigs, sheep, and all other animals that are bred in captivity are fed a variety of chemicals. Almost all vegetables and fruits are sprayed with pesticides and insecticides, and many other types of synthetic additives are put into the ground in which they grow.

The public is assured that each one of these chemicals *individually* has no harmful effect on human beings. But no one has put all the chemicals that are used in the food prepared for the average meal into one test tube, heated them to body temperature, and then examined what happens.

We are literally eating a chemical cocktail every time we ingest an average meal. What this cocktail does to us is not certain; the effects are as yet unknown. One thing is for sure, though: they certainly do something or they would not have been used to kill insects or boost growth in the first place. If your body finds any of these irritating, then it will surround them in a protective coating of fluid or fat, which will contribute to the blocking of energy.

The second consideration about what you eat is to assess the food itself. What is less known and is sometimes ridiculed by the ignorant, is that cooked food has a variety of negative effects on your body. It tends to slow down the digestive process and load up your system with deposits that become more toxic with age. An excess of cooked food will eventually make you sick and reduce your vitality.

Our digestive system consists of a series of tubes along which pass all the things that we put inside our mouth. Not all that we put in passes out. Apart from the nutrients that are drawn from the food, there is left within our intestines and bloodstream much waste matter, because the average person's body is continually overloaded with food. It just does not have the time to eliminate it all before the next batch comes in.

This waste matter is stored in the folds of the intestines and also, via the bloodstream, in the various organs and cells of the body.

Over the years, it collects and begins to weigh down our bodies more and more. The body actually stores waste matter within itself. Crusts of toxic mucus and other deposits can be found in various parts of the body during autopsies. It is also rare to find a colon that is not filled with quantities of unexcreted waste matter, that has slowly toxified the system even more.

Many diseases can be traced directly to a deteriorating state of the intestinal tract. This is why we find the medical profession promoting the eating of fiber to clean it out. Fruit and vegetables are the best source of fiber. The intestines are very similar to a blocked sewer pipe. These blockages greatly reduce the efficiency of the digestive system, causing it to have to work much harder and use more energy than normally required, so reducing the amount that you have available for other pursuits.

It seems very strange to me that we wash the outside of our skin every day, but we never consider cleaning the inside, even once in our entire lives! There are some who doubt that there is any waste matter remaining inside. They believe that their bloodstream and digestive system, even after loading them for decades with overcooked and processed food and chemicals, is a pure sparkling mountain creek of freshness.

We are all familiar with cholesterol, which causes blockages to the arteries. We are also familiar with plaque on the teeth and a coated tongue. These are all signs that there is something blocking up or constantly being deposited in our system.

What this blocking up does, in the digestive tract, is deny the absorption of nutrients from the food we eat. In fact, it is quite possible to be fully fed, yet be starving for nutrients!

The key is to clean out the body of all its waste products, while at the same time absorbing the required nutrients.

The Diet for More Energy

To my wife and I, the healthiest diet is one where about 75 to 80 percent of the food eaten is raw salads, fruit, fresh juices, raw or lightly steamed vegetables, and brown rice. Raw, freshly picked produce, organically grown, is the healthiest food there is. Organically grown means that no chemicals have been used during the growing and delivery process. If you can't get organically grown food, then use freshly picked produce.

Raw food still has the life force in it and contains a variety of other useful substances. Obviously, as science progresses, all sorts of new elements will be identified, along with the vitamins and minerals already discovered. And there is also the added effect of the "electrical" or "magnetic" power of the life force itself in raw food. As well, this diet efficiently flushes out the digestive tract of its waste matter because of its high fiber and fresh juice content. This, then, allows more nutrients to be taken in.

Sprouted seeds and grains are also highly nutritious and delicious when thrown into salads. It is well worth studying the advantages of raw eating. One of the greatest things is that you no longer constantly crave food. There are absolutely no cravings whatsoever. On an ordinary diet of cooked food, your body is always craving the next meal. This is because it is starving for the proper nutrition. On a predominately raw diet, you feel completely satisfied all day long.

The other 20 to 25 percent of what you eat should be nutritionally rich, fresh food that suits you personally. Obviously, the less processed the food, the better, but there is no need to be a fanatic. If you want to give your system a good cleansing—and this is a good thing to do every few months—then just eat raw fruits, salads, and vegetables; and drink plenty of freshly squeezed fruit and vegetable juices. You will start to feel really terrific very quickly, and you will wonder why you were not eating like this before. It is also, surprisingly, very delicious. You will find that your taste buds wake up and begin to pick up a whole range of flavors that you didn't know existed.

This is also the easiest way to lose weight. If you are overweight, you will find that a pound or two per week will just drop off without the slightest effort or feeling that you are on a diet. The advantage of this is that the skin naturally reduces itself back to the body contour without losing elasticity.

The mainly raw food diet is the most intelligent one to follow. It is simple and effective. And, perhaps most surprisingly, you are filled with energy and vitality. This is the unexpected and remarkable effect of it. You suddenly find that lethargy and tiredness are a thing of the past. You feel rejuvenated and filled with a zest for life.

If you are very toxified, you may feel headachey or sluggish on the first day. This is the unloading of toxins into the bloodstream before they are eliminated. The feeling will pass very quickly. If you eat some cooked food, the sluggishness will stop because the body will immediately cease the cleansing process and use its energies to go back to dealing with the incoming cooked food.

Raw food-eating saves time. It is very quick and easy to prepare and clean up afterwards. The poisons in your life will also fall away of their own accord. Caffeine drinks, tobacco, alcohol, and processed, tinned, and frozen food will all disappear without the slightest effort. And you won't miss them. All you will be left with is excellent health, high vitality, more creativity, and the joy of being alive.

If you are suffering from a disease and getting nowhere with it, why not try this mainly raw food diet and see what the effects are. There are many stories where diseases have been cured by medical doctors who prescribe it. Read one of the many books about raw diets. Leslie and Susannah Kenton's *Raw Energy* has many examples and covers the subject very thoroughly.

Whatever happens, you will look and feel ten or more years younger if you make a wide variety of organic raw food and juices the mainstay of your diet. Fresh juices are packed with valuable nutrients, and it is these that give energy and help to clean out your system. It is the ingestion of these additional juices that give your body what it craves for the most. Always include them in your diet.

I have found that this diet is the one that works the easiest and the best for me. It is not really a diet, but a way of eating that is great for your health and may make you feel better and happier every day.

❖ ❖ ❖

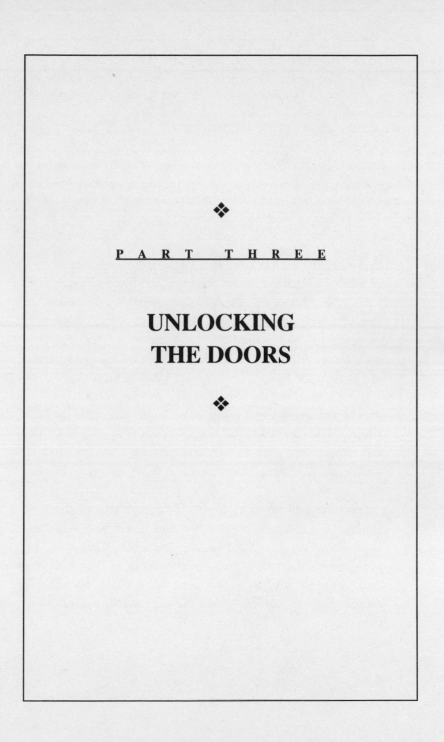

❖

P A R T   T H R E E

UNLOCKING
THE DOORS

❖

WHAT YOU CAN DO TO CHANGE YOUR LIFE

To be able to master your life, the first prerequisite is to be able to use the knowledge that has been given to you so far. Mastery of life does not happen by chance. You will have to take actions in order to bring about any changes you desire.

Ordinary happiness is the experience of being able to create your life in the way you please and to have experiences along the way that give you pleasure. It is within the grasp of anyone who is prepared to do what is necessary to fulfill their desires. It is not complex. It just requires knowledge, understanding, and techniques to bring about the necessary changes in your mind.

You now have the knowledge. The next part of the process is to structure your life and mind in a way that will bring you the benefits you seek. Life is a playground. Learn the rules of the game so that you can join in and play to your heart's content. Happiness is available. Now is the time to bring it into your life.

CHAPTER 2 7

GO FOR RESULTS!

The Best Method

The best method for changing your life is to *go for results*. Focusing only on past problems, or trying to dig them out without new goals, can last years and change little. Whatever you focus on expands, and this applies to both the positive and negative aspects of your experience. So it is vital to actually define what you want, and then go for those results.

As I mentioned earlier, be very careful about getting into ideas such as, "I'm going to sort myself out completely before I change things in my life." This is a trap because it is only the *taking of actions* that will sort you out. If you want to clear yourself in your ability to relate, you are only going to do this in a *relationship with someone*. If you want to be successful at anything, you have to become so by actually doing that thing you are interested in. The teachings given here are not for you to avoid making goals or for getting your act together in life by only doing something internally. The unavoidable reality is to realize that the making and setting of goals and the taking of the necessary steps to achieve them is the *only path to success*.

Some people want to become spiritually realized or enlightened, and they decide to concentrate only on performing spiritual practices. They misunderstand exactly what enlightenment means, and so they waste their lives by *avoiding life*. They too must take specific actions to increase their own energy and power and clear themselves of delusions by taking actions in the world (we will deal with the higher states in the final section of the book).

◆ 181

Both the clearing of contractions and the setting and activation of new goals are necessary. One without the other can sabotage your life. The reason for using goals and going for particular desires is that these actions have the effect of releasing and washing away old negative patterns. It also gives you the means to discipline your mind so that it can become a powerful tool that can take you to the highest and most exquisite experiences available for human beings.

Dissolving the Locks

What happens when you go for a result or goal is that you bring to the surface all the inhibiting belief structures and sabotage patterns that have blocked your ability to enjoy your chosen desire in the past. So, by taking actions that upgrade your life from what you were conditioned to believe were the boundaries of your possibilities, you are confronting your mindset and its blocks. Normally, when you go for a desire, you are able to go partially towards your goal, but when the point comes that would signify you had reached a new, freer expression or more success, very often you sabotage yourself in some way.

These blocks, if left uncleared, are like spring locks that jump back into place as you stretch yourself, and they cause you to lose opportunities. For instance, you meet an attractive person, but you blow it with silly remarks or the wrong response to their conversation. Or you pull back from a deal that would make you very wealthy just when it was about to go through. This happens because a fear arises, and you find yourself overpowered by it at the crucial time. Later you look back and see just how great it could have been if you had gone through with it.

Your timing may also reveal a sabotage pattern. A woman told me the story of her mother who played the lottery every week. She had used the identical numbers since the lottery actually started and had never missed a single week. One week, inexplicably, for no external reason whatsoever, she totally blanked out and forgot to put the ticket in, and, you guessed it, that was the week all her numbers came up. She would have made more than a million dollars. There is a pattern in place that causes these things to happen. The 22 x 11 will help you bring it to consciousness and remove it.

The other thing you have to be aware of is that your rational mind will be able to justify any decision you make, even when you are about to sabotage yourself. In fact, its function is to make sense of things, so justification is easy for it, even if the evidence is not complete or is faulty. We have all seen how people can justify their actions or the actions of other people. Even if the behavior is ridiculous, they are quite satisfied by their own thought processes. If they have a negative mindset about relationships, and they are rejected by a person who is attractive to them, they will not take responsibility for it, but will project the fault onto the other person. For example, they may say the attractive person was too pushy, or if the problem was a business deal, then they will justify this rejection by saying that the deal was offered by a person they really couldn't trust.

So do not be surprised if this negative response and projection onto others happens to you as you proceed towards your new goals or whatever it is you want to make you happy. As soon as you catch yourself being negative, clear it up immediately, or at least ensure that it doesn't happen again. Always be conscious of any negative reasoning or blame. You may also project this onto other areas of your life. A variety of responses may arise. You may physicalize your negativity and experience things such as exhaustion, sickness, relationship issues, projection of negative emotions like anger, sadness, frustration, and the arising of irrational and causeless fear. You will catch yourself doing this quite a lot as you proceed along the path to your own fulfillment.

If or when this happens, realize that it has to happen as the clearing of the past takes place. The techniques taught in this book will reduce the negative blocks as well as make you more conscious and aware of what is actually occurring.

The first and *unavoidable* step is to make a decision about what you want. If you don't make a decision, then you will not be awakening the power you need to create your desires. Even if you are not sure of what you want, you can make a decision to research what is available.

The Power of Making Decisions

The most powerful and creative mechanism of your mind is activated when you make a decision and stick to it. Without activating this potential, you are staying in a rut. Decision making is the expression of your personal power and reveals that it is you who is in charge of your life.

Check now in your life how you use this most powerful of your conscious mind's abilities. Are your desires undefined? Do you make haphazard choices, just accepting what's there and easily available, rather than making the effort to go for the best and most rewarding? Is there uncertainty about who you are in your life, about what you are going to do with your life or with any part of it? Do you avoid making difficult, or even any, decisions, preferring to leave them to someone else or to a later date in the hope that in some way or another everything will work itself out?

The decision power is personal power. People who have power in their lives have the ability to make decisions and carry them through. Wishy-washy or weak people who can't get their lives together have little or no personal power and are pushed around by the forces of life. They have no decision power.

Making a decision and sticking to it is a sign of strength, and it builds more strength. People who can't make decisions hand their power to someone else. And this someone else is merely someone who can make a decision.

Freedom from Fear

For many people, as soon as they make a decision to progress in their lives in some way, fear or anxiety arises. This is what we have discussed above. It is perfectly normal because, as we have seen earlier, the underlying structure of many of the programs that exist in every human being's mind is fear. Fear is the foundation, and so, when you change, the fear must be released.

All progress in life involves going through these invisible fear walls. There is no avoiding it; it just requires going through it. And surprisingly enough, once you are through one, its power over you immediately disappears, and you wonder why on earth you let that stupid fear hold you back for so long.

Your first step then is to look around the various areas of your life, and see what you want to change and then make the certain, unavoidable, and definite decision to go in the new direction.

A Great Secret for Success

For many people, it is difficult to decide what they want to experience in this life. They usually end up repeating whatever it was that Dad or Mom or Uncle Joe or Aunt Flo did. This is the easy way out, and people accept it even if those relatives did not enjoy what they were doing.

If you cannot decide what to do, or if you procrastinate, or are confused about the major steps you want to take in your life, then decide to spend six months, or a year, or more, researching what you want by seeing what other people do. Travel, try other jobs, do voluntary work overseas, read widely, study something or several things, meet and talk to people until you find out what interests you or what you enjoy.

This is a great secret of life: do what you love to do or, at the very least, what interests you. If you are uncertain about what you enjoy, then consider all your present and past involvements and remind yourself of what it was that gave you the most pleasure—family life, growing things, business, study of a subject, a hobby, the theater, movies, sailing, and so on. Then research and examine how it is that people earn an enjoyable living, or, if you want, a fortune, from this activity.

Years ago, I knew a man who wanted to live in peace and quiet doing nothing at all while he considered his future. He loved sitting in the sun and being with nature. So he got a job looking after a small plantation of trees for a doctor who was using the land as a tax loss. He was given a nice house to live in and was paid a small wage to do absolutely nothing apart from watching the trees grow. The doctor needed someone to keep an eye on things, and the man was very happy. He read extensively and occasionally traveled to town and made friends in the area. This was his method of research. After two years, he had decided on what he wanted to do next and off he went. He now owns a very successful restaurant.

People can make fortunes out of a variety of activities. Colonel Sanders made one out of cooking chicken, Paul McCartney, and countless others, out of singing and writing. Look around the world, particularly at different societies from the one you were brought up in. Drink deeply of what life has to offer. Maintain a positive and optimistic approach to everything. Educate and inform yourself of what is available on the menu of this world.

If you do what you love to do, you will live a very fulfilled and happy life. You don't have to go for great wealth, unless you really want it. There are so many experiences available. To enjoy as many as possible, and get the best out of them, you will need to structure your life in a particular way. Things rarely just happen. Those people who lead really successful lives usually have created the events and circumstances deliberately and with conscious intention. They have followed a plan or specific methods. Next, we will examine how this is done and give you the technique you will need to ensure that you are able to create what you want.

❖ ❖ ❖

CHAPTER 28

LIVING AS A CREATOR

Changing Your Life Script

There is an old saying in life that 5 percent of the people make things happen, 15 percent watch it happen, and 80 percent wonder what's happened! Only *you* can decide which group you will be in.

To help you join the 5 percent, here is the most useful of all techniques. It is the basis and foundation for every other personal growth methodology you will undertake. Without doing it, or something similar, you will be unable to really create the experiences you want in your life. Completing it makes everything so much easier. If you only use one of the techniques given in this book, use this one.

Inside you right now is your life script. It is the controlling program of your life that is a result of all your previous conditioning, and it dictates your destiny. Your future is held in your mindset, and this life script will play out forever unless it is changed. You may never have thought about this point before reading this book, but there is something within you that is driving your life. This something within you contains the whole plan of your existence and is the source of all your choices and decisions and, therefore, actions. This something is what is called your *life script*, and it creates your experiences by causing you to make conscious choices in the world.

In order to change it, you need to rewrite it and so be able to live out new experiences and choices. An excellent method for doing so, which has brought great success to thousands of people whom I have taught, is what I have called "Lifewrite." It is an opportunity to make changes to your life script so that you can re-engineer your mindset to achieve the new results you want. If you do not do this, then your only other option is to continue to live out what is programmed within you already.

Enjoying Your Desires

When deciding what you want to enjoy and what experiences you want to have, it is necessary to consider all aspects of your life. Leaving one part out can inhibit the success of the others. Your whole mind is one single interconnected organism, and each part is able to be in contact with all the others. For example, if you leave out the consideration of money and your financial realities, this may wreck your relationship. The pressure from having a lack of cash can quickly sour many seemingly positive relationships.

Or, if you leave out a consideration of your personal, one-to-one relationship from your plans, this can easily wreck your career. An unhappy partner can be a tremendous liability for you and your career goals. It is wise to ensure that your partner is included in your plans.

All the broad categories of life need to be catered for: relationships, health and fitness, career, wealth, creativity, and any other area important to you. Once this is done, then specific desires need to be chosen.

Your mind must know the desires that you want to enjoy. You need to be precise, just like a computer. If you don't know what you want, you will never get it, and you will continue to play out what your parents, school, and peer groups impressed upon you. If this was great, then keep it, but if there are any areas you would rather change, then you must concentrate on them.

Lifewrite

With Lifewrite, you are writing a short novel of your *future life*, so you need a structure to use that is practical and can be applied very easily and quickly.

What you do is as follows:

First, assemble the broad range of your desires under general headings, such as relationships, career, lifestyle (house, car, clothes), creativity, leisure activities, travel, and so on. Begin with the basics of life, and then branch out into the specialties you are interested in. This grouping together will help you form a general picture and focus on what you want. Remember to include all areas of your life.

Sort these desires into chronological order. Choose what you want to do, and when. Decide which are the most important and need immediate attention, which you need to put into place soon for long-term results, and which you can leave until later. If you want to start a business and go on holiday to South America, then there is no use in starting the business and *then* going to South America. Obviously, it is wiser to get the holiday over with first, or leave it until the business is established. Sort everything into priorities.

Once this is organized, you can then begin the Lifewrite itself.

If you are uncertain of what to choose in any or every area of life, then enter into a period of research as described in the previous chapter. It is useful to define each of the steps that will be necessary for you to take to fulfill the research and discovery process. In other words, decide exactly what you are going to do as your research. List the individual things carefully and precisely and define them in detail. Make a step-by-step plan. Clear up confusion before you start.

Now begin the actual writing of your future experiences. This is the "novel" of what you want to happen to you. You literally write out your own future as though you are telling a story.

Always write in the third person, identifying yourself by name. You may write in the present tense, for example: "In June, Kevin goes to Hawaii on a vacation," or you may write in the past tense: "In February, Joan started law school at Stanford University." (Always remember to put the year in, too.) It is entirely a matter of personal preference; both work equally well.

The experiences you wish to have should be well defined and detailed, rather than generalized. Do not go into ridiculous detail, but certainly be specific, as it is far easier to create the experiences you want when you are able to describe them with clarity.

Plan for a minimum of at least a year. Three- to five-year Lifewrites are more suitable because a year can pass in a flash. There is no limit as to how long in the future you can prepare your Lifewrite. Some people plan for 20 years ahead. It is useful to have more time available for your long-term or larger goals. Begin your Lifewrite about three months into the future. You may also give yourself a period of six months as you write and rewrite it, until it is completed.

Write out your desires in chronological order, in the form of a story. Writing out desires makes it very easy to choose which order is appropriate to fulfill them in and also to avoid self-delusion. A head full of desires, some of which conflict with each other, are quickly sorted out in the discipline of the written word. You can also live things out on the page rather than wasting a few years going for a desire that may prove unfulfilling. Writing out all the elements of an experience will often eliminate the need to undergo that experience, because you will discover that it is not what you really wanted. This will clear the decks of your mind so that you can concentrate on what will truly fulfill you rather than wasting time preoccupied with dozens of possibilities and living out none of them.

Be imaginative in your choices. You can create anything you wish within the normal range of human experience and available in the culture in which you live. Don't get stuck repeating a pattern of the past that you haven't enjoyed. If you don't change these patterns, no one will, and therefore you will continue to live them out.

Choose wisely. Research what you want to experience. Everything you focus on will come into your life as an opportunity. You may, of course, change anything you wish at any time. It is you who is in charge of your life, no one else, if you wish to take up this responsibility. (You are free, of course, to hand over the power of your life to any person you please, but they will then use you in whatever way suits them.) As things appear in your life and you see the reality of them, you can then decide to take them up or not. Be alert to opportunities as they appear. You can always change your mind if the opportunities do not look so attractive on closer inspection.

If you don't choose, and Lifewrite is a very effective way to examine and create your choices, then you will keep repeating the patterns of the past forever. This, in itself, is a choice.

The basic Universal Law is one of Abundance in everything. Look how a single seed of corn can grow into a bush that yields hundreds of corn cobs, each filled with seeds. Look to the heavens and see the stars in the sky, to the sea teeming with fish. Life doesn't hold back; it expresses its abundance constantly and continually. How much of that abundance you take up is entirely up to you. You may restrict yourself to very little, or you may choose a generous experience of life.

Once you have completed your Lifewrite, occasionally reread it and update it, including new choices and eliminating the old. It is a great idea to take a weekend off once a year and rent a cottage out of town to concentrate on your Lifewrite for the following year or more. Many people avoid this formal consideration of their lives. Make sure you don't. It is easy to become just a leaf blown in the wind by circumstances and miss the opportunity to cause your life to go in the direction you want it to.

Read your Lifewrite as often as you can, and take all the actions of your life in accordance with it. Do not contradict the contents of it with careless language or weak-mindedness. This will negate its creative power.

With regard to how often to read it, it is best in the first ten weeks to read it at least twice a week; for the next ten, once a week; and from then on, no less than once a month. This excludes any periods of revision. If you revise it dramatically, then you should read it regularly for a few weeks so that you can imbibe the new desires clearly.

Again, this is the single most important technique that you will ever do. Make sure you do it. It will change everything.

Here are two fictional samples. The first one is written by a single young man called Frank. He writes his Lifewrite as follows:

> In June (the year), Frank goes to New York to look for ideas to start a new business back home. The flight there is very relaxed, and he gets upgraded to business class, even though he only pays economy.
>
> Once in New York, he stays in an ideal hotel near the area where the businesses he is interested in operate from. The room is excellent, very quiet, and has a terrific view. He makes a point of eating in the restaurant and, while dining, he makes several useful contacts in the ten days that he is there. Many of them give him good leads and ideas that allow him to follow up on some brilliant opportunities. He is also invited out to dinner and lunch at people's homes. At one of these meals, he meets a friend of the person who invited him, who offers him a deal that he

can take home, that will make him a very successful man. He takes the opportunity and discovers that this person is honest and generous and really is committed to helping him.

In his tour of the city, he also discovers three other fabulous businesses that are available and within his range to secure. The trip, from a business point of view, is an amazing success and sets him up for many years, increasing his earnings by over $300,000 a year. He makes new friends that last him the rest of his life. Also, at one of the dinner parties, he meets a beautiful and radiant young woman, and they are both immediately attracted to each other. He finds her stunningly attractive and she willingly agrees to accompany him back to...and I leave the rest to your imagination!

And here is the other example written by a woman called Amelia. She writes:

Amelia goes to Hawaii in July (year) with her partner Paul. She has rented a bungalow with her own private swimming pool at a luxurious resort for two weeks. It is a wonderful rest, and she travels around the villages and towns, visiting the local artists. The people she meets at the hotel are very friendly and are happy to leave the couple alone. The staff are excellent. Amelia and Paul have all the privacy they want and are able to grow more deeply in love than they have ever been before. It is the most wonderful time they have ever spent together, and it enriches them both.

While there, another couple invites them both to join them on their luxury yacht for a few days as it cruises the Hawaiian islands. Amelia and Paul happily accept and have a wonderful adventure, mooring in little bays with white deserted beaches. The people on the islands invite them to join in with their festivities, and they have nights of sheer pleasure under the stars eating and dancing with the very friendly people. At the end of the trip, they return home with a new bond between them, having had the most wonderful holiday ever..."

It might seem amazing to you that people can just write out what they want, and it happens. So many people who have attended our seminars and practiced this technique have had this experience. It is amazing, but it is also just a result of the laws of life. What has happened in your life so far is a result of what is in your lifescript right now, and by changing it formally, which is what Lifewrite is, you will cause the laws of life to operate in the way you want them. What is more amazing is that so few people realize that this is how life works. Now you know, and you can use this technique as you please.

With each of the fictional Lifewrite examples above, you can see that they are only small sections of the whole Lifewrite. They are quite detailed, but not overly so. The experiences created are obviously very pleasurable to the writers.

By writing one's life script in this way, you will bring to the surface all the doubts, fears, and guilty feelings that are in your mind about having an excellent and absolutely happy life. Why settle for anything less? It's available to you. If and when any negativity does arise, such as thoughts like: "This could never happen to me," or "It's too good to be true," or "How could this process possibly work," then just write the thoughts on a separate piece of paper and throw it in the garbage at the end of your writing. The best thing you can do with negativity is remove it from your system. The formality of writing it down and throwing it away sends a very strong signal to your mind that you no longer want such beliefs polluting your mind.

You can see that these fictional people have written out their ideal experiences. You can do the same. With Amelia's, you notice that she has included her partner Paul. Now it is very important, if you are to include anyone else in your Lifewrite, that you write it in association with them. Do not expect them to do what is in your Lifewrite if they have not been involved in the creation of it.

Write your own script out, following the steps outlined above, and you will soon see why this is the most powerful technique for many, many people. It really is fabulous. Don't get too hung up about the dates. Some things will come sooner, and some later, than you wrote out. Just adjust and allow the events to happen when they are able to. Whatever happens is only just a reflection of your own beliefs and patterning. The clearer you are, the quicker things can come to you. Next, we are going to look at exactly why this technique works.

❖ ❖ ❖

CHAPTER 29

THE ATTRACTION MECHANISM

Awakening to More of Your Mind

Now that you understand the necessary concept of taking responsibility for your own life, it is vital to remember that *everything* in life appears for a reason. Nature has laws, and there is no contradicting them. Even when you are unaware of the laws, life doesn't care. It follows its own patterns, and it is up to you to discover what they are, if you want to gain the best that life has to offer.

The greatest ignorance in our society is the way that our minds create our reality. We have understood rational, logical thought and its application to the material world to create our technological society. Now we need to turn our attention to the function of the mind itself, as it is the controller of our happiness or unhappiness, our success or failure in the world.

You literally attract into your life, by this unstudied mechanism, all the people and opportunities that you are involved with. There are no coincidences. Everything occurs because of the ever-present abilities of your mind.

Let's look at some simple proof in your own life.

You may have experienced thinking about someone, and a couple of minutes later that person phones you. Or you are walking along the street and thinking about an old friend whom you haven't seen for years and you turn the corner and there he or she is. Or, you may have known mothers who knew something was wrong with their child in another part of the house or at school—they felt something, they "knew," and they were right. Or, you may have examined the studies of identical twins who have experiences of dreaming the same dreams or having the same thoughts even when they are on opposite sides of the world. Or maybe you've been able to predict which songs are coming up next on the radio and get three in a row correct.

These experiences are commonplace, and they rely on this mechanism of mind. What else could they rely on? *Coincidence*, remember, is just a word we use when we are unaware of life's laws in operation.

The Significance of Wavelengths

First of all, it is necessary to realize that we live in a Universe filled with wavelengths, both natural and those made by human beings.

The natural ones, such as infrared, ultraviolet, gamma rays, and the various radiations from outer space, we are all familiar with, and we know they exist because there are instruments to recognize and measure them. These natural wavelengths have always existed in the universe, but we only know about them because we have built the instruments to read them. Five hundred years ago, humans were unable to know of their existence because they did not have the instruments that could pick them up. No doubt in another 500 years, more of these natural wavelengths will have been discovered because more advanced and sensitive instruments will have been invented.

Today we also have the wavelengths that are a result of the inventions of human beings, such as mobile phones, television and radio, satellite information, and so on. These wavelengths fly around the world and are able to be picked up by whoever has the correct instrument designed to recognize and translate them into useful and understandable forms.

How Wavelengths Are Encoded

All wavelengths are encoded with information that comes from the *source* of the wavelength. The television program that you receive on your set at home is a result of what is being beamed out from the television channel. It can't come from anywhere else. You are tuned into that specific signal. There is no coincidence taking place. The wavelengths of the mobile phone call contain the words that are being spoken by the people involved in the call. Even though they are invisible to the naked eye, they obviously exist. What is not so obvious is that humans also are wavelength-emanating and receiving beings.

Programming Your Wavelengths

Every single person's brain sends out wavelengths. There are many scientific instruments that have been developed over the years to read and analyze them. The one that has been gaining popularity for many years is the biofeedback machine.

This simple device is basically a small box with an amplifier, a light-emitting device (an LED) and a sound speaker. It is connected by a number of wires to a headband that has some electrodes sewn into it. A special conducting cream is applied to the electrodes, and they are then placed at various points on the skin of the head and held in place by fastening the headband.

The person is then able, by controlling their brain's wavelengths, to send a signal down the wires to the box and cause the LED to turn on and off and flash at various speeds and also to make a sound tone that can increase in volume and alter its rhythm and modulation. All this is done purely by the control of their brain's wavelengths. Biofeedback machines are readily available, and anyone can learn to use them quite quickly.

These simple instruments prove beyond any doubt that the brain's wavelengths exist. What is perhaps not realized is that these same wavelengths are encoded with information. The TV transmitting tower can only beam out the program coming from the studio it is attached to and, in exactly the same way, you beam out wavelengths that are encoded with what is within you.

Your mindset, which contains your memory and all the elements that make that system up, is the source of the choices and decisions you make, which become your life experience. It also is the programmer of the wavelengths you send out into the world and to which the world responds by sending into your life the various desires that match your inner patterns and memory banks.

You actually attract into your life the things and people you are interested in. You find yourself in the right place at the right time to undergo the experiences you are holding in your mind, regardless of whether these experiences are good or bad. If you are unsuccessful in fulfilling your desires, it simply means that you have a sabotage pattern within your subconscious, which is sending out a conflicting signal.

You might have a desire to become very creative, but in your subconscious still lives a pattern or belief that says you are hopeless at creative activities. It could have been put there by a teacher in your school days who humiliated you in art class. It then lasts for the rest of your life, unless it is dissolved, sabotaging your conscious desire.

The Power of Wavelengths

The other vital fact to remember is that the power of a wavelength is not diminished by the number of receivers that pick it up. For example, a television transmitting tower beams its signals all over the city. If only one television set is on, all the wavelengths do not pour into it and blow it up. If ten million sets are on, the signal does not weaken, causing the picture to go dim. It doesn't matter how many sets are on, they all receive exactly the same quality of picture. The only variation in quality comes from the distance that each set is from the transmitting tower. This is obviously dependent on the strength of the signal.

The human brain is a surprising entity in that its abilities and potentials have yet to be completely understood. We know that it is far more complex and powerful than the most advanced computer, even though a fraction of the size. It also has abilities of a subtle nature that have yet to be discovered, even though we can glean some insights into what it can do from the teachings of the sages and mind explorers of all cultures.

There is no doubt that the brain emits wavelengths and that these wavelengths are encoded with information. What is not yet known or proven is how powerful it is in the sense of how far it can transmit these wavelengths. There is some suggestion that it has access to finer frequencies that have no limit in their ability to broadcast vast distances. The only way to know for sure is by testing your own abilities for yourself.

How Are Wavelengths Transmitted?

To understand all this thoroughly, it is useful to continue with our analogy. Imagine yourself as a television transmitting tower, beaming out your signals to the world. These signals are being received by all other living things. We are all constantly receiving and transmitting wavelength encoded messages to each other. It is all going on at a subconscious and unconscious level. You could say that we are all like mini television transmitting towers and that we live in an ocean of wavelengths, which are encoded with information relevant to us. We pick up matching signals and desires, at an unconscious or subconscious level, from other people, and it is these people who are attracted into our lives and we into theirs.

So if you have within you a subconscious pattern in your memory bank that holds the view that all relationships are boring and mundane, then you will be constantly beaming that pattern out into the world, and it will be picked up by people who have a matching pattern. They then will be attractive and attracted to you.

If you have a pattern within you that says there is a lack of money in your life, then you will be sending that out into the world; therefore, you will attract into your life the opportunities that result in a lack of money. You will not be able to attract into your life the opportunities to make a great deal of money because it is not in your patterning, and so you cannot broadcast it into the world, just like a TV station cannot broadcast a program not in its library.

By realizing this, you can then take necessary actions to change what you want to experience. You have to stop broadcasting what you don't want and start to broadcast what you do want.

It is not necessary to grow an extra brain or do anything out of the ordinary. You merely become conscious of the faculties that you have already and then apply them with full consciousness rather than from a semi-conscious or unconscious state.

This means using your wavelength broadcasting faculties deliberately by only holding in your mind the events you want to enjoy. Never forgetting, of course, that you need to eliminate whatever is within you that is sending out the wrong or conflicting signals, and which is a result of the old patterns. If you don't remove these, they will continue to send out their signals resulting in blocked or conflicting goals and, therefore, confusion and difficulty in bringing about the results you want.

Using the Power of Focus

Have you noticed that when you are vitally interested in something, all sorts of coincidences start to occur? The more intensely you are focused on that particular experience, the more you seem to attract into your life the necessary events and contacts that you need to bring that goal to fruition. If you have just become interested in certain people, you suddenly start to meet them unexpectedly, or find that people know them or their names come up in conversation, or you find yourselves at the same party. And this is magnified even more when the people are interested in each other. This is not a strange thing; it is just how life works. *The intensity of your desire* fuels the mechanism of attraction within your mind, which then sends out the appropriate wavelengths, so bringing you the experiences you desire.

Create New Mind Patterns

Your old belief patterns have created the experiences you have had so far through the use of this wavelength-emanating mechanism. How it works to cause you to take the appropriate conscious choices is as follows:

When a person or circumstance appears in your life that matches your subconscious patterns—for better or worse—you will receive a conscious thought impulse, which arises from your subconscious memory bank. This causes you to choose them or that experience, regardless of what the consequences might be. Initially, it might seem like a terrific experience or opportunity, and you dive in with excitement. Then, as time unfolds, it may reveal itself as an unrewarding and frustrating involvement. It would be this latter experience that was held in a pattern in your memory, which had to be played out. Conversely, something that appeared boring and mundane, which you may consciously feel obliged to commit yourself to, which has also been attracted into your life by your wavelengths, may turn out to be amazing and fulfilling. Your conscious choice to agree to join in with that experience, even though it seemed on the surface to be dull, was prompted by your subconscious pattern that was, in fact, always loaded with the resulting positive experience, even though you were unaware of it.

Whatever comes into your conscious mind causes you to take the action that matches the subconscious pattern. If you want to change what comes into your life, you, once again, need to change the patterns in your memory.

New mind patterns will always be needed for each new experience. To attract new goals, it is necessary to insert into your mind an exact expression of the experience you want to have. The more precise it is, the easier it is to dislodge the old, unwanted pattern and insert the new ideal instruction.

You can only send out what is already within you. You can't send out what is not within you. You have to put it in, otherwise the emanating signals from your subconscious will remain the same.

The best technique for this is one that uses the mind in the same way that it normally operates. There is no point in trying to force your mind to do something it is not already structured for. This technique is called "Vibrasonics," and it is detailed in the next chapter. Examine it carefully, and use it to help you to bring into your life the experiences you want.

❖ ❖ ❖

CHAPTER 30

VIBRASONICS

Your Power of Creation

Your mind creates your experiences using three powers: (1) The *primary power* is the use of *thoughts*, which include all sounds and language. The effects of these are profound, and we are constantly using them to program and reprogram our systems.

(2) The *strongest* power is the use of its own *energy*, which sometimes translates as emotion or as a flow of the life force.

(3) And the *clearest* is its *visual power*. This can be seen in the dream world and in the realms of deep meditation. The visions and adventures of the inner worlds are far more profound and significant than those of the external world. The language of the deep mind is visual. A picture tells a thousand words in the mind as well.

Now you will be given a very potent, yet very simple technique to assist you in achieving your goals. This technique only takes five minutes to do, once a day. It uses all three of the mind's powers and matches exactly the way your own mind works. Many people have had dramatic and amazing results from this technique. The key for you will be to use it and to *keep practicing* it until you achieve what you want. This technique is "Vibrasonics."

The purpose of Vibrasonics is to assist you in changing the patterns of your mind so that you can broadcast into the world the experiences that you wish to attract. In other words, all you will do is to change the patterns and beliefs, and your higher intelligence, which is already in operation 24 hours a day and brings you all the events of your life, will actually attract to you what you want. It will use the wavelengths to do this. It is all an automatic process.

Follow the steps below precisely, and practice regularly for results. As always, no practice equals no results.

1. Decide on an experience you would like to have.

2. Encapsulate it into a scene, similar to a movie or video. The scene should be approximately 30 seconds long. It is as though you have gone into the future and become a "fly on the wall," *watching yourself* experiencing this particular scene. You always see yourself, your body, acting out the desire in the scene. It is exactly as though someone has filmed you actually living out this scene, brought it back from the future, and you are looking at it on a screen. Remember, you always see yourself in the scene; you are never looking through your own eyes at what is happening.

3. The scene should encapsulate the *fulfillment of your desire completely.* Go as far into the future as you can. Do not create a scene that is only a partial way to the fulfillment of your desire.

An example: Let's say that you are the sales manager of a company, and you want to become managing director. What you would do is invent a scene that would encapsulate this desire perfectly. You would see yourself in the managing director's office, performing the tasks that the managing director would do in his or her day-to-day activities. You would be giving orders to staff, making arrangements with clients, or having discussions with members of the board. Pick any of these normal activities *that only the managing director could do*, and make that your 30-second scene. In other words, it is a slice of the life of the managing director, and you see yourself in this role. There is no way that you could be playing out this scene without actually being the managing director. You must create a scene that encapsulates you doing exactly what it is that you want.

You would not invent a scene that had the chairman of the board congratulating you on your appointment as managing director, because much can happen between being appointed and actually doing the job. This is why it is important to go as far along the track into the future as possible, to a point where you are actually living out your desire to the fullest extent.

For instance, if you wanted to marry someone, you would not have a Vibrasonic where you were being proposed to; you would have it set at sometime *after* the wedding, for much can happen between a proposal and the wedding day. Instead, set the scene at a party celebrating your first (or 50th!) wedding anniversary.

What this does is to give a clear image to your mind that you want to live out this experience. It now has a new and precise instruction encoded into its system that it will automatically run with.

4. The sound track of the scene is "actual." It does not involve any repetition of affirmations or statements, such as "I am managing director, I am managing director, I am managing director." It is a "true" soundtrack, with the words that would actually be said by a managing director in that particular situation.

5. Once the scene is decided upon, prepare yourself for its implantation into your mind in the following way:

Sit comfortably in a chair, with your back straight. It is important to formalize the implantation by sitting in this way, rather than lying on a bed or slouching on a couch. Vibrasonics is an action that you take, and it requires concentration and focusing, rather than daydreaming. This is not fantasy time, where the feeling is "Wouldn't it be nice if ..." It is *decision and internal action* time. Only the discipline of a deliberate intention will bring you the results.

Once seated, and this is where you take a potent diversion from things like visualization, you must *turn on a positive energy*. This means you must feel as good as you can. There are many ways that you can activate a positive energy, such as deep breathing, listening to music, exercise, and/or remembering a past event in your life that was fulfilling or exciting. Perhaps you can think back to when you won a prize for something and you were very pleased and excited. Or perhaps you can think of a romantic evening where you felt love and happiness. Maybe you remember an exhilarating natural vista that you witnessed when you were on vacation that filled you with a great joy of being alive. You can use any of these sorts of memories. Perhaps you are able to turn a positive energy on at will already. It doesn't matter what you use to activate this energy, as long as you activate it somehow. It is the addition of this energy, coupled with the details below, that will eliminate the negative patterns.

If you use music, then be sure to turn it off *before* you begin the Vibrasonic. If you are remembering a past successful event, then *hold on* to the energy that has been activated, and *let go* of the memory that brought it up, leaving just the positive energy within you, and then *insert* the Vibrasonic.

Whatever you use, you will soon learn how to be able to turn on a positive energy by your will alone. There is just a knack to it, and you will soon pick it up and can dispense with the other methods.

It is *vitally* important to bring this energy into action, as the whole success of the technique depends on it. Whatever degree of good feeling you can activate will do. As time progresses, and you practice more, it will become easier and easier and then automatic. The good energy will also become more powerful.

6. Having turned on the energy, now bring the 30-second scene onto the screen of your mind. Run it. Even if it is hazy or seemingly nonexistent and you only see darkness, keep going. If you find it difficult to see yourself, your body, in the scene performing the actions, don't worry; it is still working. A flash of the clothes you are wearing is enough. It is the intention behind it that is the motivating factor.

If you have difficulty visualizing the scene within your mind, again, don't worry. If you could see it as clearly as you do a film in the theater, then it would be coming into your life very quickly. It is natural to have difficulty seeing the scene clearly, for the negativity and sabotage patterns are blocking you. Anything new that is contradictory to an old pattern will be resisted by those patterns. The removal of the negativity loaded into them is the only method of dissolving them and so allowing the new desire pattern to become firmly programmed into your memory.

The way to increase your ability to visualize is very simple. You can look at any magazine photograph of a living room. Gaze at it for a minute, then close your eyes and see how much of it you can remember. List all the different objects mentally, try to actually see them in your mind. Then open your eyes and check, then repeat. Do this for two weeks with different pictures, and you will find that your ability to visualize increases remarkably. An even more useful suggestion is to take a recent photograph of yourself and stick it on a collage of pictures that sum up the goal of your Vibrasonic. Then you can use it to practice on. It has the additional effect of reminding you of your goal as you practice. Naturally, you do not merely use it as your Vibrasonic. You must use the specially created 30-second "motion picture" scene.

Keep running the 30-second scene again and again, at least ten times. But, if you lose concentration and your mind wanders to something else or the scene changes or you lose the positive energy, *then immediately stop and open your eyes for a second or two, recharge the energy, and start the process again.* Any negativity, lethargy, or emotions you feel are a result of the release of those factors that are sabotaging and hindering your ability to achieve the experience that the scene encapsulates. It is appropriate and correct that these negative releases come out. It is one of the major functions of the technique and the only way that you can release the negativity.

7. Continue to perform Vibrasonics at least once a day. You may also run one just before you go to sleep or when you wake up while still lying in bed. But this must not replace the formal sitting once a day for at least five minutes.

8. You may also do one for far longer—an hour or more if you want. These are very effective for removing deep-seated, old patterns that have been hindering you for a long time. You still open your eyes and reset the process every time you lose either the image, the positive feeling, or when your mind wanders. It is also a good idea after a long Vibrasonic to rest a while and fall into a semi-sleep to access the dream world of the unconscious and perhaps receive a signal or information from that deeper source. This was the technique used by the man whose story I told you earlier, who had, while in the womb, experienced his mother falling over and embedded into his mind the concept "If I love a woman, I will die."

9. Continue your Vibrasonics until you have achieved your goal or until you have lost the desire to have it. Be alert to the signals from life itself that advise you of the need to take particular actions to achieve what it is that you want. Become aware of the opportunities that will come your way as a result of the instructions you are sending to your mind and the encoded wavelengths that your mind then sends out.

10. Finally, remember that it is necessary, as with all the other techniques, to take the actions in the world that are in tune with your desires. No actions means no result. These techniques are not an opportunity to sit at home and have the check come in the mail, or the perfect partner knock at your door, while you just sit on the sofa using your mind. Actions are the key. But actions without mind techniques run the risk of the wrong or no result. So do both.

Once you have completed your Lifewrite, use the Vibrasonics and the 22 times 11 and the declarations to achieve each of the goals you have written. By doing so, you will become the creator of your destiny. You will be taking complete responsibility for your life, and you will be strengthening your will power, concentration power, and intelligence. In short, you will be becoming a more conscious being. And this is the certain way to absolute happiness.

Consciousness is the real key, and in the final section we are going to look at the great mysteries of life: the unconscious, higher states, the realm of higher powers of the mind, karma and reincarnation, your true identity, and the state of enlightenment.

This will be the icing on the cake, the reason for, and the meaning of, life, and here you will be given the means of discovering your most essential and blissful self.

❖ ❖ ❖

❖

THE ULTIMATE EXPERIENCE FOR A HUMAN BEING

❖

THE STATE OF ABSOLUTE HAPPINESS

There is available for you, a state of being that sur-passes every other experience possible. It is so pro-found, so totally fulfilling, so exquisite, so blissful, that when you are in it, all questions are answered, all desires satiated.

To find this experience, it is only necessary to know where it is and the methods of how it is achieved. The beauty of this state of being is that it is closer to you than your own breath, and the way to it has already been tried and tested by countless others who have gone before you.

Here we will examine the ultimate goal of every human being. Know this and you will have forever what it is that you truly want, that you truly need, and that will give you everything.

C H A P T E R   3 1

WHAT YOU TRULY ARE

Meeting with a Great Being

I have been very fortunate to have had experiences that have totally transformed my life from what I was conditioned to become. The most profound of these were all due to meetings with a most remarkable man. He was known as Muktananda, which translates as "The Bliss Liberator." Bliss is a way of describing absolute happiness. The experiences that I had in his company were both liberating, in the most total sense of the word, as well as ecstatically blissful.

Muktananda lived in Ganeshpuri, a tiny village a couple of hours from Bombay, India, and he traveled all over the world for the last few years of his life, transmitting his ancient wisdom and power to millions of people, both in India and the rest of the world. He was an Enlightened Being, a *Siddha*, which means *a perfected master*. This means that he had transcended, or gone beyond, the normal state of consciousness that 99 percent of the population live in.

He was truly extraordinary, as the half a million or so people he initiated outside India will confirm. In the West, we have little knowledge or tradition of people such as this. These beings are like a flash of lightning that come into your life, revealing the true power that lays latent within you. Unpredictable, indefinable, uncontrollable, incomprehensible, Muktananda was filled with an awesome, loving energy. Just to be in his company altered your state. You literally felt different. You were filled with such bliss, divine ecstasy, all-consuming love, euphoric joy—such absolute happiness—that your mind stopped its constant chatter, and you were drawn radically into the present and saw, usually for the first time, exactly what life truly had to offer. It was as though you had woken from a deep sleep, and your senses had become totally fulfilled, enlivened, and exhilarated.

Most people are bound to a lower state of consciousness, which we call ordinary life, with its struggles and limitations. But in this staggering and seemingly infinite Universe in which we live, there is obviously much, much more than we can possibly comprehend with our tiny, personal consciousness. In fact, we have no grasp of even a hundredth of the capabilities of our own individual minds. Muktananda had. He was a fully self-realized being. He no longer held beliefs about how life worked at its deepest and most profound level; he knew, from direct, personal experience. He was also able to apply and demonstrate these unknown opportunities of life for the benefit of millions of people.

Muktananda was an author, poet, musician, singer, artist, master gardener, cook, and an authority on most of the scriptures and spiritual paths of India. He administered an ashram (which is a school for attaining higher states of consciousness and discovering the true source of happiness) of thousands of residents. He was visited by, and gave advice to, astronauts, physicists, actors, artists, business and government leaders, rock stars, psychiatrists, doctors, lawyers, and millions of everyday people. They came to him because he knew the truth of how to become ecstatically happy.

So it is to Muktananda that I will always be truly grateful. Without my seven years studying and practicing under his auspices, my life would be an intellectual exercise, an uncertain search and a normal seeking of satisfaction in the objects of life rather than in the essence of life.

His main teaching was to know your Self, to look within, understand the mechanism of your mind, master it, and free all blockages from your system. He lived his whole life in this way, studying under the greatest sages of India for 25 five years and finally, for an additional 9 years, was the leading pupil of the great Nityananda, who was recognized all over India as a fully enlightened being.

To experience your highest potential and awaken to experiences that will bring you ecstatic joy and total fulfillment, you will have to know your Self. So what is it, what is the essence of who and what you are, what are its limitations and boundaries, and how can you access the whole of it and live your life in the best way possible?

Considering Yourself

The basic premise of all spiritual and personal growth is that most people suffer from *avidya*, a Sanskrit word meaning a *misconception about reality*. It is this particular misconception that is the cause of almost all confusion, suffering, and lack of success in life.

Right now, as you read this book, there is held together in your consciousness a whole collection of faculties that you call "me," and everyone else calls "you." Most of these faculties you are unaware of, even though they are vital and necessary to your being. If you examine this "youness," you quickly become aware of the fact that you have a body and senses, and there are also thoughts, imagination, and feelings present. This tends to be the limit of self-examination for most human beings.

Many people do not believe that they are anything other than a physical body. They have not given any time to considering the possibility that there may be more to them than being just a bag of skin and bones with a few organs and some blood. They also presume that their mind is a sort of chemical or electrical by-product of the physical body, rather than the body being a result of mind.

Self-examination and introspection is a vital activity for anyone who wishes to access their full potential and discover all the secrets of themselves and life itself. In the culture of the so-called developed world, this is not recognized as a useful or productive thing to do. The main push is to raise the standard of living and to educate everyone. These are excellent goals and should continue to be pursued, but it is also necessary to focus on what you truly are if you are to know absolute happiness.

What Is a Human Being?

Have you ever wondered how you found yourself in this predicament of being a human being? Who or what put you here, and how did it actually happen? Did you exist in some way before you were born as a physical body? Did you agree to be born as a human being or ever make a decision that you would come to Earth? How can you remember this, if it was actually the case? Or are you just a physical entity that had no consciousness and did not exist as an individual before you were born and will not exist in any way after the body dies? How do you really know what you are? How do you decide? Does anyone really know the truth?

These are, of course, the major philosophical questions of human life and have been pondered by all the great minds over the centuries. It is relevant for us to look briefly at them because as you proceed to your goal of absolute happiness, you will discover that your whole mind will reveal its contents to you. This is a wonderful and stunning experience, but it can also be confusing unless you understand what is going on. Your mind contains undreamed-of realms of experience. In fact, in your dreams when asleep, you explore these realms, but rarely are conscious of more than a tiny fraction of what is available. The dream world is really a dream Universe because it is filled with such an incredible array of experiences.

What Is the Nature of Your Individuality?

You realize, as you explore your inner nature through conscious intro-spection, that your personality or "personness," which you so strongly identify with as yourself, really is only a mask you wear. What you truly are is far deeper and far more profound than you have ever realized. This is why the great sages have always instructed their pupils to "know thyself."

Because of the "busy"-ness of life and, in some cases, the weakness of concentration and will power, most people are focusing on the external world, or the physical reality, as it is commonly referred to. There are obviously other levels of reality that exist even though we may not know of them, which are beyond the reach of the physical world. The activi-ties of the mind are one of these. You cannot grab a dream, for it is not physical. You can see its physical *effects* in rapid eye movements (REM) and skin responses, but it belongs in the non-physical realms of life.

It is in these internal realms that you will discover what you truly are. And, as you search for your true self, the mind will unfold its contents, and you will see and experience all sorts of internal revelations that will cause you to draw some extraordinary conclusions. This is why I will be giving you an outline of the probable experiences you may encounter, so that you can assimilate them and not allow them to drag you from your goals into the infinite realms of the mind. It is such an attractive movie that you will find yourself enthralled and amazed at what it can do, as you examine it internally. This whole, or higher, mind is a biocomputer game of phenomenal power that contains all the possibilities of the Universe.

As you go for your ultimate goal—your absolute happiness—you will discover that the mind will show you who and what you are and what you have been. You will find that you are far more than a body with a mind. You will unravel the secrets of your identity and seem to experience past lives.

Past Lives, Present Realities

The theory of past lives is one that you will have to confront as you proceed to absolute happiness. As your mind unfolds itself, it will give you experiences that you will identify as being a past life. You will genuinely feel that you have lived it and that you know, with complete certainty, you were the person living that past life.

There are three possible explanations for this experience. First, that it is absolutely true: past lives do exist; or second, somehow you have accessed a Universal memory where all the events that have ever happened are recorded, and you have tuned into a particular past life that someone, somewhere, once lived. In other words, you have accessed their memories. And third, that it is all a hallucination of your mind.

In a Universe such as this, I believe anything is possible. So you can take your pick, because you will eventually, if you follow a path of introspection and self-examination, experience yourself as something that has lived before as another identity and as something that does not require a physical body to be conscious and aware and remember what is going on. I personally prefer the theory of reincarnation, and so do the vast majority of people who have pursued the path of absolute happiness. If it is a hallucination, then it seems to be a very powerful one that has gripped some of the best minds who have ever lived.

Almost every lasting philosophy and spiritual path, even though it may not agree with the theory of reincarnation, teaches that you are not just a physical body. There are various ways of saying it, but the central theme of all of them is that you are a being, an entity that is independent of the physical body. This entity is sometimes referred to as your *spirit, soul*, or *subtle body*. Occasionally, it is called your *higher self*. Let's call it a subtle body from now on so that we won't get caught up in the various disagreements involving the different belief systems.

The Existence of Your Subtle Body

According to the teachings of reincarnation, and from now on we will presume that they are correct, this subtle body has existed prior to your birth. It continues to live within the physical body for the duration of the body's life and then departs from the physical when it has served its purpose. When the energy body leaves the physical body, the physical dies, but the subtle body continues. The subtle body wears a physical body in a similar way to how your physical body would wear a body stocking.

Prior to birth, you slipped into the envelope of the physical body and are always totally independent of it, even though temporarily imprisoned within the fleshy walls. You brought into your present life a series of memories and impressions that you have collected over eons of time, from previous lives. For a variety of reasons, most people have no consciousness of these past lives, even though they can be accessed by regressive hypnosis and appear as a by-product of correct meditation (meditation is a specific, concentrated way of looking within that I will discuss shortly).

You will never know for sure until you directly experience yourself as a separate entity, alive, or conscious, and independent of the physical body. Some people say that they "astral travel"; that is, they are aware of themselves in an astral body floating around a room looking down at their physical bodies or flying all over the world and even to other planets, while they sleep. In this experience, they are always connected to their physical bodies by, so they say, a fine silvery cord. They say that they do not know whether the astral body would survive or not if the cord was to break.

One of the Chinese systems has another approach. They believe that through special exercises it is possible to create a "spiritual body" from the physical and that this can then become an independent energy body that no longer requires a physical body. When the physical body dies, this self-formed energy body remains alive and can explore the universe.

Some people like to spend time trying to discover what their past lives were and even attempt therapy to elicit these past events. This may or may not be helpful. If they feel better and are able to proceed more pleasurably towards their goals, then it is useful. I personally believe that the past is the past, and it is the present and the future that should be of concern.

This particular work is all about results and achieving your desires and creating the life you want here and now, although it is useful to be informed about the philosophy of reincarnation. Whatever has happened to you in the past has happened, whether it is in this present life, when you were a child, or in some past life when you were occupying a different body. It is no use dwelling upon it. You have already lived it. Everything that you have experienced in the past is encapsulated in the identity that you are living right now, from however deep in the past it has come. It is the only thing you have to deal with. It is vital to get on with this present life. It is your vision for your future that will give you personal freedom and allow you to come most powerfully into the present. If there is anything to clear or that you need to know or remember from the past, it will come up quite naturally during the methods you will learn here.

The Law of Karma

The law of karma is closely intertwined with reincarnation. It basically states that "whatever you do comes back to you." It is absolutely precise. If you hurt someone, then you will receive back hurt in exactly the same quantity, but not necessarily from the person you hurt. It can come from any source. So if you punched someone in the face, the law of karma would operate for you to receive the same back. You may find that you are in a football match and hit your own face on the goal post as you slip while running for a goal. Or, if you are truly loving to someone, then you will receive back the same love, but again not necessarily from the same person.

All the actions that you take in each life are stored in your memory as impressions. These stored memories are known as karma. Therefore, it is wise to perform good and generous actions so that you can enjoy the fruits of these in the future, whether in this life or the next. The law of karma continues through all your lives, and it may be that you are living out in this life the results of actions that you took in a past or several past lives.

I have found that the law of karma works flawlessly in my life and in the lives of the people I know, regardless of whether or not reincarnation exists. In the Bible, it is said that "as you sow, so you shall reap," and this is basically an explanation of karma. It seems that the more you develop yourself and increase your awareness and consciousness, the faster the law of karma operates. In fact, after intense periods of meditation, I have found that it can literally become instant, which is an amazing experience. You really do get back what you give out. Keep this in mind always, whether you believe in karma or not. It is a very useful rule to live by.

Without any doubt, there is a subtle, or energy, body within you right now. You can actually feel, sense, and see it, by the application of correct practices. It is not an unusual thing, and it has been codified by every single spiritual path since time began. Sometimes it is wrapped in the shrouds of myth, and at other times it is revealed in an allegorical way. It certainly exists within you, again, whether you reincarnate or not.

It is certainly worth examining because it is the key to really understanding what you are and being able to access all the hidden talents and potentials that exist within you. There are tremendous states of consciousness and powers of the mind that can only be accessed by clearing your subtle body.

The subtle body, as you shall see, is the vehicle of the mind. Free it and clear it, and you will truly empower yourself.

❖ ❖ ❖

CHAPTER 32

YOUR COILED POWER

The Myth of the Serpent

If you examine the myths of all cultures and religions, you will find one common image in them all. It is that of a snake, usually called a serpent. From Adam and Eve in the garden of Eden, the Australian Aboriginal Rainbow Serpent, Moses and his serpent staff, Quetzalcoatl, the Mayan feathered serpent, the Indian Kundalini, or coiled serpent; to the Greek Caduceus or staff of Hermes, which is a staff with a serpent, or sometimes two, coiled around it; and on and on, you will find numerous descriptions and stories about these reptiles.

In ancient times, before the written word was available on a mass scale, people would have to communicate and pass on their knowledge by telling stories and by painting. Anything that someone had discovered or had been told by their elders had to be transmitted to the next generation to ensure their well-being. Many of the dances of tribal peoples around the campfire were expressions of useful information about where food could be found, or warnings about dangerous animals, or where rivers could be crossed, and so on. Their dances and paintings were their "textbooks" for survival and knowledge, as well as a means of celebration.

What is interesting about the myth of the serpent is that, like all else in these tribal stories, it symbolized something to do with human life.

If you look at the symbol of the medical profession, you will see they have used variations of the staff of Hermes, the Greek Caduceus. Caduceus, in literal translation, means a *Herald's Staff*. But the reason that it was chosen as the symbol of the healing profession is because it signifies something far more profound, as do all the serpents in every culture and age. This "something" was, of course, completely understood by those who chose the symbol. It was explicitly relevant to healing. They didn't just choose it because it looked nice.

What the medical profession's Caduceus signifies and parallels is the human nervous system—obviously an appropriate symbol for doctors, as the spinal cord and brain are the most vital elements of a person's life.

Imagine a human spinal cord sitting up straight with a brain on the top. If you look at it face on, you will see that it is very similar to a snake with its head flared open. A cobra is the most familiar representation of this shape. If you poke a cobra with a stick, it will stand upright and flare its head, ready to attack.

So the serpent, or snake, was probably the clearest representation tribal people could use for a human spinal cord and brain. Snakes would always be around, and every tribe would be familiar with them. So any information that was tied in with such a strong and familiar symbol would be easily remembered by the succeeding generation.

Now the reason that the human spinal cord is so important is because it is the most important part of the physical body. It transmits all the signals from the brain to the rest of the body. But what is less known is that the serpent myth was pointing to the subtle spinal cord, called *sushumna*, in the Indian system, which is the central structure of the subtle body. The real knowledge these myths of the serpent were aiming to reveal was of the subtle body. The native peoples did not have a medical profession as we know it today. There were no autopsies or surgeons who examined the physical body after death. What they saw internally during their "dreamtimes" and meditations were the activities of the subtle body, which is why they chose the symbol of the serpent as the means of communicating the knowledge to succeeding generations. It is also the subtle body that the symbol of the medical profession is pointing to, which is rarely known by modern doctors.

The Experience of the Subtle Body

The subtle body exists in the same space as your physical body, except that it is made of a finer material. It is larger than your physical body, and you feel it as an energy rather than something physical. If you close your eyes and bring your index finger close to the point between your eyebrows, you will sense it before your finger touches the skin. What is happening here is that you are feeling the two points of your subtle body connecting before the two points of the physical body actually touch.

The subtle body is something that you will experience within yourself as you explore your own mind. You will see it internally, you will experience its energy flows, and you will feel it releasing its blockages. It also contracts itself, along with the physical body, as a result of suppressing emotions and feelings. You will have experiences of it letting go, accompanied by surges of energy flowing powerfully through you, as you become more conscious and strengthen your mind and release the past.

The energies are experienced as blissful, empowering, and immensely enjoyable. They seem to operate from a higher intelligence within you, often curing diseases and healing psycho-emotional scars from the past. It is important you know of this intelligence, so you understand what is going on. People who do not understand sometimes believe that there is something wrong with them, when in fact it is tremendously fortunate to become conscious of, and awaken, this more intelligent part of themselves.

We all have a subtle body, even though it cannot be seen or measured by instruments except, perhaps, by the use of Kirlian photography. This is a system that can photograph, with a special process, the emanations of energy from a living organism including humans. On a photograph, it shows an aura of energy coming out from, say, a hand, for a few feet. People who see auras around other people are seeing the emanations of the subtle body.

Let's look at exactly what the subtle body is.

The Structure of the Subtle Body

Most cultures more than a thousand years old have accepted the existence of the subtle body. The subtle body is most clearly defined in the systems of India, particularly yoga. For thousands of years, countless people from all parts of the world have studied its teachings and followed its methods so they could access their inner selves. Basically, yoga is a system of increasing concentration. These people, who extended their concentration, were able to turn their attention within and explore the realms of their minds. Many of them then codified, through writings, paintings, and verse, what it was they had experienced.

As these works built up, it was discovered that there was a body of experience that was consistent for each of them. The primary knowledge they all shared was of the existence of the subtle body. It was experienced as an energy body independent of the physical body. In fact, they discovered that the physical body was dependent on the subtle body for its life.

This subtle body has a specific structure that they all became aware of and codified. It is similar in size and shape to an adult human being. It is pulsating with energy and light. It is said to have 72,000 *nadis*, which are subtle nerve channels, along which its energy flows travel. If you can imagine a human nervous system standing on its own, without any other part of the physical body present, you would see a mass of tiny nerves running out from the spinal cord along where the rest of the body, limbs, and trunk would have been. Imagine now these being filled with a bright energy, and you will have an idea of what the subtle body looks like.

The emanations of the subtle body stretch out from the physical and encase the physical. You may be aware that for people who have had a limb amputated, the feelings remain, even though the physical part has disappeared. They feel an itch in a foot that no longer exists, and it is very frustrating because they cannot scratch it. These sensations come from the subtle body, for the subtle body is the blueprint for the physical body and remains whole throughout your entire life.

The brilliant Chinese system of acupuncture uses the energy meridians of the subtle body, as well as other physical energies to heal and strengthen people. My experience is with the Indian Kundalini system, so it is this method that I will briefly mention.

Kundalini and the Chakras

The central subtle spinal cord, called *sushumna*, is a fine tube, along which an energy called the *Kundalini* travels. Kundalini means *coiled energy* and is often represented as a serpent in myths because it takes the shape of the subtle spinal cord and brain. Kundalini is said to be suppressed at the base of the sushumna, which parallels the location at the base of the physical spinal cord, and can awaken by the practice of concentration. The Kundalini energy then travels along the sushumna through various energy centers called *chakras*. It is in these that many of the emotional blockages are held.

A chakra is a meeting point of a series of nadis. It is like an intersection on a road, where several roads meet at a single point. The individual nadis are the "roads" coming in, and the intersection is the chakra where all these energies meet and pass through. Each chakra, and there are thousands of them, can be contracted and can hold in blocked emotional (and other) energies. When the kundalini energy moves along the sushumna, the subtle spinal cord, it clears out these blockages and heals and harmonizes the whole system.

It will also free up the whole nervous system and remove all stress from the physical body. As it is allowed to flow more freely through the system, all sorts of powers of creativity and intelligence awaken and become available for the person to use as he or she pleases.

The subject seems to be very esoteric, but does have a basis in biology and physics. The understanding of these subtle energies is a great key for healing and empowering people, as well as awakening levels of genius. There is so much information to give you about this subject that it would take up another large book even to give a general outline.[1]

If you find you are having some experiences of the energies of the subtle body, then find someone who has experience with them. Make sure they are intelligent and have studied with a kundalini master. There are members of the healing professions, even some medical doctors and psychiatrists, who understand what is happening. Be wary of people who have been trained in the art of meditation who have no understanding of the kundalini energies. Certainly do not ask anyone who knows nothing about the kundalini for help with your progress. This would be very unwise. And, of course, beware of those who have studied a few yoga postures and who say that kundalini is dangerous to get involved with. It is only dangerous if you do not have an experienced teacher. If your kundalini energies do awaken, a sincere and qualified guide will be able to

---

[1]In a later work, I will be giving you the whole story on the kundalini and the chakras. If you are interested in receiving information about it, then write to me at the address on the "About the Author" page in the back of the book.

give you advice for what is the most brilliant and fortunate happening in your life.

If you believe in reincarnation, the subtle body is the vehicle of the soul or individual spirit or entity as it reincarnates from body to body over countless centuries. If you don't believe in reincarnation, then the subtle body still exists, and you will experience its existence if you pursue self-exploration, but it will seem to be associated with the physical body in some way. Its revelation is the great adventure of life and also the gate through which you must pass to enter all the higher states.

Looking Within

It is possible to see within your physical and subtle bodies with your inner vision. This is the same faculty you use to see in your dreams. Everybody knows this from direct experience. There is obviously an internal seeing faculty within you, even if it is impossible to find it, in the way that you can find the physical eyes. Even if they open up your brain, no surgeon could see it, but it is still there. You use it every night when you dream, or during the day when you are visualizing something. It is a great idea to awaken and use your inner vision even more, as it is a sign that you are becoming more conscious.

Our problem is that when we start to look within, we tend to fall asleep and only have occasional glimpses of our inner universe, which we know as dreams. The ancient and present-day mind explorers are able to remain conscious while they look within. This is what is called *meditation*. It means *looking within while increasing your concentration*. Meditation is the unavoidable master technique for those committed to learning the truth about who and what they are. You cannot know yourself without it; all you will know, if you do not apply it, is your personality and ego.

What the mind explorers found, and what you too will find if you choose to examine your self to its deepest level, is that you will start to explore and open up that part of you that is known as the unconscious. This is truly the realm of the most extraordinary and amazing experiences of all, and it is to this that we will now turn.

❖ ❖ ❖

CHAPTER 33

UNIVERSAL MIND

The Limitless Mind

The exploration of mind is the last frontier in anyone's life. For when you start to work with it, then, and only then, can you pierce through to the answers to all questions about your life and life itself. Knowing mind and its abilities will grant you absolute knowledge and absolute happiness.

We have already looked at the conscious and subconscious mind. The third section of mind is referred to as *the unconscious.* Now we really become aware of the great secrets, known only by the few explorers of the inner realms.

Actually, to use the word *unconscious*, I find a gross error, because it implies that this part of the mind is not aware, but asleep or "out cold" in some way. In other words, it is *not functioning.* For, this third part of your mind is extremely conscious. It is, in fact, supremely intelligent and functions 24 four hours a day, 7 days a week. If it was unconscious, that is, "not aware of its actions" (which is what the word *unconscious* means), you wouldn't be alive.

Your unconscious is the supreme intelligence within you, that took your body from being a tiny seed and grew it into a full adult human being. The unconscious knows exactly what it is doing. It is the blueprint of your physical system. This is the part that keeps all the organs of your body working, digests your food, and heals you. It is also the source of your conscious intelligence. It is not limited to the physical body.

This "unconscious mind" is, in fact, the Universal Mind. It is also known as *Universal Consciousness* or just plain *Consciousness.*

Carl Jung, the brilliant psychiatrist, found in the later years of his life that he was confirming everything that had been known for thousands of years by the ancient sages of the East. He spoke of a Universal Mind that the whole Universe was contained in, like fish are contained within an ocean. This is a most useful way of understanding exactly what this Universal Mind substance is. *Mind* is a word that we normally associate with thoughts and images so, from now on, to clarify this greater part of it, we will call it "Consciousness." Our ordinary everyday consciousness or awareness is only a tiny part of something far greater.

There is much confusion about what Consciousness is. There is a belief that it is a result of the activities of the physical body. The physical emanations are not what we are talking about here. Personal consciousness is only a fraction of the absolute Consciousness so, to differentiate between your ordinary, personal consciousness and the Universal, we will spell the Universal aspect of it with a capital "C."

This substance that we call Consciousness contains the greatest secrets of all. Literally the methodology of all creation, both in your personal life and of the Universe itself, is totally controlled by Consciousness. Understand and tune in with Consciousness, and you can fulfill with ease any desire that arises.

Let's look at exactly what Consciousness is.

Consciousness

The true function of all mystical, spiritual, and personal growth paths is for the sole reason of experiencing other levels of consciousness and the expansion of personal consciousness into the "transpersonal" realms. The transpersonal realm involves experiences beyond, or greater than, the personal.

To understand this more fully, we need to grasp exactly what Consciousness is and how it functions in our lives. First of all, we will detail the various elements and then put them all together at the end of this description. As these elements are listed, you may not understand them fully. Just continue, and all will be made clear at the end. The descriptions you will be given are based on the direct experiences of countless people and are the basis of many spiritual paths in the world today, particularly in the East. I will also include my own experience in the next chapter, so that you can see why I have adopted this understanding as the truth. In the end, it is only your own experiences that count for anything in your life, because they cannot be denied.

Naturally, your understanding of what happens to you is defined by your intelligence and the perceptions of your rational and logical functions. Some people have an experience and come to incorrect conclusions and then defend them as the absolute truth. A few hundred years ago, diseases were often believed to be the result of demons or punishment from some god. Now, of course, with the application of rationality and scientific attitudes, we can see that genetics, bacteria, viruses, bad hygiene, blocked arteries, and the drinking of alcohol and the smoking of cigarettes and other such causes are to blame. When you get into the realm of other states of consciousness, many people's beliefs about how life works are severely confronted. There is a lot of resistance to change. This is why, with all these things, I keep a completely open mind. If there is a better explanation, I am quite willing to examine it. But, after many experiences and examinations over more than 25 years, I have yet to find a more precise and accurate understanding than the one I will detail below. I am convinced that knowledge of Consciousness is the key, and I am certain that it will give you the means to access the highest in your own Self.

So, according to my discoveries, what is Consciousness?

It has various qualities or ways of describing it. As you will see, we are examining something that has almost infinite variations and complexities, but at essence is extremely simple:

1. First of all, Consciousness is a substance, a "thing" that exists and is objectifiable. It is something that can be examined, like anything else that has form.

2. It has the ability to be conscious or aware. Within yourself you can be conscious of the mind—imagination, feelings, thoughts, sensations. Externally, in the world, you are conscious of all the events and circumstances of life. This is the most familiar aspect of Consciousness.

3. The less familiar aspect is that this substance called Consciousness is supremely intelligent. It knows what it is doing, and it needs no brain

to work through to manifest this supreme intelligence. So this is a quality beyond your own individual consciousness.

4. Consciousness, in its absolute nature, is an unbroken field that exists in all places at all times. It is everywhere in the Universe. It contains the Universe, like an ocean contains all sea life.

5. Consciousness is also the material from which everything in he Universe is made. It is the ground from which the Universe grows.

Let's use an analogy to explain this a little more clearly: imagine you have a table filled with various objects made of gold. There could be rings, necklaces, cutlery, ornaments, statuettes, and so on. Now each one of these is an individual item and is easily described as such. Each has its own name, shape, characteristics, weight, and size. But they are all, even though individuals, still made of the same substance—gold. In the same way, everything in the Universe is made of this substance called Consciousness. Energy and matter arise from Consciousness, and the objects of the Universe—the planets, stars, and all that is on them—are a result of interactions between these three—that is, energy and matter as it is manipulated and directed by Consciousness. You can say that Consciousness is the original material and source of all expressions of creation. It is the clay from which the bricks of the Universe are made.

6. It is, therefore, constantly creating, sustaining, and destroying the contents of the Universe. From the largest objects, such as stars, right through to a tiny ant, everything has its life cycle. Each item arises, or is born, in the field of Consciousness, lives within it, and then dissolves back into it, in the same way that an iceberg dissolves back into the ocean.

7. It creates all objects in the Universe by the power of vibration. Vibration is its manifesting power. We know that everything is in vibration, from the most dense to the most subtle. The word *Universe* reveals the truth of this to us. If you divide it, it becomes *uni-verse*, which means *one rhythm*.

In other words, there is one single, unbroken conscious substance, almost infinite in size, causing rhythms within itself, which then are created and manifest as countless different objects. It is similar to the way icebergs are formed: there is water, then a change of temperature occurs, and the water contracts into a different form—that of ice—and a whole new completely different form arises, an iceberg. If you look at the Universal field of Consciousness in a similar way, you can understand just how it can alter its one substance into an unimaginable variety of individual objects.

To sum these first seven points up, we can say that Consciousness, through its supreme intelligence, creates this almost infinite variety of vibrations that appear as the various objects of the Universe, from the largest to the smallest. So the creative force and power of the Universe is entirely aware of what it is doing. Now to the eighth and most important point for humans.

8. Your personal consciousness, that part of you that is aware right now, reading this page, is made of exactly the same substance as the absolute Consciousness. The substance that is conscious in you is identical to and inextricably interlocked with the substance from which the Universe arises. Your personal consciousness, because it is inextricably interlocked with the absolute Consciousness, is the means and the way by which and with which you create your life. Let's now look at it with some analogies that will give you a clearer understanding.

The Ocean of Power

We can call Consciousness "the Ocean of Consciousness," for it contains all life in the way that the ocean of water contains all sea life. The ocean of water "contracts" itself to form icebergs, which then melt and disappear. It is made of trillions of individual drops of water. Imagine that you are on a beach and you are able to take a single drop of water from the ocean and hold it between your fingertips. You could sense all its qualities: it is warm or cold, wet, shaped like a pear, soft, and so on. When you threw it back into the ocean, it would join the other drops and essentially disappear into the body of water. It hasn't, of course, disappeared; it is still there somewhere.

Now let's say, just for this analogy, that that individual drop you hold in your fingertips is self-conscious and has a mind. It would then be able to say to itself: "I am an individual drop, I'm warm, wet, shaped like a pear, soft, my body stops at the skin, etc." It would have a sense of identity as an individual, as an ego. The real meaning of the word *ego* is "a sense of individuality." It is nothing to do with pride or ambition, even though most people associate those and similar qualities with it.

If you then put this "self-conscious" drop back into the ocean, it rejoins the body of water and merges with the rest of the drops. But it is still self-conscious. It still knows who it is, and its awareness of itself is still limited to its skin, even though it is now surrounded by other drops.

This is very much what has happened to us. Our perceptions of ourselves, of who and what we are, tend to stop at the skin. We have no awareness beyond the skin, in the sense that we can feel nothing that our skin does not touch. (Here, I am obviously not talking about emotional feelings, just physical things.)

Now back to the drop of water in the ocean. Let's say that now it is in the ocean, touching other drops all around its own skin, and it can suddenly experience itself as *all the other drops* that it comes in contact with *and* all the others that they come in contact with. Its awareness joins with the awareness of the other drops and makes a single, unbroken expanding body of awareness. In other words, it now can experience itself as the *whole ocean*, as a single body of water.

Its experience of itself has expanded dramatically, and it has now lost its *sense of individuality*, even though it has not lost its "body," the original drop, which still exists somewhere in the ocean. Its sense of self has become the whole ocean, and it is not separated from any part of the ocean. It was always made of ocean material—water—and all it has done is merge with what it was made of. It is now in an expanded state of "ocean consciousness."

The Limitless State of Being

The above experience is very similar to what is available for human beings. Your individual consciousness, which seems to be contained within your skin, is made of exactly the same material as the ocean of absolute Consciousness, which contains the Universe and from which all the objects of the Universe are made. You, by the application of correct techniques that have been known for thousands of years, can directly experience an expansion of your own personal consciousness beyond the limits of your body, just like the drop can expand its awareness into the vast expanse of the ocean.

You already exist within the field of absolute Consciousness. Your own personal consciousness is *exactly* the same substance, just like the drop is made of sea water. By letting go of your ideas and beliefs about being an individual bag of skin and bones wandering around a planet, you can experience yourself as expanding into the environment and eventually to the edges of the Universe. This is the true spiritual path and the experience that will free you from the problem of *avidya*—wrong identification with the body as the limit to who and what you really are—the ultimate "misconception about reality."

The ancient sages give many hints about this state. They say things like: "Instead of experiencing yourself as a tiny cog in a vast Universe, you can experience the Universe as a tiny cog in you." They also say, and this is traditional in all the major religions and paths, "The way to directly experience the highest is through transcending your ego." Often this has been misinterpreted and translated as "You have to get rid of your ego." You don't have to get rid of it, just like the drop in the ocean does not have to get rid of itself. You just have to transcend it—that is, go beyond the limits of your sense of individuality. The individuality remains, but you have one foot in the absolute and the other in the individuality.

And it is here that you will experience the states of Absolute Happiness. But to begin experiencing them, with the bliss, increased intelligence, creative brilliance, and divine, ecstatic love that accompanies the expansion of personal consciousness into absolute Consciousness, you have to deal with the factor that at present you call "me."

❖ ❖ ❖

CHAPTER 34

TRANSCENDING THE EGO

The Cause of Limitation

It is our own particular mindset that separates us from directly realizing these higher or expanded states of Consciousness that are available for us. Our collection of beliefs, described earlier in the book, has been stored and recorded into our memories since conception. These beliefs control our experiences.

Remember what happened as you grew up. You were told you were a boy or a girl, what your nationality was, whether you were good or bad, clever or stupid, beautiful or otherwise, and so on. These remarks, coupled with all the other experiences of your life, embedded in your psyche the limits to your experiences. What went in tells you what you are allowed to do in your life.

If you were told, and therefore believe, that you are only a body, then your experience of yourself *cannot* go beyond your body. Your mind, your biocomputer, will restrict your experience and awareness of what you are to your skin. You cannot expand your awareness into the ocean of Consciousness because there are too many psychological locks in your mind.

For instance, if you had a program inserted by, for example, your religious conditioning, which states that you cannot experience yourself as anything other than an individual body with a mind, then it will be impossible for you to go beyond that program, because of all the fear that would arise as you contradicted these religious beliefs. All of the more advanced religions give people permission, through their doctrines, to aim for experiences of higher and expanded states of Consciousness.

Unfortunately, they usually also dump a whole lot of unnecessary baggage on the minds of their followers, which would cause the founders of these religions to turn in their graves at the misinformation that is being perpetrated in their names.

Beware of dogma; much of it has been put in place by the bureaucracies that have built up around religions. Often the sole function of this dogma is to feather the nests of those in positions of power and authority. Question deeply and intelligently before accepting anything, and rely on the experiences of living people to confirm your beliefs, rather than books or papers written by people who you have no reliable knowledge of and no proof that everything that they have said has been accurately recorded.

Removing Fear Is the Key

Unfortunately, fear is the basis of many beliefs. Fear of death or some sort of hell or some personification of evil stops people from examining the deeper parts of their own mind. What happens, in these situations of personal exploration, is that when you start to awaken yourself from the semi-conscious state that most people live in, you are accessing and releasing all the hidden fears and anxieties that are within us all, buried in the subconscious mind.

As these are flushed to the surface, they are often projected onto something else. So, for instance, if you had a fear of the dark as a child, which was too overpowering at the time, and so you buried it, as you grow up it still exists inside your memory. It was actually tied up more with being afraid of what might happen when it was dark, rather than being a fear of darkness itself. Maybe you feared attack or even death. Children's imaginations are very vivid.

When you begin to awaken yourself to your own power, this fear re-arises, and if you don't understand or are unaware that you are clearing yourself, then you have no option but to project it onto something. As a child, you may have had the experience of thinking that there was a bogey man in the cupboard, or there was someone under the bed. This probably terrified you. This fear, which remains within you until cleared, might be projected onto another country, or a race of people or types of individuals, or it can turn into a religious hate, a distrust of men or women in general, fear of loss of a relationship, fear of economic circumstances, or of anything at all, even mice! On the other hand, if you are aware of what is going on within you, then it is easy to breathe through it and dissolve it forever.

At the time, these irrational, projected fears can be completely justified and rationalized. But you will always need to be alert and realize that fears or other negative emotions, as they arise, are usually old storehouses being released and cleared out. Just be conscious and breathe through them. Unless there is actually a threatening circumstance occurring in your life there; and then, where fear would be a normal response, be wary of negative emotion as it arises, without the justification of something actually happening to cause it. And be very wary of "generalization fears," which are those that involve prejudice, racial and religious hatred, and all the other types of overall negativity. The projection of one's own fears onto others or other objects always keeps you where you are.

The journey to higher and more expanded states of Consciousness requires the elimination and dissolution of all old fears, particularly the fear of death, which is held in the abdomen as a tight ball or fist. Most people are entirely unconscious of this. It will be released and dissolved by the process of becoming more and more conscious. True meditation dissolves all fears slowly and surely.

Expanded States of Consciousness

When I use the term *expanded states of Consciousness*, I am referring to the release from the prison of personal fears and beliefs of individuality. This obviously requires an open mind. Check out your beliefs, because many of the convictions about how life is and how it works are based on delusions or misinformation or a lack of facts. Anyone who vigorously or desperately defends their beliefs without a clear logical understanding of what is actually going on, and whether or not what they are saying can be proven, is operating from a basis of hidden fear. *Convictions*, which are beliefs without proof, imply a meaning similar to the word *convict*. So be careful that any convictions you hold are not making you into a convict, locked in the dark prison of a misinformed or deluded mindset—a useless place to be, even in the best of times.

Once the healing, harmonizing, and balancing of your system has taken place—that is, you have freed yourself from old negativities, deloaded blocked emotions and energies, let go of incorrect or unnecessary beliefs patterns, and matured in your attitudes and abilities in the world, then the force of evolution can recommence with its main work: to proceed to take you to higher and higher states of Consciousness. One only has to check the state of consciousness of people who lived in the Middle Ages to see just how much the human race has evolved. The developments of electronics and technology are witness to this constant growth and expansion of Consciousness throughout the human race.

This is the nature of life. This is what has happened in the past, is happening now, and will happen in the future. The evolutionary force is a force that is evolving your being so that it can experience all the levels of Consciousness.

Expansion of Consciousness

I had an experience of Consciousness in 1978 that clarifies and illustrates how this expansion can occur. It happened while I was spending time following the instructions and teaching of Muktananda, the meditation master whose teachings I followed over a period of seven years, that I mentioned in the beginning of this section.

On one occasion, in Melbourne, Australia, I had been staying in his ashram, his meditation college, for several days. It was at the beginning of a three-month-long period in his company. I had been doing the practices he taught for several hours every day. The main hall was in a building ten minutes' walk from the house that I was staying in. That evening I was returning to the house, walking along the street, when I started to feel a most unusual sensation. It was as though I was growing taller as I walked along. I didn't think much about it, but it persisted and became so strong that I literally felt that I had grown twice as tall as normal. I felt absolutely huge and very, very strong. It was such a powerful experience and felt so real that I looked up, fearing that my head would hit the awnings of the shops under which I was passing. But of course I was still the same physical height that I had always been. So I stopped on the corner of the street, at an intersection.

It was then that the most extraordinary and amazing experience that I had ever had in my life occurred. As I stood still, there was an explosion of energy within me, in the center of my midriff. It moved up towards my head and expanded in all directions throughout my body, spreading through every pore of my skin and then out into the dark night. Accompanying this release of energy was a feeling of absolute and inexpressible bliss. My hair stood on end, and I was filled with a divine ecstasy, a euphoria of unprecedented proportions. The energy then continued, expanding out in all directions at once, like an inflating sphere, with me at its center.

But most amazing of all, was that as the energy sphere moved out, "I" moved with it. In the same way that I always experience my hands, feet, head, and the rest of my body as "me," this direct experience and sense of "me"-ness, this feeling of aliveness and existence, expanded along with the energy to a distance of about two to three hundred yards. I experienced myself as the road, the pavement, the street lights, the gas station, the light rain, the trolley lines, and everything else. It is impossible to describe in any other way. I "became" everything. I realized that everything had consciousness or rather was Consciousness. I was aware of no longer just being my body, but of being something that existed *independently* of the body and yet at the same time, still having a body. The drop had become a larger part of the ocean.

I stood there for about 20 minutes, enjoying the extraordinary nature of what was happening, and then a little voice inside my mind drew my attention to the time and that I had to be back in the house before 10:00. Muktananda had instructed all doors to be locked by then, and anyone not back would not be let in. I walked along the street and just made it. I tucked myself into bed. When I woke the next morning, I was back to my normal state of contraction into the physical body, with my consciousness contained within my skin.

I had this experience many times during my study and work with him, as did many tens of thousands of other people. I believe that it is, in fact, the *natural state* of human beings who are free of all negative conditioning and who are fully alive. The ability to have one foot in individuality and one foot in the absolute (like the drop in the ocean) is obviously available all the time, but to be able to open up to that experience permanently requires a complete and total release of all beliefs that bind you to individuality and all negativities that close off your heart.

This expansion of energy and consciousness may seem an incredible and even ridiculous idea. If you haven't had it, it can be hard to understand what I am talking about. But just consider the simple atom. When the energy of an atom is released, as in an atom bomb, the explosion of energy that follows can destroy a whole city. If a single atom can contain so much energy, why should it be such an impossible thing for you, who are made up of billions of atoms, to be able to release an extraordinary amount of energy as well? Of course, don't take the atom analogy too far. Humans don't blow up, as an atom bomb does. Their release is an opening and steady expansion of Consciousness.

Become a Rare Being

It is a rare being who can surrender to his or her own power and so experience an expanded state of Consciousness, and it is even a rarer one who can consciously develop the unshakable will power, intense concentration abilities, freedom from ego, and the necessary warrior mentality to drag him- or herself out of the delusions of ordinary existence and into the highest realms of human freedom and transhuman Consciousness. It is within the grasp of all, but very few hear about it, and even fewer make the decision to do it. Many are called, but few choose.

It is hard to devote yourself to such a life if you have not mastered the material world and created a role that you are comfortable with. It is necessary to be happy in a career and be free of craving for money. It is very helpful, if not vital, to be in a loving relationship or know how to constantly express love. It is also useful to be in good health. These are all nothing more than signs of a free mind. And without a free mind, there will still be negativities to deal with. Let's now see how you can most efficiently free your mind.

❖ ❖ ❖

CHAPTER 35

STEPS TO HIGHER STATES

The Ultimate Technique

People who are devoted to the path of expanding their Consciousness and clearing out their negativity are usually enjoyable to be around. There may be times when the release is very strong, and they are going through a particularly powerful unloading, that they have some difficulties and will appear antisocial. But they always become more intelligent, perceptive, responsible, kind, generous, reliable, truthful, and aware in all areas of life. They are more able to listen and give appropriate responses. They are less and less likely to be radios without an "off" button, blabbering on only about things that are self-centered. Those who are increasing their perception and intelligence find that the practices of raising Consciousness dissolve any narcissism.

To enter into higher and expanded states of Consciousness, the first requirement is the *clear and unshakable intention* to actually do what is required to master yourself and your life. Once you have made this decision, you then take the appropriate and deliberate actions that will bring this desire for mastery into reality.

The ultimate technique to speeding up your own evolution is meditation, when correctly taught. If it is incorrectly taught, you can be involved in a long path to nowhere and find yourself back where you started, with the only thing gained being a lighter wallet and/or precious time wasted.

Choosing the Best Teacher

There are many well-meaning yet misinformed people teaching meditation. The easiest method to ascertain whether they know what they are talking about, is to check their lives. Meditation, as I said earlier, is nothing more than increasing concentration on the essence of your own being, so resulting in an obviously excellent life.

Check if the answer is yes to the following questions: Do these people have loving relationships? Are they successful? Have they mastered something? Have they studied under a true and recognized master? Are they easily accessible? Are they obviously in a better state than you? Are they friendly and generous and full of humor? If you can answer yes to these, then you should be okay.

Make sure that there is no insidious cult around these people that drags you into its web, so you are stuck there. Also, make sure they do not charge more than a fair price for their teachings, and be wary of the ones that give their teachings away for free. You will discover that very little comes for free. You eventually pay in some form or another. In my experience, most things offered for free can end up costing far more in the long run—either in the sense you pay with your time as a volunteer, or the information and techniques they offer you are so paltry and insufficient that you are unable to make any progress.

I have found that it is much better to pay in cash for information, either as a straight fee or as a donation. You know exactly where you are in the deal, and there are no strings attached. If later you want to give some of your time free of charge so that you can spend more time with the teacher or be able to contribute to the running of an establishment that supports the art of meditation, then that is fine. A rational, fully informed decision can bring tremendous benefits. But in the beginning, pay cash.

The reason for this is that meditation is a warrior's art, not in the sense of going to war, but in overcoming the obstacles within one's mind and in the world. It is not for those who are unable to become responsible and reliable. To access higher and expanded states of Consciousness requires you to go through and release your own negativity. The concentration and persistence needed is never found in unreliable or vague people, those who avoid taking complete responsibility for their lives. It requires courage, the desire for certainty and true knowledge, and the explorer's attitude to life. It is not for those that want to remain weak; it is for those who realize their weaknesses and are determined to translate them into strengths.

Increasing Concentration

Meditation is extended concentration. It means to concentrate on that which you are interested in. A lawyer will meditate on his or her brief, doctors on their patients, an artist on his or her art form, and the general on the battle plan. It is obviously unwise to meditate on TV soap operas, fast food, drugs and alcohol, negative emotions, and so on. Wise individuals will meditate on things that uplift and inspire them or improve their lives. A seeker on the spiritual path will meditate on that which will stop all seeking and reveal the truth about life itself, which is, of course, Consciousness.

If you want to understand Consciousness or your own mind, then you must concentrate on it, pay attention to it, and it will reveal all its secrets. Shortly, I will give you the means by which you can begin this process. First of all, it is important to know what happens when you do focus on Consciousness.

The Release of Contraction

The first thing that becomes apparent when you meditate is that you directly experience that you are holding on to your physical body. It is as though there is an attitude of tension running right through you. You suddenly become aware that you have been like this nearly all your life and that it is an unnatural way to be. It is as if you have clenched your fist very tightly and then held it behind your back and forgotten all about it. Then, some years later, you begin to feel this tension in your back, and you bring your fist forward and look at it. You can't feel it, but as you concentrate on it, it starts to open up, and it becomes painful as you reconnect with the tension. Then, the pins and needles start as the blood and nervous energy enter and the life come back into it, and you are able to use it again. You are amazed that you had this behind your back all those years and were totally unaware that it was there.

It is the same with your whole bodymind. You become aware of just how tightly you are holding onto yourself. This has come from the conditioning process and your reactions to the events during your childhood, which have been stored in your memory, both physically, psychologically, and emotionally.

This tension must be released before you can proceed to higher states of Consciousness. In fact, the process of expanding Consciousness includes becoming aware of this "bodymindset" and releasing it. It is a central part of the growth process. This is why all the greatest spiritual paths have included some sort of body release work in their systems. Paths that don't involve this can be long, arduous, and unrewarding experiences, unless you have no tension to release, which is impossible.

Once you do commence on a path of release and increasing of concentration, many pleasant surprises await you. For instance, you will become aware that you are tuning into your higher intelligence, which is constantly at work, and you realize that opening to it more and more is the most sensible thing to do and the best approach to life, because you are dealing with the very life force itself.

You understand just how you have been hindering its attempts to do its work of evolving you and how you have been slowing down your own growth. Unnecessary things, such as bad habits, drop away spontaneously and naturally. Much in life becomes effortless, and you find that the path is always humorous and never a somber or cold-hearted event.

This is because you are dealing with the very principle of life, and as you go with it, your personal consciousness starts to open up in the most delightful ways. You find your ability to relate to others becomes deeper and more profound as various higher faculties awaken. There is a realization of the connectedness of all of life.

The more conscious you become, the more effective and powerful you are in your daily activities. It is as if you are opening all the reserve circuits of your mind. You find, as you transcend the rational mind, that you become more intuitive. The more you trust, the more will become available. Intuition is extremely useful. Without it, the mind can be a maze with no exits.

The Natural Power

There is nothing more natural than the free flow of the life force. It is, after all, the clearest expression of life's creative power. Like a pristine stream unmuddied with the pollution of civilization, when the life force is unhindered, there is the purity and power of a wild, free river. This is what you will become aware of within you as you meditate and what will clear you of delusions, fears, and negativities.

It is not necessary to belong to a religion, nor is it a barrier. Meditation has nothing to do with religion. It is a science to exercise and strengthen your mind. Religion can be a help if it focuses you in the right direction. It should guide you to a direct experience of the life force and your own essence. Awakening to and allowing more of the life force to flow within you is not an intellectual process, a head trip. It is more a feeling, energy experience.

The internal method of meditation must be learned from a living teacher, as there are other ramifications that need to be explained, as well as individual questions to be answered that come up from the student. It can never be learned from a book, because it is something beyond the intellect; it deals with pure mind, of what is beyond thoughts. Instead, I will give you an external method of meditative concentration. This will give you the means to live your life in the finest and most rewarding way possible. It truly is brilliant in its simplicity and amazing in its results.

❖ ❖ ❖

C H A P T E R   3 6

LIFE AS A WORK OF ART

The Path of Actions

All the greatest sages, enlightened beings, and meditation masters had one thing in common, regardless of the age and culture they lived in: they treated their whole life as a work of art. This means many things, and all of them are relevant to the ideal technique for you to use as you proceed to higher states of Consciousness in your daily life.

Regardless of the life path and lifestyle you choose, you can make it a work of art. You do not need to be an artist in the traditional sense of the word. You can be anything: a street sweeper, a laboratory technician, a painter, a computer operator, a driver, a doctor, a nursing mother, a banker, or a judge—in other words, anything.

You will find that only by making your life a work of art will you be truly satisfied. Be very aware of what is being explained from now on, because it is a very powerful way to speed up the whole process of your growth, and it has astounding results in your life.

This way of life is known as *Karmayoga*. Yoga means to integrate with your highest essence, and *karma* means actions. So, Karmayoga means to use actions as the way to integrate with your highest essence. This highest essence is, of course, *absolute Consciousness*, which is synonymous with *absolute happiness*.

Another way of describing it is to say that Karmayoga is the yoga of action in the world that will take you to your deepest and most euphoric bliss, both in the material world and in your relationships, as well as to the higher and expanded states of Consciousness.

So what exactly is a life lived as a work of art?

Let's first define an artist. A laborer is a person who works only with his or her hands. Professionals are people who work with their hands and their minds. Artists are people who work with their hands, their minds, and their hearts. In other words, they work, they perform their actions, with their whole being.

Entering Higher States

Most people, once they have tasted a higher state of consciousness, will find that they have enjoyed the best and most fulfilling experience that life has to offer. *Enjoyable*, as a word, hardly scratches the surface of the depth, profundity, mind-blowing, and stunning states that are available. In fact, it is impossible to communicate verbally or in pictures more than a hint of what you have within you. It is like trying to explain or communicate to a deaf person what a symphony sounds like. There is no common ground of experience to lock into. Even so, it is still latent within us all. I have known many, many people who have had numerous experiences of higher states of Consciousness. The following stories will give you some idea of what they are like.

An actor I once knew in Melbourne had such an experience. He was a very good actor and well known as one of the leading lights of his generation. One evening, while on stage, he had an extraordinary experience. He described it as somehow transcending or going above his body, yet while still remaining in it. It was not astral traveling or anything of that nature. He found himself looking at the other actors as if from a far greater height. He felt much taller, even though he, obviously, physically remained the same height.

He also felt stronger and was filled with an amazing strength and confidence, as well as an indescribable bliss. The acting became exquisitely simple, and the performance that he gave was the finest of his career. The other actors, after the performance was over, asked him what had happened. They had never experienced working with such an accomplished person before. He had raised the quality and intensity of the whole play to undreamed-of heights. He, of course, had been meditating for the first time in his life.

I asked him about it later on, and he told me that it was the finest experience he had had in his whole life—far greater and more fulfilling than falling in love, winning awards, and any thrill sport. It transformed his life, and he spent time finding out if any other actors had had similar experiences. He discovered that there have been quite a few. He told me that it was the type of experience you may get three times in your whole life, but it is so brilliant that you devote yourself to your craft in the hope of attaining it again.

This altered state of Consciousness is also the secret of great classical music. The music you hear at a concert is only the medium through which the energy of the pianist and the "soul" of the composer is transmitted to the audience, so raising their level of Consciousness. The great classical pianists play from the heart, and it is this emotion that raises up the audience to their level. The whole action of playing the music is an exercise for them to raise their own level of Consciousness. Of course, they rarely speak about it because so few people understand. This is why people go to such concerts, even though they may not realize what is actually going on. It is the same with any great work of art.

Increased Physical Power

Another experience I know of is relates to a young man and his girl-friend, whom I used to share a house with many years ago. These two had a motorcycle, and they used to travel around everywhere on it. One day they were coming home, along the winding, built-up road. A car backed out of its driveway too quickly, and the bike swerved to avoid it and fell over, just before it collided with the rear of the car. The girl was thrown clear, but the young man fell under the car, and the back tire drove onto his back. As the bike hit the car, it stopped immediately. He was pinned there. The girl, a very slight, thin person, screamed and ran forward. In an instant, some huge force of energy and strength came up from within her, and she lifted the rear of the car off her boyfriend's back and he was able to roll clear. Fortunately, he was not badly hurt.

I am sure you have heard similar stories, for there are many of them around, and it is not such an unusual event. In times of great stress or fear, it seems we human beings can exhibit great feats of strength. The girl mentioned above tried later to lift the car again and was unable to even lift it a fraction of an inch. We all have these powers, but they are latent and unused and locked away.

Another man I knew, was a lawyer. He had gone to the mountains to do some skiing. He had only been skiing a couple of times before and was still a beginner, still trying out the gentlest of slopes. This time, he and his friends had gone to a new and unfamiliar location and were skiing along an unmarked slope that ran through some trees. They were making a little race of it, and he decided to go around a large rock to overtake them, as he was at the rear. As he rounded the rock, the slope became suddenly steeper, and he found himself going too fast and then, totally unexpectedly, as he tried to make a run for what he thought was a bank, the ground dropped away from him, and he plunged over an edge and down the steepest slope he had ever seen.

It was as steep as those used by professional downhill racers. As he did so, he had a unique experience: he totally freaked out, a terrible fear gripped him, and he thought he would tumble over and fall to his death. As this total terror washed over him, he felt something suddenly "snap" inside. Everything that he knew to be himself, every shred of personality he held so dear, was dismissed instantly to the back of his mind. Then, in a split second, an incredible peace swept over him. All the chatterings of his mind were silenced, and he found himself in an altered state of Consciousness. In this state he felt fearless, absolutely confident, and completely centered. It was a state he had never been in before. He discovered that he had perfect balance and, as he skied down the steep slope, he found that just by minuscule movements of his body, he could easily keep upright. He sped down, faster than he had ever gone before and blissfully enjoyed what was happening. At the bottom, he came to a halt. His friends had watched him go down from the top and later, when they got to him, were amazed and in disbelief over what they had seen.

There have been many other reports from a wide variety of people, in a range of different activities, who have had similar experiences. I am sure that people such as mountain climbers, race car drivers, parachute jumpers, and other thrill seekers do their respective activities because the act has the ability, when they are pushed to the edge of risk, to put them into these types of states.

Some painters also find that the action of painting puts them into these higher states. They find that the intensity of their concentration actually alters their state of consciousness.

What they are all doing, without realizing it, is practicing the technique of Karmayoga.

Karmayoga

Karmayoga is traditionally described as follows: *the unbroken concentration in the present through the actions that you are taking.*

It does not matter how mundane the actions are, anything involving physical actions is appropriate: washing up, driving the car, raking the garden, exercising, athletic activities, playing with the kids, brushing your teeth, or taking a shower. You can choose any activity whatsoever as long as it involves physical actions. Thought- and image-based activities are not appropriate for this exercise. The simpler the action, the better, when you are starting.

All you do is *concentrate on the physical actions of your chosen activity to the exclusion of all else.* This means you do not pay attention to thoughts or other external events and circumstances. So, if you are washing up, you do not think: "I am picking up the plate, and I am scrubbing it with the brush." You do not involve yourself with any deliberate thinking. Thoughts may flash into your mind, but you observe and let them go; you do not get involved or lost in the thoughts. You merely continue to concentrate on the physical actions.

If you are washing up, put all your attention into your hands. Really feel the brush in your hand, the pressure of the plates and saucepans as you pick them up. Watch what is happening, feel the water (through rubber gloves if you want) as the plates dip into it, concentrating only on what you are doing. Do not have the radio on or any music playing. Do not enter into conversation with anyone else. Let nothing distract you. Do this for at least 15 minutes. If you are doing something else that takes a shorter time, such as brushing your teeth, then merely use the normal time that it takes. Do not extend it unnecessarily. The key to the whole thing is to continue to pay attention to the actions you are taking to the exclusion of all else. Obviously, if an emergency arises, then you behave as you normally would; otherwise, avoid all other things that would normally distract you. Naturally, it is wise to tell those whom you live with what you are doing. Don't ignore them or, if they are not supportive of your efforts to increase your concentration abilities, do this exercise when they are not around or when you are away from them.

It is really very simple, but you will be amazed at just how much your mind grabs your attention. Some people misunderstand what this technique is. They believe it is something to do with stopping your mind or stopping thinking. It is not; it has to do with transcending the thinking mind. You can't stop the mind; you can only rise above it. Don't waste your time trying to stop thoughts. Just pay attention to something *other than* your thoughts—that is, the actions you are taking with your chosen activity.

The benefits of this excellent technique are identical with, and then far greater than, those mentioned above for the actors, musicians, and those who are involved in high-risk sports. What these people actually do causes them to focus intensely, but they are unable to enjoy the higher state when they have stopped their activity. It is the desire for this higher state that causes them to continually take up those activities. A person who practices Karmayoga can do it all the time, regardless of what it is that they are doing. They can do it with any and every activity whatsoever. The intensity of concentration will increase with practice. It is a much faster and more efficient way of achieving those same ends, as well as being a way to take you to far deeper and more profound states permanently. It is deceptively simple, but the essential core of it is that you are constantly focusing your attention on pure Consciousness and by doing so, you are automatically making yourself available for experiences of expanded states. Whatever you focus on you become.

❖ ❖ ❖

C H A P T E R   3 7

INCREASING WILL POWER

Extension of Concentration

Essentially, what people who practice Karmayoga are doing, and as you will be doing if you are interested in gaining control of your mind and your life, is extending the duration of their concentration. By applying this method, you will always be developing the ability to concentrate for ever-increasing periods of time. These periods of unbroken concentration will, as a side effect, give you an unshakable will power. It will also give you the most useful attribute of being able to use the increased powers of concentration in any area of life you choose.

As you focus on your simple acts, you will find that you are actually placing your consciousness on one focal point. What this does is drag all contractions and blockages from all parts of your being to the surface of your awareness. This is the way you will become more aware of your whole being.

Extending concentration is the only means for clearing all the internal psycho-physical blockages and raising your level of consciousness to ever-expanding heights.

What happens for most human beings is that as they concentrate on something during their daily lives, their surface mind continues to function and occupy their awareness. Thoughts, images, memories, fantasies, and daydreams are constantly arising and being given attention. This focusing on the activity of mind keeps the blockages in place. People find they cannot go deeper into mind or transcend it, because they are using only the surface of it. You can't dive deeply below the waves of the sea if you are swimming on the surface. It is the same with the mind. This is why concentration on the activities and movements of mind will never take anyone deeply into their own self. To dive deeply means to leave the normal activities behind for some time.

When practicing Karmayoga—that is, concentrating on physical actions rather than on movements of the mind, you will find that your ability to retain unbroken concentration on what you are doing is severely limited. Most people can do it for short periods, but then the mind wanders. How many times does your mind wander from one thing to another during an hour? The reason why it is very hard to retain concentration on a physical activity is because, by concentrating fully, you start to bring up the blockages from the subconscious for clearing. Focusing your attention fully and continually, in the unbroken way just described, on a physical activity, however small or insignificant, will cause your attention to dive deeper, below the surface of the normal chatterbox mind.

It is similar to what happens on a physical level when you want to build muscle. Those who work out with weights know that it is necessary to contract the muscle as hard as possible to cause the muscle fibers to grow, so resulting in a larger muscle. What also happens is that the harder you contract it, the deeper it can relax. The actual growth takes place during the relaxing phase. In Hathayoga, the *asanas*, or postures that are practiced, use the same principle. By holding the body in a particular posture for extended periods of time, the muscles become strongly contracted, so that when the posture is released, there is a tremendous relaxation and letting go. This release is not only of the contraction that took place during the posture, but also of any long-held tension and stress from the muscle fibers and any other parts of the body that are involved. All these old tensions that normally are untouched during the everyday use of the body and its muscles are contacted by the posture and so cleared out. These pockets of stored tension and stress can be unnoticed for life, and it is only the specialized physical exercise that contacts and releases them. The contraction of the muscle is the trigger that causes the release of old blockages. It is exactly the same with the mind.

As you concentrate and hold your attention on the one activity, the focusing brings up any old contractions from within your mind. They can be emotional, such as suppressed anger or sadness; or psychological, such as a belief about life, or both. A contraction, just before it gets to the surface, is felt at a subconscious level as a negative. This is to be expected, for it is, after all, an old block that was originally suppressed because it was negative. Usually, rather than let it rise to awareness, our mind flips or jumps to another surface thought or image, the concentration is then lost, and the negative then sinks back again, because the concentration power that was magnetizing it to the surface has been dissipated. It no longer has the power to draw it to consciousness. It would happen in the same way if you were trying to build a muscle. If, as the tension increases, you let go of your muscular contraction, you will be unable to build any new muscle, nor will you be able to relax the muscle deeply enough and so remove any old, long-held stresses. As with the mind, the ability to let go deeply is determined by how concentrated you can be.

This is why the mind is always moving around and chatterboxing on continually during the day. It stops itself going deeper, by avoiding concentrating for extended periods. Because if it does concentrate in this way, it brings old negativities to the surface that are normally buried. So the mind has no option but to jump to something else. Ordinary concentration is like this. You hold your attention on something you want to do, but your mind is always coming and going from what you are concentrating on.

Through extended concentration, great minds such as Einstein were able to make their amazing discoveries. Einstein would go into a deeply relaxed state where he would retain consciousness but let go of paying attention to his surface mind. By retaining consciousness—that is, concentrating—he was able to go deeper into his own intelligence and come up with the brilliant insights that have changed the world.

In all the great monasteries and ashrams, when a person arrives, they are given a simple task to do, like sweeping the courtyard or preparing food. They are instructed to do it perfectly without losing concentration at all. What this specific act of concentration does is focus their attention in the now and drag them out of a semi-conscious state where their mind is wandering from this to that to the other. This is Karmayoga.

If you apply Karmayoga to your actions, you will draw old negativities to the surface and, by retaining concentration, you will integrate them at a conscious level. As you do so, you will find that, by not allowing your mind to wander, all sorts of emotional reactions may appear. You will always be in control of them and can bury them again for later processing if you choose, by relaxing your concentration. If you decide to allow them to surface, you can expect something like the following to occur:

The Layers of Release

1. *Personality:* The first response you will become aware of in your mind, as you concentrate, is the desire to think about your personality or "personness." Let's say you are using the washing up as your simple action to practice this technique. As you do it, inevitably your attention will be drawn from paying attention to the actions with the plates and saucepans to the thought and imagination processes. You will think about what is happening in your life, what you did today, your plans for tomorrow, the relationship, job involvements, and so on. So each time you become aware that you are paying attention to thinking rather than the actions, you must bring your attention back to the actions.

2. *Boredom:* The next layer of your mind that appears, if you choose to continue concentrating, is boredom. This always occurs when you dig below the surface personality. The personality does not like to be bored, the reason being that you are getting closer to the things that are stored in the next level down from it. Boredom drives many people to fill up their time with trivia. They aimlessly socialize, enjoying the sound of their own voice as it rambles on with irrelevant and low-grade conversation or, worse, they get into ego and power games with their unfortunate family, acquaintances, and work associates.

   Boredom is the state you enter just before you find out something about yourself that you have been burying for many years—for example, awareness of any unpleasant behavior patterns or negative characteristics. It is the state we enter into which layers over the blocked emotions. Boredom can also manifest as avoidance or resistance to taking any conscious actions, in other words, remaining concentrated on what you are doing. Even causing yourself to pay attention to the washing up can bring to the surface this type of blocking action of the mind.

3. *Anger:* If you continue with your concentration on the simple actions, the next layer you are likely to encounter is anger. Anger is the emotional state felt by people when they can't get what they want, or the world isn't working in the way they want it to. It is sometimes known as rage. It is often a childish response to a situation where the person is confronted either by their own lack of power and/or their inability to accept the reality of a situation. Children demonstrate it on a regular basis as a temper tantrum. Naturally, there are many other ugly scenarios that people can find themselves in that also cause anger. Rarely though, have people figured out how, or even felt it was appropriate, to express anger, and so have learned to suppress it in the subconscious mind and to contract their physiology. It remains there for life or until processed out of the bodymind system.

As you continue with your simple actions, you may become angry for no reason at all. It may "steam" out of you. Looking back after such an event, it will seem rather amusing. If it happens while washing up, it is difficult to get angry with the plates and saucepans, but the anger still arises.

Now if or when this happens, merely be aware of it, and let it go by breathing deeply through it. Our normal response, when we experience an arising of old, stored anger, is to automatically project it onto something or someone outside ourselves. If no one is around, we may get angry with the government over interest rates or unemployment or the environment. Or, we may project that anger onto some section of society or a relative. For most people, what they project it onto is irrelevant, just so long as they do not have to face the reality of, and take responsibility for, their own suppressed anger. Nearly everyone is performing this particular "avoid"-dance. If we can remain conscious through the release of this situation, then we can go even deeper.

4. *Sadness:* Sadness is usually buried more deeply than anger and appears next. It is a strange experience to be washing up, concentrating carefully on what you are doing, only to find waves of sadness surfacing. Some people even burst into tears. Again, as this feeling arises, it is very important not to project it onto something, such as the

starving people in Africa. You must own it for yourself, as it is coming up from you. Only then can you process it out of your system and really be of help to those in dire need.

Sometimes it even comes up as despair, a particularly intense form of sadness. This can be overpowering, and it will require all your attention to retain concentration. This feeling will cause you to project very forcefully onto the major issues in your life, even onto life itself. Just keep breathing and retain concentration, and it will be processed out. It is a very rare event to dig this deeply early in the practice of such exercises, but it has been known to happen. Remember, no emotion can control you unless you let it. And if one arises without an outside circumstance causing it, then it is just coming up to be released. It is merely a clearing of an old loading, which is better out of your system. Whatever you do, don't fall into the trap of continually playing out an old emotion again and again. Just let it go, and move on by concentrating on your actions.

5. *Fear:* The most unusual and unexpected emotion to arise when you are washing up or concentrating on an activity is fear. Fear is the basis of all negativity. It is the underlying layer of much of the personality and the subconscious mind. You will inevitably release old fear on your journey to full Consciousness. But, when approached with awareness by the practice of Karmayoga, it is easy to handle and is released carefully, just like the valve on a pressure cooker which, when opened, allows the pressure to just steam away until it is all gone. Again, always remember to breathe through it.

6. *Love:* Finally, under all these emotions, you will get to the free flow of energy from the heart that we call love. Love will just start to bubble up, and you will feel it as a blissful and euphoric feeling. It also does not require an outside source to prompt its arrival. Your true nature is love, and it is felt as an energy. So when the blocks are cleared, the energy you feel is known as love. This is the goal of all clearing work.

Sometimes you may find, as you are doing your Karmayoga practice, that the emotions arise in a different order. You may bypass anger and go straight to sadness, or you may go straight to fear. Some people find they are drawn into a blissful, loving state very quickly.

Just continue with the practice, and you will find that all will be cleared and appear quite naturally. You don't have to worry about it, as it is your own higher intelligence you are contacting, and it is quite capable of clearing you.

Karmayoga is a brilliant technique. It will bring you tremendous benefits from the moment you start to practice it. You will find that your mind will become very strong, and you will become more intuitive, more in synchronicity. Your creativity and self-expression talents will increase, and you will find a new self-confidence developing. Success, in any venture, will become only a matter of applying yourself and enjoying the fruits of your actions. It is a brilliant method to integrate into your everyday life, as it takes no time at all because you are applying it to all the normal things you do anyway.

Now, let's put the whole work together so you can take yourself to absolute happiness and stay there.

❖ ❖ ❖

WHAT NOW?

Moving to Your Future

The first step in any new venture is the decision to do it. It is the same with being a Life Artist, a person who uses the technique of Karmayoga in all of his or her activities and who is interested in expanding personal consciousness into the higher states of absolute Consciousness. This practice, as I am sure you have understood, brings the greatest rewards and the most fulfilling experiences for a human being. It encompasses the most pleasurable experiences of life and allows you to appreciate all the powers of your mind.

Decision nearly always brings up negativity and resistance to be cleared. This is to be expected. Just go through it. If you don't make the decision to express your highest potential and enjoy your life to the fullest—which are one and the same thing—then your only other choice is to live your life *without* access to the other 99 percent of what you have inside yourself. All those talents, hidden powers, skills, and abilities will remain unused. You will always be playing victim in some part of your life, such as having poor relationships, an unsatisfying career, lack of wealth, psychosomatic diseases, and the inability to express yourself fully and communicate what you truly mean.

In short, you will be dedicating yourself to the life of a victim. The sounds that a victim makes are: blaming others, complaining, confusion, procrastination, dependence, aggression, neurotic need, uncertainty, guilt, patterns of continual failure, self-image problems, inability to commit or persist when it comes to making a choice or achieving a goal, and so on.

If you recognize any of these qualities in yourself, then there is some serious "re-engineering" to do within your mind.

On the other hand, here are the expressions of Life Artists (those who have made the decision to keep growing in life): personal responsibility, intelligent research into the means to obtain what is wanted, continual personal growth and education, growing awareness of themselves and their patterns, the ability to manifest the experiences they wish to undergo, and an ever-increasing love in their lives.

Consciousness Brings All Rewards

Check yourself out to see whether you have set yourself up as a victim in any area of life. The first place is often the body, with improper dietary habits, the ingestion of cigarettes, excess alcohol, and other drugs. Or, maybe it is a total lack of fitness. If any of these habits apply to you, don't tell yourself off, do something about it.

Just run through all the other areas of your life—money, relationships, career, leisure activities, social responsibility, and so on—and see what is there. It is not actually hard to *do* something about these things. What is sometimes difficult is to *start*. By just taking it one step at a time, you can make any goal achievable and seem effortless.

Use your Lifewrite. Make sure that it is detailed in all areas. Maybe you can focus on one large area of life at a time—such as relationships or money—for a year or two. My wife and I did so, and we eliminated the hidden negativities that could have come up later in life. We took about a year off and just concentrated on relating to each other. It wasn't just a case of spending time together and carrying on with life as though we were on vacation; it was a matter of applying the techniques I have described here for you. To be able to do that cost us money, but it was worth every cent. We both worked only about six weeks that year. We lived off our savings for the rest of the time. It was a wonderful experience, filled with all types of expression of ourselves, a clearing of the subconscious and, therefore, an ever-deepening understanding of each other and our relationship. Love, closeness, and a deep friendship was the result.

The most interesting thing about being a Life Artist is that as soon as you embark on the path, life itself responds. It clears out the old beliefs by presenting you, in ways that seem amazing, coincidental, and even magical, with unavoidable information and experiences that sift out the old garbage and open a variety of opportunities.

The Real Opportunity of Human Life

Human life is an opportunity to have something to do, a purpose or a mission to fulfill. And the measure in which we avoid doing something with our life is matched in the same degree by a feeling of emptiness. The only satisfaction comes from dedicating ourselves to something and doing the best we can to succeed at that choice.

We can dedicate ourselves to anything whatsoever, as long as it is coupled with the decision and intention to master it. This is the attitude of the Life Artist. It can be a happy family life, an invention, research into something, perfection of a skill or athletic ability, teaching, artistic pursuits, a spiritual discipline, a business or profession, or learning how to love to the fullest extent possible.

What you do doesn't matter. You will find whatever is appropriate by researching what is available for human beings in this age and culture. Of course, you are not limited to just one choice. For instance, you can learn to love, have an excellent family life, and master an art form or career. It is the karmayoga attitude that you put into it that matters.

There is no satisfaction in having no purpose. *Satisfaction in life is the fulfillment of the purpose you have chosen.* If you have no purpose, if all you are doing is drifting through life aimlessly, if you are sitting back waiting to see what happens, then you will live a life of mediocrity and deluded self-importance, at best, and a depressing, lost-sheep, victim-type life, at worst. Purpose gives strength. The choice is always yours. Just working to earn enough money to pay the bills will never satisfy you because you will be denying too great a part of yourself, your powers, and your abilities.

Taking Control

Decide to create an ideal life and then do it. As things appear, deal with them—don't avoid or put them off. Do everything to become stronger and more concentrated and more loving. These three go hand in hand. You have in this book the techniques to get you moving. Now it is only a matter of putting them into practice.

Don't worry about past lives (if you believe in them) or the past in general. It has already happened. Whatever has happened in the past cannot be changed. You are a result of your past, and so all you have to deal with is who and what you are right now. Go for results in the present circumstances you live in.

The keys to the major areas in life are as follows:

- **Wealth**—Understand and master business, whether it be in products, services, art forms, or investments. Don't be frightened of it. Form a relationship with it. Anything to do with attracting money into your life involves the principles of business and the marketplace.

- **Relationships**—Look on them as an opportunity to express love, generosity, caring, responsibility, and growth for all concerned. The ability to relate deeply is extremely rewarding and offers countless opportunities for love to be expressed.

- **Spiritual Knowledge**—Practice Karmayoga. Learn to meditate properly with a genuine teacher who has the qualities described earlier. Do the techniques. Fill your mind with information and stories of great beings. Spend time in the company of spiritual warriors. They will always appear in your life when you are ready or when you truly desire this knowledge. Don't avoid the world; master it to the degree you require. A simple life is the easiest to assist you with focusing on the highest knowledge. *Simple* does not necessarily mean *poor*, it means having plenty of time to pay attention to your own essence.

Your Own Growth

The only person that you are ever going to be stuck with during your whole life is YOU! Have you ever considered this before? Let's hope that it's not a depressing thought! It is, therefore, intelligent to make sure that you are the person you want to spend the rest of your life with. This means that you will have to continually grow and improve your abilities.

If you stay the same, you may become dissatisfied with yourself and probably become unsatisfying to everyone else.

The only sure way to make changes in your life is to follow a path of growth, both personally and in the world. Just like a mango tree grows bigger with time, and is able to give off more and more fruit, be certain that your life is spent in the same way. Growing is not just a matter of becoming successful and working on yourself. It's the *fruit* that you give off, the things you contribute to the well-being of your family and society that represent the true measure of your success.

These fruits of your success should be enjoyed by those around you. Generosity of spirit is recognized by a quite natural, uncontrived state of being. You are no longer interested in your personality and its machinations. Your output in the world is more and more "fruit," in the sense that you are giving off what others want or require. You are able to do this because you are fulfilled internally and therefore no longer in narcissism. Blowing your own trumpet is no longer on your agenda.

Continue to grow and live your life like the mango tree. Unless your life is filled with the full and total responsibility as the creator of what happens, then you will be leaving the experience of life up to the conditioning that is already in place in your subconscious mind. You will be unable to contribute and give back to life.

Your whole mind is an amazing instrument. Its powers are awesome, and when you explore your mind, what is in there will stun you. And the beauty of it is that it is entirely under your control, if you wish to take that control. It will need your constant attention to bring these latent abilities and potentials to full fruition, but it is worth it because inside you right now are undreamed-of powers of intelligence, mastery, and faculties of creativity that are all lying dormant. It is your choice to activate them or to let them sleep.

What Now?

Now is the time to make the choice to create your preferred reality. Reread this book and master the techniques and principles. Don't merely put it down and say, "How nice." Get on with the job. Only *you* can do it, no one else can do it for you. But you are not on your own. There are other more powerful forces and energies in the Universe that are not only keeping you alive and bringing you your present experiences, but are very willing and able to create for you your preferred reality. All that is required is that you consciously understand and join in the game.

Keep the process of growth going. Read, listen, and attend anything that will educate you and raise your intelligence. Take the help of outside sources to assist you with your own awakening. Develop the attitude of a warrior. Train your mind and body.

You have a body, the body doesn't have you—but you must know what "you" truly are. You are a free spirit, a spark of the life force, the creative power of Consciousness, that is totally and absolutely free. But for the moment, you have become bound in a physical form in this particular realm of creation we know as the world. Pause, take some time, and see how true this is.

Life can be looked on as a game, as a play of Consciousness. The goal is to be a creator, an actor on the stage of life, a liberated being who can enjoy any experience you want, within the realm of life that you live in.

What you are experiencing in your world is always a reflection of what is in your mind. You create your reality from your conscious and subconscious. You always have and always will. Life has set us up in this way. The game, or the play of life, is to escape from the maze of the mind and realize who and what you truly are.

You have no option but to master your mind if you wish to master your life in any area at all. It is easy to see that in those areas of your life that are working well, you also have control of your mind. So it is obvious that the key for a rewarding life is to control your mind and direct it to where you want to go. The easiest path to success is to become more and more conscious of your behaviors, your mind and your Self. There is, in fact, no other path.

It is a great help to bring everything into a particular order. You will discover that a disciplined life is truly pleasurable. It is impossible to create any new desires and bring them to fruition without bringing order and discipline into your life. Nor is it possible to access the realms of absolute happiness without the same.

The word *discipline* can often bring up all sorts of negative reactions. It can imply punishment or hardness, it can suggest doing something you don't want to do because you are impelled to by some outside authority. This is not the sort of discipline I am talking about. The only discipline worthy of consideration is self-discipline. You, and only you, can bring your mind and your whole system under your conscious control. Even the word *control* tends to freak some people out. They would rather live a life in which there is no control. This is usually due to some difficulty in childhood. *Control* is a positive word if it is you who are taking control of your system.

Consider now, is your life an orderly one in which you are the creator of all that you do? Or are you merely reacting to external circumstances and doing what is necessary to survive and having a few minor enjoyments?

Pause for a few moments and identify immediately the areas in your life that are disordered. These are the ones that are not working in the way that you want them to. Check the areas where there is frustration, craving, need, and want. Look deeply, see what they are, and write them down. If you don't write them down and just leave them swimming in your mind, telling yourself, "Oh yes, I know what they are," then it is most unlikely you will ever be able to do anything about them, and they will stay in your life, possibly forever, in one form or another. Remember, identifying a problem is 90 percent of the solution. Writing it down gives you the ability to observe it in a detached way and then take intelligent action.

There is so much that the world has to offer, so many enjoyable and exciting adventures available, regardless of your age, wealth, background, or past. You can change it all, and you can have it all, once you have identified what you don't want, decided what you do want, and truly made the decision to become absolutely responsible, absolutely conscious, and absolutely happy.

Make the decision, and then take the actions. Now is the time. This is the place. Become the person you know you really can be. Become fully alive. Maximize your potential. Know your Self. Start immediately.

THIS IS IT!

❖ ❖ ❖

S E L F - H E L P
R E S O U R C E S

The following list of resources can be used for more information about recovery options for addictions, health problems, or problems related to dysfunctional families. The addresses and telephone numbers listed are for the national headquarters; look in your local yellow pages under "Community Services" for resources closer to your area.

In addition to the following groups, other self-help organizations may be available in your area to assist your healing and recovery for a particular life crisis not listed here. Consult your telephone directory, call a counseling center or help line near you, or write or call:

American Self-Help Clearinghouse
St. Clares-Riverside Medical Center
Denville, NJ 07834
(201) 625-7101
(8:30am - 5:00pm Eastern Time)

National Self-Help Clearinghouse
25 West 43rd Street, Room 620
New York, NY 10036
(212) 642-2944

AIDS

AIDS Hotline
(800) 342-2437

Children with AIDS Project of America
4020 N. 20th Street, Ste. 101
Phoenix, AZ 85016
(602) 265-4859

Hotline
(602) 843-8654

National AIDS Network
(800) 342-2437

Project Inform
19655 Market Street, Ste. 220
San Francisco, CA 94103
(415) 558-8669

Spanish AIDS Hotline
(800) 344-7432

TDD (Hearing Impaired) AIDS Hotline
(800) 243-7889

The Names Project - AIDS Quilt
(800) 872-6263

ALCOHOL ABUSE

Al-Anon Family Headquarters
200 Park Avenue South
New York, NY 10003
(212) 302-7240

Alcoholics Anonymous (AA)
General Service Office
475 Riverside Drive
New York, NY 10115
(212) 870-3400

Children of Alcoholics Foundation
P.O. Box 4185
Grand Central Station
New York, NY 10163-4185
(212) 754-0656
(800) 359-COAF

Meridian Council, Inc.
Administrative Offices
4 Elmcrest Terrace
Norwalk, CT 06850

National Assoc. of Children of Alcoholics (NACOA)
11426 Rockville Pike, Ste. 100
Rockville, MD 20852
(301) 468-0985

National Clearinghouse for Alcohol and Drug Information (NCADI)
P.O. Box 234
Rockville, MD 20852
(301) 468-2600

National Council on Alcoholism and Drug Dependency (NCADD)
12 West 21st Street
New York, NY 10010
(212) 206-6770

ANOREXIA/BULIMIA

American Anorexia/Bulimia Association, Inc.
418 East 76th Street
New York, NY 10021
(212) 891-8686

Bulimic/Anorexic Self-Help (BASH)
P.O. Box 39903
St. Louis, MO 63138
(800) 888-4680

Eating Disorder Organization
1925 East Dublin Granville Road
Columbus, OH 43229-3517
(614) 436-1112

CANCER

National Cancer Institute
(800) 4-CANCER

Commonweal
P.O. Box 316
Bolinas, CA 94924
(415) 868-0971

ECAP (Exceptional Cancer Patients)
Bernie S. Siegel, M.D.
1302 Chapel Street
New Haven, CT 06511
(203) 865-8392

CHILD MOLESTATION

Adult Molested As Children United (AMACU)
232 East Gish Road
San Jose, CA 95112
(800) 422-4453

National Committee for Prevention of Child Abuse
322 South Michigan Avenue, Ste. 1600
Chicago, IL 60604
(312) 663-3520

CHILDREN'S AND TEENS' CRISIS INTERVENTION

Boy's Town Crisis Hotline
(800) 448-3000

Covenant House Hotline
(800) 999-9999

Kid Save
(800) 543-7283

National Runaway and Suicide Hotline
(800) 621-4000

CO-DEPENDENCY

Co-Dependents Anonymous
P.O. Box 33577
Phoenix, AZ 85067-3577
(602) 277-7991

DEBTS

Debtors Anonymous
General Service Office
P.O. Box 400
Grand Central Station
New York, NY 10163-0400
(212) 642-8220

DIABETES

American Diabetes Association
(800) 232-3472

DRUG ABUSE

Cocaine Anonymous
(800) 347-8998

National Cocaine-Abuse Hotline
(800) 262-2463
(800) COCAINE

National Institute of Drug Abuse (NIDA)
Parklawn Building
5600 Fishers Lane, Room 10A-39
Rockville, MD 20852
(301) 443-6245 (for information)
(800) 662-4357 (for help)

World Service Office (NA)
P.O. Box 9999
Van Nuys, CA 91409
(818) 780-3951

EATING DISORDERS

Food Addiction Hotline
Florida Institute of Technology
FIT Hotline
Drug Addiction & Depression
(800) 872-0088

Overeaters Anonymous
National Office
383 Van Ness Avenue, Ste. 1601
Torrance, CA 90501
(310) 618-8835

GAMBLING

Gamblers Anonymous
National Council on Compulsive Gambling
444 West 59th Street, Room 1521
New York, NY 10019
(212) 265-8600

GRIEF

Grief Recovery Helpline
(800) 445-4808

Grief Recovery Institute
8306 Wilshire Blvd., Ste. 21A
Beverly Hills, CA 90211
(213) 650-1234

HEALTH ISSUES

Alzheimer's Disease Information
(800) 621-0379

American Chronic Pain Assoc.
P.O. Box 850
Rocklin, CA 95677
(916) 632-0922

American Foundation of Traditional Chinese Medicine
1280 Columbus Avenue, Ste. 302
San Francisco, CA 94133
(415) 776-0502

American Holistic Health Assoc.
P.O. Box 17400
Anaheim, CA 92817
(714) 779-6152

The Fetzer Institute
9292 West KL Avenue
Kalamazoo, MI 49009
(616) 375-2000

Hospicelink
(800) 331-1620

Institute for Human Potential and Mind-Body Medicine
Deepak Chopra, M.D.
973 B Lomas Santa Fe Dr.
Solana Beach, CA 92075
(619) 794-2425

Institute for Noetic Sciences
P.O. Box 909, Dept. M
Sausalito, CA 94966-0909
(800) 383-1394

Natl. Health Information Ctr.
P.O. Box 1133
Washington, DC 20013-1133
(800) 336-4797

The Mind-Body Medical Institute
185 Pilgrim Road
Boston, MA 02215
(617) 732-7000

World Research Foundation
15300 Ventura Blvd., Ste. 405
Sherman Oaks, CA 91403
(818) 907-5483

IMPOTENCE

Impotency Institute of America
2020 Pennsylvania Avenue N.W., Ste. 292
Washington, DC 20006
(800) 669-1603

INCEST

Incest Survivors Resource Network International, Inc.
P.O. Box 7375
Las Cruces, NM 88006-7375
(505) 521-4260

MISSING CHILDREN

National Center for Missing and Exploited Children
(800) 843-5678

RAPE

Austin Rape Crisis Center
1824 East Oltorf
Austin, TX 78741
(512) 440-7273

SEX ADDICTIONS

National Council on Sexual Addictions
P.O. Box 652
Azle, TX 76098-0652
(800) 321-2066

SMOKING ABUSE

Nicotine Anonymous
2118 Greenwich Street
San Francisco, CA 94123
(415) 750-0328

SPOUSAL ABUSE

National Coalition Against Domestic Violence
P.O. Box 34103
Washington, DC 20043-4103
(202) 638-6388
(800) 333-7233 (crisis line)

STRESS REDUCTION

The Biofeedback & Psychophysiology Clinic
The Menninger Clinic
P.O. Box 829
Topeka, KS 66601-0829
(913) 273-7500

Rise Institute
P.O. Box 2733
Petaluma, CA 94973
(707) 765-2758

The Stress Reduction Clinic
Jon Kabat-Zinn, Ph.D.
University of Massachusetts
Medical Center
55 Lake Avenue North
Worcester, MA 01655
(508) 856-1616

ABOUT THE AUTHOR

Michael Domeyko Rowland is a writer, researcher, and explorer of the human mind and consciousness. He lives in Northern New South Wales, Australia, on a farm with his wife, Paulina, and dedicates himself to communicating information that will uplift, inform, and inspire people to improve their lives and raise their level of consciousness. He was born in the United Kingdom, of an English mother and an Anglo-Indian father. He came to Australia as a teenager and worked in the film and television industry, starting as a runner on the series "Skippy the Kangaroo," and ending as a director of the series "Return to Eden."

During this 20-year period, he intensely studied the newly emerging Western disciplines of freeing the mind and unlocking personal power. He also formally trained as a teacher of various ancient methodologies of mind and consciousness exploration and ways to increase concentration. He now runs one of the most successful personal development companies in Australia.

To contact Michael, or to receive information about his seminars and audio- and videocassettes, please write to:

P.O. Box 1000
Bondi Beach
NSW 2026
AUSTRALIA

❖ ❖ ❖